UNCERTAIN TRAVELERS

BRANDEIS SERIES ON JEWISH WOMEN

Shulamit Reinharz, General Editor
Joyce Antler, Associate Editor
Sylvia Barack Fishman, Associate Editor
Susan Kahn, Associate Editor

The International Research Institute on Jewish Women, established at Brandeis University in 1997 by Hadassah, the Women's Zionist Organization of America, Inc., supports interdisciplinary basic and applied research as well as cultural projects related to Jewish women around the world. Under the auspices of the Institute, the Brandeis Series on Jewish Women publishes a wide range of books by and about Jewish women in diverse contexts and time periods.

UNCERTAIN TRAVELERS

Conversations with Jewish Women

Immigrants to America

Marjorie Agosín

Edited and annotated by Mary G. Berg

Brandeis University Press

PUBLISHED BY UNIVERSITY PRESS OF NEW ENGLAND

HANOVER AND LONDON

Brandeis University Press

Published by University Press of New England, Hanover, NH 03755

Printed in the United States of America

5 4 3 2 1

CIP data appear at the end of the book

Contents

Acknowledgments

First, I wish to thank the uncertain travelers with whom I conversed in this book. They offered me an intimate look at their lives, and I am grateful for their trust and friendship. Mary Berg, friend, translator, and editor, has been intimately engaged in shaping this project from its beginnings. Stephanie Carter, Kevin Findlan, and Leslie McIntosh were enthusiastic researchers and fact checkers. My editor, Phyllis Deutsch, believed in *Uncertain Travelers* at an early stage. Her vision was instrumental in creating this book.

Finally, I wish to thank my parents, husband, and children, whose love continues to make my journey possible.

December 1998   M.A.

UNCERTAIN TRAVELERS

MARJORIE AGOSÍN

Introduction

1909	Paternal grandparents flee Czar Nicholas II's pogroms by crossing the Carpathian Mountains on foot to Istanbul, then Marseilles, and sail to Chile; in 1922 they settle in Quillota in the Central Valley of Chile
1920s	Maternal grandfather, Joseph Halpern, emigrates to Valparaíso
1939	Great-grandmother Helene Halpern leaves Hamburg for Valparaíso
1940s	Maternal grandparents settle in southern Chile
1948	Parents marry
1951	Parents come to the United States for father to study at the National Institutes of Health, Bethesda, Maryland
December 1, 1952	Sister, Cynthia, born in Bethesda
June 15, 1955	Marjorie born in Bethesda
September 1955	Parents and sister return with Marjorie to Santiago de Chile
January 7, 1963	Brother, Mario, born in Santiago
1971	Moves with parents, brother, and sister to Athens, Georgia, when father begins work as professor of biochemistry at the University of Georgia
1972	Returns to Chile to visit (and every year after)
1973	Spends a year in Jerusalem on scholarship
1977	Bachelor's degree in philosophy at University of Georgia in Athens
1977	Grandfather Joseph Halpern dies in Chile. Marjorie marries John Wiggins in Athens, Georgia, and moves to Bloomington, Indiana
1982	Doctorate in Latin American Literature from the University of Indiana. Moves to Massachusetts and begins teaching in the Spanish department at Wellesley College
January 10, 1988	Son, Joseph, is born
July 25, 1993	Daughter, Sonia, is born
1995	Named full professor at Wellesley College. Wins Letras de Oro Prize with book, *Noche Estrellada* (North/South Center, University of Miami) and Latino Literature Prize for *Towards the Splendid City* (Bilingual Review Press)
1996	Publishes *A Cross and a Star: Memoirs of a Jewish Girl in Chile* (University of New Mexico and Feminist Press) about her mother's life in southern Chile

1997	Reissue of *Dear Anne Frank* (University Press of New England)
1998	Publishes *Always from Somewhere Else: A Memoir of My Chilean Jewish Father* (The Feminist Press). Chosen by *Scholastic Magazine* as outstanding Latina leader

I've been told the story of my own journey to Chile so many times that I no longer know whether it really happened or whether I invented it all myself.

My genealogy includes many generations of travelers. My paternal grandparents, Abraham and Rachel Yagosinsky, fled the pogroms of Czar Nicholas II, crossed the Carpathian Mountains, and arrived on foot in the city of Istanbul. They continued on foot all the way to the port of Marseilles. There they changed their name to Agosín and embarked for Chile, a destination that must have seemed at the world's end. They settled in Quillota in the Central Valley of Chile in 1922. My father, Moisés, born in Marseilles, was an infant when he arrived in Latin America.

My maternal grandfather, Joseph Halpern, left Vienna in the 1920s at his mother's urging; he had become involved with a Viennese cabaret singer not to the family's taste. He chose Chile as his new home, where he was joined by my great-grandmother Helena in 1939. (Certain that she would return to her home in Austria once the Nazis departed, she carefully locked her house, and left the key for safekeeping with the Viennese police!) Grandfather Joseph Halpern met and married my Argentine-born grandmother Josephina, herself the child of Russian Jews from Sebastopol. My mother, Frida, was born to Joseph and Josephina Halpern in Tacna, Peru in 1929.

My mother met my father at a family gathering in Valparaíso when they were teenagers (my father was the first cousin of my grandmother Josephina) and they were married in 1948. In 1951, they moved to Bethesda, Maryland, for three years, where my father, training to be a biochemist, studied at the National Institutes of Health. My sister, Cynthia, was born in Bethesda in 1952; I was born there three years later. My family returned to Chile three months after my birth. My sister and I thus hold dual citizenship, an emblem of our bifurcated identities.

When my mother was expecting me, her English was precarious, and she decided to call me Marjorie because she was a devoted fan of Herman Wouk's novel *Marjorie Morningstar* and of the television series "My Little Margie." My second name follows the Jewish tradition of naming children for deceased family members: I was named after my aunt Stella Broder, murdered in Auschwitz. Thus my name is Marjorie Stella; had I been born a few months later, it might well have been Margarita Estrella.

The story of my naming is amusing, but names matter, and mine has been a

---

4

source of real irritation over the years. Chileans did not know how to pronounce "Marjorie," and often I wished I were "Margarita" instead. Twenty years later, in the United States, "Marjorie" was no longer a problem, but "Agosín" became one: every time I go through an airport, offer a passport, pass through customs, someone comments on my foreign last name. When I apply for grants, I become a minority (Hispanic—a category thrown out of kilter as soon as someone realizes that I am a Jew). The dual citizenship that marked my birth, complicated by my religious identity, has made me an uncertain traveler, a person obsessed with questions of personal identity. I am convinced I became a poet and storyteller in order to participate in inventing my history and, in so doing, to invent myself.

My childhood was that of many girls growing up in Latin America in the middle of the twentieth century. My life in Santiago de Chile was, for the most part, a happy one. I lived amidst an extended family of grandparents, great-grandparents, generous and eccentric uncles, and loving aunts. There were many nannies, women of Amerindian descent, whose clothing always smelled of smoke from the kitchen fires. The most beloved of these women, Delfina Nahuenhual, was an Araucanian Indian of noble descent, whose family owned vast tracts of land. Yet she spent her life in service to white people, cooking and serving food at my family gatherings. At these gatherings, my European-born relations regaled us with their tales of harrowing escapes from Russia and Central Europe, of arrivals on the Valparaíso shore, of treks on muleback across the Andes between Argentina and Chile. These stories, though glorious and thrilling, were weighted with unanswered questions. What did it mean to travel on women's trains? Why didn't my mother's aunts come back, and if they did come back, why were they so changed?

These strange gaps in my family history lent both mystery and tension to these largely joyful occasions. As an adolescent, I was haunted by a familial past that remained unresolved and unsettled. I felt I never had the full story, or the story quite right. And in the absence of what then seemed a coherent past, how could I know who I was? In Chile, my sister and I were U.S. citizens who spoke no English, while my grandparents, who spoke Spanish, were called "gringos." (All foreigners were "gringos" in Chile and all Jews were considered Arabs, Turks, or Russians.) We felt like outsiders, but this feeling had reality only within our family circle. There was no national debate about people like us, people who didn't fit. It was not until we returned to the United States that I began to feel like a complete "immigrant."

In 1971, when I was sixteen, my family moved to Athens, Georgia, where my father had been appointed professor of biochemistry at the University of Georgia. We did not cross the Andes on foot this time, but flew on a Canadian Pacific plane to Savannah. We knew no English, and had no notion of the culture of the American South. We had left behind all the grandparents, nannies, and

Sunday gatherings of our brightly-colored Latin America—a place where I had fallen in love with the Spanish language and with poetry. In North America, I had to invent myself all over again in order to survive. I clung desperately to my memories even as I struggled to reinvent myself in this strange, new environment. In North America, I was a blond Jewish Latina who spoke Spanish and liked to dance *merengues*. But having to explain myself, to repeat the story of our emigration, was like having an open wound.

In the United States, being a foreigner marked me like a deep scar. The rules had changed, yet I remained an outsider. In Chile, I was different because of my fair skin. In North America, I resembled other blond Americans, but my language, Spanish, and my thick accent set me apart. For many, many months, I had no voice. I slowly learned to speak, and to be, in a new language, but yearned for conversations in Spanish. If I could have recreated something from Chile then and there, I would have chosen the conversations of women street sweepers, gossipy exchanges with neighbors, chatter with my father when he had finished playing the piano, or talks with my mother just after sunset, as she rubbed me dry after a bath. Conversations imply confidence, trust, and intimacy. They open avenues of exploration and tap fountains of feeling.

Uncertain Travelers is a book of conversations with women like myself—educated Jewish women with complex itineraries who have traveled much and landed at last in the United States in the second half of the twentieth century. They have come from different places and for different reasons. Latin American travelers like Matilde Salganicoff, Renata Brailovsky, Silvia Testa, Ruth Behar, and me left our homelands to escape political turmoil or to pursue economic opportunities in the United States. Travelers of European birth like Zezette Larson, Elena Nightingale, Susan Bendor, Susan Suleiman, and Katherine Wenger either fled Europe just prior to World War II, or, having survived the war in hiding, or in concentration camps, immigrated to the United States once the war had ended. Some came as children, others as adults; some arrived well-off, others as veritable refugees. Each interview necessarily reflects the very personal response of the traveler to her own distinct set of experiences. But what I found most amazing as I grew to know these women was that despite such profound differences, we all shared something greater: the experience of exile and the quality of being foreign.

In recent years, writing about immigrants and immigration has been spurred by new waves of Hispanic, Asian, and African refugees, people fleeing political or economic instability in their homelands and, like the uncertain travelers of a century ago, hoping for a better life in the United States. Sociologists discuss the processes of acculturation and assimilation; politicians worry about whether these new immigrants are good or bad for the economy. Scholars in many fields now acknowledge the importance of memory to survivors of personal or historical trauma, and investigate its role in tying the past to the present. This book contributes to this growing literature in a very specific way. By allowing its travelers to speak for themselves, and by retaining many of the silences, ellipses, and repetitions of the conversations, *Uncertain Travelers* offers the reader the *experience* of remembering. Itineraries, which open each chapter, convey the subjectivity of individual memory: no two itineraries are exactly alike. The chapters themselves, arranged chronologically, with the older women speaking first, also provide a multigenerational history lesson. Here is a collective reminder of how history and chance have conspired to make the twentieth century a century of displacement, diaspora, and loss for millions of people.

Years ago, during a snowy winter in Rochester, New York, at a middle school where I was speaking, a Cuban child came over to me and in her melodious Caribbean accent said, "You know, I can tell you my story. I traveled on a raft with my parents. The sharks chased us. My newborn brother died while we were crossing." Then she paused, and asked me, "How are books made?" This book, created to answer this child, was made as a guide to our personal and collective past. I hope you enjoy the journey.

ZEZETTE LARSEN

February 21, 1929	Clemence Zezette van der Sluis born in Brussels, Belgium
1929–1943	In Brussels, and a couple of years in France. In Brussels, near maternal grandparents
1941	Brother, Marcel, is sent to hide in a Trappist monastery in another part of Belgium
1942	Zezette hides, with the help of the Belgian underground, in a Catholic convent and boarding school in Overies, Belgium, under the pseudonym Marguerite Michaels
1943	Returns home to see parents who were in hiding. She and parents are captured and deported to Auschwitz-Birkenau
1943–1945	Auschwitz-Birkenau
Spring 1945	Escapes from death march (Birkenau to Ravensbruck) near Leipzig, Germany
May–July 1945	Hospitalized in U.S. military hospital near Leipzig
1945–1950	Lives in Amsterdam, Holland, with uncle's family, which she visited before the war, and studies social work at University of Rotterdam
1951	Moves to New York City and works at Macy's; marries Sven Larsen
1954	Moves to New Jersey and becomes social worker, then supervisor, in child care agency (foster care and adoption)
1956	Marriage to Sven Larsen ends
1958	Receives master's degree in social work from Rutgers University
1968	Moves to Israel
1970	Moves to Newton, Massachusetts, and works for Combined Jewish Philanthropies. Becomes executive director of Jewish Community Housing for the Elderly
1981–1992	CEO of Barkan Management Co., Boston, Massachusetts
1976–1998	Active involvement with Facing History and Ourselves (board member and recipient of Humanitarian Award)
1992	Marries Stephen Black

When Hitler's armies invaded Belgium on May 10, 1940, the Belgian government declared martial law. A nationwide "black-out" occurred. Industries shut down and immediately shipped goods and workers to France as a means of avoiding future service to the Nazis. When the Nazis arrived in Brussels on May 17 it was deserted; bridges and public transportation were sabotaged and abandoned, canals were blocked by barges purposely sunk, and the city lacked power and water. The Belgians, though in flight, had nonetheless made their defiance clear.

Belgian refugees flooded the cities of southern France. As a result, the population of Toulouse grew from 150,000 to 700,000 in under a year. The French government initially issued a ration of ten francs per day to the refugees, charged to the Belgian national trust, which was just sufficient to keep a person alive. Many refugees, facing starvation in France, returned to occupied Belgium. There the Nazis diffused Belgian resistance by favoring the Flemish-speaking Belgians and pitting them against Belgians who spoke French.

The occupation was a serious threat to Belgian Jews and to Jews who had sought asylum there. The Nazis instituted anti-Jewish legislation in the fall of 1940. The first Jews were deported to Auschwitz-Birkenau, concentration camps located in Poland, in August 1942; deportation then continued regularly through 1944. Zezette Larsen and her family were deported from Brussels to Auschwitz-Birkenau in the spring of 1943.

I first met Zezette Larsen in the spring of 1993 in Boston. The occasion was a meeting of Facing History and Ourselves, a national educational organization whose mission is to develop programs that examine racism, anti-Semitism, and violence in order to promote a more humane citizenry. Zezette has often volunteered her service to this organization. At that gathering, Zezette came over to me and said, "You and I have a great deal to talk about." I liked her eyes, very green and deep. She seemed a blend of fragility and strength; her smile conveyed a profound sadness that she carried deep within her, like a scar. After dinner, Zezette asked me to read some of my poems about Anne Frank, who had been a friend of hers in Amsterdam. I began timidly, fearfully, not only because I was in the presence of Zezette, but because I was reading to people who would truly honor Anne Frank's life. When I finished reading, Zezette wept, and the room fell silent for more than ten minutes. After that Zezette began, for the first time in over forty years, to remember her terrifying wartime experiences.

I persuaded Zezette to let me interview her. She began telling me her story in the spring of 1996, a year in which Easter and Passover coincided. Zezette does not like either holiday because they remind her of Easter 1943. That year she returned to Brussels from her hiding place in a convent outside the city; it was then that she and her family were captured and deported to Auschwitz-Birkenau.

Our conversation took place on a sunny and clear spring morning on the Wellesley College campus, near Lake Waban. Students strolled past the lake, confident in their youth and privilege, secure in what lay ahead of them. Seated next to me, Zezette turned to the past, her eyes clouding over like a storm, contradicting the peacefulness of our surroundings.

Zezette: I will tell you when I was born. I was born in Brussels, in Belgium, in February of 1929. I lived my very early years in Brussels. We moved for a couple of years to France. My mother was French, my father was Dutch. Then they went back to Brussels where we lived until 1943.

Marjorie: What was your name when you were born?

Zezette: My name was actually Zezette. That's a name that is not common. I have another first name, actually it's a second name, Clemence. It's a name that . . . both my names are pretty difficult for English-speaking people to pronounce. It was changed during the war and I am sure we will discuss that a little later. My first name is Zezette, which I use and is mispronounced continuously. But that's one of those things.

Marjorie: Did you have a Yiddish name or Hebrew name?

Zezette: No. I did not. I came from an absolutely nonreligious family.

Marjorie: Can you talk about your parents back then? Your mother was French . . .

Zezette: That's correct.

Marjorie: And she was . . . can you give me some information about her? Where was she born and how did she come to marry your father and settle in Belgium?

Zezette: My father was Dutch. I am not sure I recall how she met my father. I am sure it was in a very wonderful way. They were both very warm, very caring and protective parents. She was born, as I said, in France. At one point her parents moved to Belgium. My father's business was in Belgium. They met and married. There is a tendency, I am sure, to idealize what you don't have anymore, but I think that I am saying it with a great deal of conviction. They were very loving and caring. They were overprotective and maybe rightfully so, because I am talking about the beginning of the war and they are trying not to involve me in some of the torture. They must have suffered knowing what was going on, but I was a young child and so maybe it was a natural reaction which I now label as being overprotective. It was no more than a natural kind of reaction for any parent. My father had a great sense of humor, so did my mother. I think that carries through still in the family. A love for life. I remember my mother loved to sing. I have inherited that from her, except for the fact that she could sing and I cannot. But I love to sing. I love music. And my father was just a nice person. I think that the eleven years they gave me, and I am saying that with lots of conviction too, because I have done a lot of thinking about it, must have been very, very good, because it gave me a great deal of strength and left me, even though there were some very hard years, I think they left me as a caring person. I do believe that I am not imagining this. It is real.

Marjorie: What do you think or feel when you remember your parents?

Zezette: Sadness. What really comes to mind is sadness for my family, who is no more. I would have liked to have the kind of youth where I could have enjoyed my parents . . . I wish I could have chosen to come to this country rather than being pushed to this country. I miss my family. To me, that's what I understand as nostalgia, but I need to think. I think nostalgia is, is all the things that could have been. When you have suffered losses, I think that it is very easy to idealize, and to lose perspective and fantasize as to what could have been and maybe that . . . that is happening to me too. I am sure it has happened. I think, nostalgia is having had to become sixty-five years old before I really truly felt happiness. And so I am nostalgic for the . . . all the years that have passed and will not come anymore.

Marjorie: Did you have any siblings?

Zezette: Yes. I have a brother. My brother is still alive. My brother was not in a concentration camp. He has a long story all by itself. He is older. He was not at home when we were picked up in 1943. I adore my brother. Up to this day . . . You are touching upon a hard subject. I think that Marcel—his name is Marcel—suffers so much of the guilt of the survivors. He and I have never, never, ever talked about the past, about our parents. It is just probably during the past two or three years as I have been able to talk more, that he is able to refer to it. When he talks about our parents, he talks about "your" parents, which is so significant. He cannot and will not talk to me about the war years.

Marjorie: Could you tell me a little about your father?

Zezette: His name was Henri. He was born in Holland and he was in the textile business. He was a salesman and had to travel quite a bit, but distances are not far in Europe. Most of his business was between Holland and Belgium. So there might have been some evenings when he did not come home, when he was in Holland, but most of the time he was home. I think he was a relatively successful salesman. We certainly never wanted for anything and lived in reasonable comfort. I am not sure I am answering your question. As I am thinking I lost your question. I'm sorry.

Marjorie: Had your grandparents lived in Holland and their ancestors before them?

Zezette: Yes. His parents, my grandparents on my father's side, yes, they were Dutch. I have no knowledge or recollection of where their parents were born. I don't remember.

Marjorie: Now, tell me about your mother. What was her name?

Zezette: Esther de Roos. She was from France.

Marjorie: Was she a Sephardic Jew?[1] Do you know anything about that?

Zezette: Yes, yes they were. But again, not at all religious. Religious isn't the right word. We were definitely Sephardic Jews, but Jewish education, in the formal sense of the word, was not part of our lives.

Marjorie: Did you have a sabbath?

Zezette: No, we did not.

Marjorie: Did you celebrate any Jewish holidays?

Zezette: To a minimal degree.

Marjorie: So you would say that you were assimilated into the life of Brussels?

Zezette: Absolutely. Yes, completely. I certainly knew that I was Jewish, but being Jewish did not necessarily mean going to temple. It was a way of life and a conviction, but not being part of the congregation.

Marjorie: So you went to public school?

Zezette: I did. Again, I am trying to give you an answer that makes more sense. We knew we were Jewish because everybody knew their religion. But we had no connections at all with any synagogue.

Marjorie: Do you remember any of your childhood friends? Did you keep in touch with them after the war?

Zezette: There was this one girl, a former friend of mine ... still a friend of mine, from before the war. Her name is Magda. She is now a grandmother. Two years ago, at the fiftieth anniversary of the end of the war, she decided to search for us.

Marjorie: Was she Jewish?

Zezette: No. She decided to search for us. It took her two years to find us. She found my brother and wrote him a long letter. She called him. Actually, she was his girlfriend, long ago in Belgium. Not a real girlfriend . . . we were all so young. I was the kid . . . the little sister who was taking little notes from Magda to my brother and from my brother to Magda. I was not supposed to tell my parents and that kind of stuff. She found him. My brother, who seldom writes to me, wrote me a letter saying, "You can't believe who I heard from." That was just two weeks before we went to Europe, so I picked up the phone and called her.

Marjorie: Magda?

Zezette: Yes. She was very happy that I was coming to Europe and we had lunch together. It was a very, very nice experience, but it was also very strange because this was somebody I hadn't seen in fifty years. First of all, how can you ever catch up? Secondly, suddenly you look at your childhood girlfriend and she is now an older woman . . .

Marjorie: Did you see yourself as her age?

Zezette: No. I did not want to. No. I was still a little kid. She was the older person. I regret we did not have enough time together because she knew stories about me from before the war that I did not remember at all. I will see her again when we go to Europe next. I definitely . . . she wants me to come and stay at her house.

Marjorie: Will you?

Zezette: Yes, yes, I will. She wants to meet my husband, Steve, of course. I said to her, "Magda, why now? Why after all these years?" And she said to me "You know, there is the fiftieth anniversary and somehow it gave me the freedom to think about it and to start looking for you."

Marjorie: Tell me more about your family.

Zezette: Lien was my father's sister. She lived in Holland with her husband, David, a banker. They never had kids and were definitely richer than we were. They were my rich aunt and uncle. They were very kind, very musical—at least my uncle was very musical. They were the people that I always stayed with when I went on school vacation in Holland. It was a real treat because they spoiled me and I loved it. They both were fun people to be with. You know how kids can look at adults and think they are boring, in most cases, you know, adults are very boring, but they were not boring and I did not see them as boring. I saw them as fun people and always loved going to Amsterdam to them. She was one of the first women in Holland, I have a picture of her, to drive a car. One of those big convertible cars, you know, you used to have to step up to get into the car. She was open and fun and a very good sport. She was caught and taken to Bergen-Belsen with my uncle. I don't recall which year, but Steve may know because he looked at the papers when we were in Bergen-Belsen. She came back, but he died there. I think I told you she came back to my uncle, who was my father's brother.

Marjorie: Was your father's brother deported?

Zezette: No, he was in hiding. He was lucky. He was hidden in the northern part of Holland. After the war my aunt, who was pretty sick, went to live with my uncle. She was bedridden. I was not bedridden. I had been in the hospital for so long, I was perfectly capable of walking and doing things, but she was not. Her legs were very much affected. She was in bed for a long, long time. One of the things I remember was she had a picture of my father in her room. Everybody who came into the room would turn the picture around. They did not want to talk about him. But she, I think . . . we never talked about our experiences . . . but she knew I knew and I knew that she knew, which made a big difference. Therefore, the closeness that we had before the war was only fortified. I have never called anybody mother or father after that. I could never have called her mother, but I loved her like a mother.

After she was able to move out from my uncle's house and I moved to the United States, she was always the person . . . and I went back to Europe just about every year, she was always the person that I went back to. She was my medication, she is the person that I corresponded with. She was very close to me and she then moved into a housing for the elderly—a condominium for elderly people, a very beautiful one, in Holland, in the country—and it was a beautiful apartment. She was getting old and she still had beautiful things that had been hidden during the war. You know, before dinner we had a little glass of port or sherry, very elegant, and when she was getting older she still did these things, and I would look at the glasses and I could see that she had washed them but couldn't see that there was still spotting. Anyway, she was a great lady until the day she died. She was a great lady. I have a very nice picture of her. There is a picture of us in the living room, that's not a good picture. I have a beautiful picture of her. I don't know where I got it from, from before the war—no, not before the war, but when she was better, after the war. So she died in . . . I did not go back to the funeral. It was much too painful. Another good-bye, you know, I just could not do it. I think . . . I am sorry about that, but that's the way it was. She died and had a tough life. She had a wonderful life before the war, but a very tough life afterwards. I think it's quite different after you come out of a camp and you were a kid when you went in and you come out and you still are a kid, but something inside you has died.

Marjorie: How did you meet Anne Frank?

Zezette: We met in Amsterdam. She was the daughter of a business acquaintance of my father and uncle. I think to me she represents youth. Her name could be anything. Because she was so special . . . because she wrote . . . she was able to put things on paper, she left a legacy that nobody else did. But as a human being, she was no different than some of my other friends.

Marjorie: Do you remember things about her that were special or different?

Zezette: I just remember having fun! Laughing. You know, when you are at that age, I mean . . .

Marjorie: Yes. What do you remember? Was it reassuring seeing someone who reminded you of the fact that you were once a "normal teenager"?

Zezette: I think so. I have, you know, had this real block from the moment I went into the camp. I never really think much about what happened before that, when I was a "normal" teenager, playing in the streets and living with my parents and going to school.

When I was with my cousin in Brussels this year . . . He is seven years older than I. He was in England during the war. He is a real family buff. He knows a lot of history. He kept telling me things and I kept on saying, "I don't remember! I don't remember!"

Marjorie: He remembers?

Zezette: A lot of things. Finally he looked me in the eye and he looked a little mad. He said, "What is the matter? You don't remember anything?" And I started to cry, just like that, and I said to him, "Don't you understand that I went through a trauma, a very big trauma? So no, I don't remember." That block . . . that's where my life started and ended.

Marjorie: Has your cousin ever gone to Auschwitz?

Zezette: No, no he has not. He would like to. I think he wants to witness it. I think people go back for different reasons. For him, I think it's trying to pull the pieces together. That was the first time. I heard, when I was in Brussels last week, that he recently went to Dachau. So there is a search going on, in his mind, trying to understand what happened . . . that fact that one never understands, but that's another story. I think that it's important for him to understand where he came from.

Auschwitz, though, I feel is my responsibility. As soon as I have enough financial freedom to do it, I am going to do it. I would like to . . . I really would like to take him . . . I don't want him to pay for it.

Zezette Larsen

Marjorie: What are some of your childhood memories?

Zezette: First of all, I had a big brother—I have a big brother—who was a pain in the neck and took a tremendous amount of enjoyment in teasing me. I think that one of the things I remember very clearly is that I very much served as a conduit for him. When he liked one of my girlfriends and he wanted to make some contact with them, then of course I was the best sister ever. Otherwise, if I had to take medicine at a certain time of the day and my mother might forget it, suddenly I would forget it consciously. He was always the one reminding my mother that it was time for me to take my medicine. That's something I still remember very, very clearly. The reason I mention to you the very affectionate woman my mother was, and this may have to do with the pain of separation, and that may be the reason why I remember this so clearly, is that there was a ritual that took place every single day. We lived on the second floor of an apartment building and I remember very, very clearly that my mother had to say good-bye at least ten times and then had to hang out of the window and wave and see that I was, you know, down the street walking. It was very reciprocal from my part because I can still, in my mind, see myself turn around and wave at her. That was a ritual. It was something that was like getting up every morning. She was an exceptionally warm person, and so was my father.

Marjorie: Was your mother an educated woman?

Zezette: I don't know exactly how far her education went, but I do remember very clearly that my mother was involved in a number of activities while we were in school. She was always home when we came home, but she was involved in a number of activities. My father was politically very curious. He was not active, but very curious, very involved, at least mentally. And I remember many, many conversations at home that were on subjects that were way beyond anything I was interested in. As a matter of fact, I found them very, very boring in retrospect. I know they were political conversations or philosophical ones. So, yes, I think they were both intellectually curious and reading was very much part of my family. My family life . . . I can remember loads of newspapers and books around the house. That's the picture that I have. They were inquisitive people. They were also people who took education very seriously. They were both very helpful in doing homework or whatever we were involved in.

Marjorie: Did you have any aunts or uncles or other extended family living nearby?

Zezette: Yes. In Brussels I had several aunts. I had one aunt and then several other people that I called "aunt" as all kids do. My father's family was mostly in Holland. He had two sisters and one brother. I had cousins. There were forty-nine people within my . . . not immediate but . . .

Marjorie: Aunts, uncles?

Zezette: That's right. Who just never came back.

Marjorie: None of the relatives in Holland survived?

Zezette: Yes, yes, yes. My family in Holland, my father's family, his brother and one of his sisters were hidden during the war in the northern part of Holland. That's a long story which we can touch upon whenever you wish. One of his sisters went to Bergen-Belsen with her husband. Her husband died there and she came out very sick. She was a wonderful lady, one I was very close to. She died about ten years ago.

Marjorie: You spoke French at home?

Zezette: French and we also tried to speak some Dutch. But our common language was French.

Marjorie: You were a young girl when the situation started deteriorating. What do you remember happening at school or with friends?

Zezette: I think this is where I probably . . . I said that my parents were overprotective. At the same time, I said their behavior was really no more than any other parent would do. I was very, very conscious of their listening to the BBC [British Broadcasting Corporation], trying to be sure that we, the kids, were not listening. My brother, of course, shared and tried to explain to me certain things that he understood. But basically, in 1940, when the Germans invaded Belgium, I was so young that the whole thing . . . I knew it was frightening. I knew there was a lot of pain at home. I knew that my parents were very troubled. Did I understand? No. I did not understand. We tried to leave in 1940. We left Brussels and started trying to leave the country. I am not sure . . . my recollection is not very clear on this, trying to move away from Belgium and Holland and walking towards the border with France. Did I really understand what was going on? No. I did not. I knew it was very, very frightening. I knew that the routine that kids get so used to and is so comfortable, was completely . . . what's the word I am trying to . . . was completely . . . yes, gone. And that there was terror. I was scared. I think that is the best way to say it. The events occurred so quickly, so quickly that I see the whole thing as being very frightening and realizing that we were all being dislocated and that I suddenly had a family and parents whose attention was focused not only on their children, but on many other things.

Marjorie: Did you continue going to school after the Germans invaded Belgium?

Zezette: I continued to go to school for a very short time. When the Jews were asked to start wearing the yellow stars is when things in my life started to change completely. This is the first time when I saw that no, I was not like the other kids. I was different. I was wearing a yellow star. I have a very clear memory of walking in Brussels with my father and wearing a star. There were German officers or soldiers coming down the same sidewalk as we were and my father was pushed off the sidewalk. It is very vivid in my mind and obviously it was quite traumatic. I have spoken about this on other occasions. It was shortly thereafter that a decision was made that we had to separate. My parents moved into another neighborhood in Brussels—I don't know if you want me to get into that at this point—and rented the lower level of a house in a suburb of Brussels. It was also the time that I was separated from them for the first time. It happened in a matter of moments, and I am not sure it is true, but that's my recollection. I was told that my name was not Zezette, but Claire, and my last name was not van der Sluis—by the way Larsen is my married name, because I have been married and divorced. Wait, I am sorry, I made a mistake. The first time my name was changed it was Marguerite Michaels.

Marjorie: Van der Sluis, is that a recognizable Jewish name?

Zezette: Probably, yes. But I was told my name was Marguerite Michaels. I was going to a Catholic convent, a boarding school, outside of Brussels, and I was told to simply do exactly what the other kids did and to be quiet, not to talk about my parents.

Marjorie: Who told you this? Was it your parents?

Zezette: My parents, yes. And that was a very quick separation.

Marjorie: What year was this?

Zezette: It was the end of 1941 or beginning of 1942. My brother was sent to another part of Belgium, a Trappist monastery. I was brought to the Catholic convent by some friends who were not Jewish and was registered as Marguerite Michaels. I lived there until 1943. Doing what? One of the things I remember is the separation from my parents and the entrance into a world that was absolutely, completely foreign to me . . . it's so vivid. I arrived there late afternoon and, at one point, heard a bell being rung throughout the convent. It was a boarding school, a Catholic boarding school. So all the kids were lining up on two sides of the corridor and putting a veil on their heads—which I did, as I had been told to do—and we went into the chapel. Prayers were every afternoon and every morning. I was very conscious of kneeling when the others did, getting up when they got up, and moving my lips although I did not know what they were saying. I had absolutely no idea what they were saying. I think then the trauma of that particular day, again, is what makes the memory so vivid in my mind. In any case, I became Marguerite Michaels.

I was an isolated kid. I did not do much talking. Although I had been . . . I had had a good childhood and so I had a lot of joie de vivre, however it was sort of . . . it disappeared pretty quickly, being in this environment. I went to confession and had nobody to talk to. I did not know what was going on. I did not know what was happening to my parents or my brother. And I, in many ways as I think about it, I think that in many ways it was a beginning, the beginning for me of a sort of . . . [laughs]. I think it was the beginning of my becoming a robot. I was doing what I was supposed to do. That is why I don't like people telling me what to do. That's a good reason . . . I should use it sometime. But it was really . . . I had to do it and I was doing it.

I don't recall exactly if it was three months after I entered the boarding school or five months, or six months. I spilled my story out to one of the priests. I just had to share . . . I think really what was behind it, as I look at it now as an adult, was I have to tell somebody the truth because if I tell someone the truth then maybe they will tell me where my family is. The result of my telling this priest was very simply that I was baptized. I guess that was their way of making me "legitimate." I had been taking communion every day because everybody else did and thus I had to be made legitimate. And so I was baptized Catholic. There was a sort of small ceremony that took place where a few sisters were present and this particular priest.

And my life did not change. I did not learn where my parents were. I just became legitimate in their eyes. To me, the interesting thing was that there was this group of people who knew that I was Jewish and hiding in a convent and they really put their lives at risk having me there. That is something that is to be remembered. It could have turned out to be a very, very different situation. I did not realize it then, but I do today. In 1943, the people who had brought me to the convent, friends of my parents, came to see me. And I begged them to let me go see my parents. They told me about my parents, but it was all so strange and unfamiliar to me and I needed to see them. So I went home on Easter of 1943. I went back to Brussels and I went to see my parents. [Pause.]

I am smiling now because I remember it as such a wonderful reunion. I knew that I had to go back. I was so young, I did not understand what was going on. I only suffered the trauma. I mean, even today I don't understand it fully. So it's hard to . . . Easter Sunday, my father decided that we should go fishing, the three of us. We left at dawn before first light. The three of us spent a wonderful day fishing and I remember this very vividly too. We came back when it was dark, but we were followed. That night the knocking . . . [long pause.] That night the knock came and we were picked up. We had been followed and picked up. Again, I remember that knock very clearly.

Marjorie: Why were you followed? Did you have a yellow star on?

Zezette: No. We did not have our yellow stars on. I think that we were . . . what is the English word . . . We were "denounced."

Marjorie: Someone knew that you were Jewish?

Zezette: That's right. And that my parents probably had been . . . it was just a co-incidence that I was home. Had I not been home, they would have been picked up. They also did not go out very much. They only went out very, very seldom, if at all. The word is not really "denounced." I think "betrayed" is more appropriate.

Marjorie: And is that why they moved from their apartment to a different part of town, so that people would be less likely to know who they were?

Zezette: No. They went into hiding when they were called to report to Malines.[2] I don't know if you ever heard of Malines, but it was a holding camp for Jews before they were sent further, mostly to Auschwitz and Dachau. So they were registered as Jews and went into hiding. Maybe I missed that sequence as I was telling you. When they were called, they were wearing a star. They went into hiding. I did not explain that properly. They went into hiding, I went to boarding school. My brother went to the Trappist monastery. The day we went out fishing, I could not tell you for sure if we were wearing our stars or not. I probably would say we were not. And we were denounced. As I said before, the knock came and we . . . we were transferred to Malines. Luckily, my brother was not home. Luckily there was not evidence, apparently, of his address at my parents' home. Although the Germans did not search the whole apartment. The whole thing went so quickly. But there was no evidence of where he was.

Marjorie: They just pulled you out right then and there?

Zezette: That's right. Yeah. Again, it's a very vivid memory which mostly related to their pain, their tears, their complete sense of helplessness because they knew where they were going. I had no idea. But they knew. We stayed in Malines for four or five days . . . [weeping] I'm sorry.

Marjorie: How did you get to Maline? How were you transported?

Zezette: By bus, or camion . . . you know, a truck but you close one end of it. The days, the days in Malines . . . my parents could not protect me from other people's conversations, other people's tears, their own tears, their desperation. And so, although I did not understand what was going on, I was surrounded by suffering people. And so we went out and we went . . . [long pause, sobbing]. The week after Easter, 1943, we went out on the train . . . that was that. There is a lot of literature about those trains and things that happened on those trains. My memory is that suddenly my parents had become two very, very old people. Your parents seem old anyway. But they were very old people now. The memories are of the stench. Again, screaming. My mother putting a spoon through the bars to collect rain so she could give me water. Also, where she had gotten it, I have absolutely no idea, but we had cans of condensed milk, the rich heavy stuff, and she fed me condensed milk constantly. I guess, hoping to . . . I don't know. I am sure you know as well as I do.

Marjorie: Do you have any idea how long you were on the train?

Zezette: Days. Days. And then we arrived at Birkenau. As you know, I have gone back three times to Birkenau. I call it the end of the line and in many ways it was . . . it is. It certainly was for me. At that point I was holding on to my mother's arm for dear life and vice versa. In hindsight, it was probably the biggest mistake in the world. Although she . . . I have often thought of that. She would never have survived it. But the fact is that we were holding on to each other. They made her go to the right and I went to the left. My father went to the men's camp. She went straight to the crematorium. And I went into the camp. I have very vivid memories of inmates . . . I don't like to use the word inmates . . . prisoners, coming up to the train and looking like skeletons, walking around and trying to grab whatever we had. I said to you earlier, I had become somewhat of a robot, doing what I was supposed to do, talking very low. I think at that point I really became a robot. [Long pause.] Seeing . . . being pulled from my mother . . . [long pause] I have made it a practice . . . practice is not the right word . . . I don't talk about the years at Birkenau.

First of all, there is a lot, again, that has been written about it by people who are much more eloquent than I am. My vocabulary does not contain words that . . . my vocabulary does not contain words that describe those years. I don't think that . . . to be very honest, I don't even think that those words exist in the English language, or any language. I also don't think that that's the object of us talking together. I see the object as very different. The fact is, the reality was that because I was Jewish . . . because I was Jewish, my life was stopped.

My mother was thrown into the crematorium when we arrived. She never even went into the camp. She was shown to the showers, which were actually gas chambers. Two absolutely wonderful beings who were of the "wrong religion," whose life stopped because of the insanity of the regime. My father did go into the camp and I saw him once. I saw my father one time while in Birkenau. He gave his ration of potato peels to come to the women's camp and to be . . . to see me. We did not talk. [Long pause.] We did not talk and we both had shaved heads. We were both very thin, to say the least. But again, I remember us looking at each other. That was the last time I saw him. The suspicion . . . suspicion is not the word . . . my assumption is that my father died in the death march when we were evacuated.[3]

Marjorie: You went in 1943, so you saw him . . .

Zezette: Sometime in 1944. I have to tell you that I think this interview will be of value for younger people. I think that one has to find reasons or has to . . . the absolute lack of knowledge about his death or where he died is so hard to bear, that . . . I am telling you he died on the death march. I have no idea. But for me it makes more sense to think that that's when it happened, rather than not to know. I came back in July of 1945, came back to Belgium. I spent three months in a hospital in Leipzig. Actually, what happened is that from Auschwitz we marched to other camps.

Marjorie: You marched?

Zezette: Yes. I marched.

Marjorie: What time of the year was this?

Zezette: Spring.

Marjorie: Spring of 1945?

Zezette: That's correct. Early spring. You are asking me a question that is hard for me to answer because there were no calendars.

Marjorie: The weather was getting warmer?

Zezette: Correct. That's the basis for my answer. On one of the marches, the last march . . .

Marjorie: The last march from . . . ? The first march was Birkenau-Auschwitz to Ravensbruck?

Zezette: That's correct. The last march . . . at one point . . . I just sat down and I knew I could not move anymore. I was a pretty sick kid by that point . . . and it did not matter or not that I even think about the consequences of staying there. I was going to die . . . I was going to die. I never thought . . . it was beyond . . . I was much beyond that stage. The march went on. There were very few SS around us at that point. There was just a relatively small group of . . . It's so hard for me to say "people" because they were skeletons. They were such pitiful bodies who continued to march. I did not. And after a while, I got myself up and started walking in the direction opposite to the one we were walking in. I walked for a while and I fell right into the arms of two American soldiers. That's how close we were. That's something that's as clear to me as two and two are four. And then I don't remember. For three months I was in a hospital in Leipzig. I was transported back by the Red Cross to Belgium.

Marjorie: In 1943 you were thirteen or fourteen, right?

Zezette: That's correct.

Marjorie: That's a very young age.

Zezette: Yes.

Marjorie: Why do you think you were considered to be an adult?[4] Were you tall for you age? Did you look mature?

Zezette: No. I mean, not unusually so. It's hard for me to say. It's hard to answer that question. How do you come back, you know? What happened that you came back? I don't know the answer to that.

Marjorie: What happened when you returned from Auschwitz and Birkenau?

Zezette: I don't know the answer. In my better days, in my better mood days, I would tell you that it was pure luck. Pure luck, coincidence, pure whatever. Yes, I was one of the youngest ones. I don't think that I looked more mature than anyone else, but honestly, I cannot give you an answer. I have never heard anybody, nor do I know anybody . . . yes, I do know a cousin who is still alive . . .

Marjorie: Was there anyone who took care of you while you were in Auschwitz or Birkenau?

Zezette: I think that the emotional shock, the environment, the people who walked around there, the continuous noise and stench were such that I didn't take care of anybody and no one took care of me. I don't think that is unusual, it just . . . I've been asked, "Did you try to survive?" Maybe the answer is yes, but certainly not consciously. I am not aware of it. I don't remember. That's my honest answer. Oh, yes, I tried to find roots and potatoes in the fields that we walked through. I tried to find anything that could provide nourishment. My mouth, by then, and that's a very vivid memory, was in such deplorable state that I could not chew anymore. All I could think of, literally, was putting one foot in front of the other.

Marjorie: There was no attempt to care for each other in Auschwitz or Birkenau?

Zezette: My youth, I think, is what really gave me strength. I don't like being one to say that no one tried to help the others. Sure, there were people trying to help. Very clearly when we had to stand in the main square of the camp, there was a concerted effort by other prisoners to make sure that everybody who was in the barracks got out of the barracks, because you knew that if somebody did not stand up that would be their end. So yes, there was support in helping people stand up on their feet and go out, but there were not lasting attachments or connections. It was all in passing. I would never want to give the impression that people did not try to be human to other people, but there was no connection, no. Maybe that was an unconscious way of protecting one's self because there had been so many losses. Why should anybody get attached to anybody else? I don't know. It's all hindsight at this point.

Marjorie: What have your thoughts been about the separations in your life? What were the lessons learned there?

Zezette: I think . . . I have done a lot of thinking about it. The early separation, the first one being when we were called in and I went to the boarding school. The second separation was at the railroad. This was so traumatic that my defense mechanism was to stop feeling. It's just as simple as that. Also, as difficult as that. I am so involved with young people, and so deeply committed in the fight against stereotyping, to try to look at people as people and to learn the right lessons from our history as it relates to all people and not to become desperate in watching what's going around in the world, and become desperate because, in many ways, we have not learned at all, not at all. I have to really convince myself and try to do my own thing, in my own circle, and do as much as I can as an individual to find some peace. To bring it back to what we were talking about, I am . . . communication and explanation and being explicit with people and frankness are important to me now, because I have suffered so much from the consequences of not being told, not knowing, living in the dark. Being open and frank with people, with young people, is so much healthier as far as the future is concerned.

Marjorie: Did you have to work in Auschwitz or Birkenau?

Zezette: For a while I worked—some of it I will touch upon, some of it I won't. I worked in the kitchen, peeling potatoes. I also, for what seems an eternity, moved stones from one spot to another, and then from that spot back to the other spot. For a long, long time. I also worked in a factory for a short time— ammunition. And that's about as far as . . . it's not relevant at this point. I'm not sure where I ended . . .

Marjorie: Did you have a sense that . . . were there rumors that the Americans were approaching or that the war was being lost by Germany?

Zezette: Yes. I do remember that. This brings up a point that is very impor- tant—my language barrier or handicap kept me much more distant than other people.

Marjorie: You did not encounter many Dutch people?

Zezette: Very few Dutch- and French-speaking people. When we evacuated Bir- kenau it was very, very clear that the soldiers, the SS, were desperate. This was quite obvious. There was great disorganization in their very organized life. Something unusual was going on for us to have to leave Auschwitz. We knew that the war was . . . at least that the Germans did not have the upper hand any- more. Was I—and I can only talk about myself—at that point conscious that maybe I was going to be liberated? No. I was too sick. I did not think that I would survive. [We stopped talking at this point. After a pause, I gently asked Zezette to talk more about her imprisonment in Auschwitz-Birkenau.] The humiliation of other human beings, the torture of other human beings, what is happening in Bosnia[5] or Rwanda,[6] this is all a continuation of what happened to me. For a very, very long time, I used to blame myself for not being more of an activist. You know, I felt, for instance, with the Russian Jews,[7] that I was sitting in my comfortable living room talking about how terrible it was, what was happening to the Russian Jews, but that I was really a faker because what I should have been doing was marching in Moscow. And that I had a responsibility that was much greater than the responsibility that I feel today. I know that I don't have the power to change the world. I know, very sadly, that hate and people destroying each other and themselves is something that will continue and continue. I think that—and maybe that's what is different between me and the Jews in Paris and other survivors—that the Holocaust is not a single, unique event, but that some form of holocaust is happening continuously, between people or countries, or people destroying themselves by behavior that is destructive. And it's just a very sad realization that I cannot take care of everything. I cannot. There is no utopia.

Marjorie: Do you think material objects, or our attachment to them, play a role in all this destruction?

Zezette: Yes, I think this is important. I say so to Steve, my husband, very often. I very often think about the fact that my parents could not leave Belgium when the Germans came. People were going to England or somewhere else and I think we could not leave for two reasons: First of all, it required a great amount of money, which my parents, as simple people, did not have. Also, I think, right or wrong, at least in my mind it was because my mother was very attached to her things . . . what little she had. And poor Steve gets into a lot of difficulty because I hate things, I don't want things. I don't want to be attached to . . . you know, I love our home, and I love our candlesticks, I'm just saying I love this, but I never want to be attached to things because I think that in the back of my mind I feel that it was because of those things that she could not leave and if she had been able to leave . . . for instance, I go downstairs, in my own home, and see that workroom with all those fixtures . . . if it was up to me, I could take half of what's in this house and get rid of it. When my aunt died, she had always said that whatever she had was for me, so, as I said to you before, I didn't go back to bury her because I just couldn't do it . . .

Marjorie: Tell me more about life in Belgium, the convent you were sent to. What do you remember about the nuns?

Zezette: There was one sister who, when you were in her class, if you looked her in the eye and if you took a button and kept turning the button, she would start to stutter. So we had a pact, between five or six kids, to look at her and start turning our buttons. It just threw her. We did that very often. And then the best one was, we were sleeping in dormitories. Each bed was separated with partitions that did not reach the ceilings, but gave you some sense of privacy. And, in that space, there was a bed and a night table. That was the extent of it. I remember that at least once a month we would take a cord and tie it to the first chamber pot in the room, under the bed, the first bed, and then to the second and third one and so on through the whole room. Then we would go to bed and wait. This was just a group of us, the bad kids. We waited until somebody had to go to the bathroom at night. Obviously when they tried to pull the chamber pot from under their bed, they would get a whole string of chamber pots coming at them and the sisters were very upset.

Marjorie: What else can you remember?

Zezette: I also recall waiting after going to bed . . . before going to bed we each had to say our prayers out loud so that the sister who was leading at the end of the dormitory could hear them, and then we went to bed. One of our greatest fun things was to wait and hear that the sisters would then pray and they would start getting undressed and it made a lot of noise because all of their skirts would make a lot of noise. We loved to wait until we knew they had taken most of their skirts off, or dresses, and then say, "Sister, could you come look at this?" And then you heard all those garments being put back on. Somehow, I remember this. I don't know why.

So, that was life, I am sure that was it. I mean I do know that there was tremendous fear in me. I think that the separation was a tremendous issue for me. It shadows my life still today. I don't like any type of separation. I don't like to say good-bye. I hate it. I never say good-bye. I never want to go places because I never want to leave places, it's too difficult. I think that separation is just a very big issue, the first one being the one where, you know, I was separated from my parents to go to the convent, but the main one being in Auschwitz, when I was separated from them forever. I know that is an issue, unfortunately, in our marriage, because I don't like being separated from Steve, although sometimes I like it very much, but in general, seriously, I don't like being separated from the people I love. I don't like to see you go. I hate to say good-bye to friends; it's very difficult for me. It's a reminder of things . . .

Marjorie: Have our conversations reminded you of many things?

Zezette: I think that in many ways I remember this because I read some notes yesterday . . . I am going to cry . . . but that's all right. Before the convent, it was just a close attachment to my parents. I am sure that many kids do that, girls especially. I remember our ritual good-bye very clearly. I don't like separations, and I am trying very hard not to . . . One of the consequences of being afraid to separate is being afraid to connect. That you can work on, obviously. I have worked on that and done a very good job at it. I certainly, you know, connect with people, but a strong connection, like I have with the Facing History staff, is something that has really taken . . . I mean, it's only because you were all so open to my pain that I have been able to do this, but otherwise, it's mostly . . . you know, I just go that far and I don't want to go any farther because it's too painful for me.

Marjorie: Have you kept in touch with any other relatives in Europe? What happens when you go and visit them?

Zezette: Yes. There is something I wanted to share with you, one of the things that happened during my last trip. My oldest nephew is almost the age that my father was, his grandfather was, when he died. I kept on looking at him. He looks a lot like my father did. A lot. Not his character, but physically . . . A couple of times I wanted to tell him this, but decided not to. It's so sad, you know. It just struck me, suddenly. I had become the older generation. I was suddenly very aware of that. I don't know. It was really an interesting experience . . . being very aware of the kids, my three nephews, and them not being kids anymore, but men. They are a new generation. Suddenly, they were creeping up to be the age that my parents were . . . This only made me feel older. And I was very . . . I still have not put it into place, psychologically, that is.

Marjorie: Tell me a little about leaving Europe to go to the United States.

Zezette: Well, with hindsight, I believe that leaving Europe was for me an attempt to leave my past behind, but I took that past with me. You take it wherever you go and . . . I very much know that now. At the time, all I knew is I was coming to the United States, the country that believed in the Declaration of Independence, where all people were supposedly equal, at least that is what I had learned, and thought about a lot as I was put on a boat by my family in January of 1951. I left without the understanding that I was going to try to find a new life here. I thought I would try it here for six months and then I would see what happened. And so, as I said, they put me on a first-class boat and the reality was, I was seasick during the entire voyage and certainly did not enjoy the privilege of being first class, the one and only time in my life. When we approached New York, after whatever number of days it took to cross the Atlantic, I remember very clearly going on deck and being absolutely hysterical with joy at seeing the Statue of Liberty. I was hysterical with fear, as well. I didn't know where I was going and, as I told you, I didn't speak any English. I landed in Hoboken and was met by a friend of my family's, a kindly older gentleman who attempted to find me a job in New York City. I stayed with friends of my aunt and uncle who lived in Manhattan and that was certainly not a good match. These were people who were quite aged and for whom I felt I was a burden. So I did not stay with them very long. I came with a nice degree in social work and I landed a job stuffing envelopes for Macy's, the biggest department store in the world, I think. I earned very little money.

Marjorie: What was your life like at this time?

Zezette: I was lonely and I was afraid. I remember trips in the subway going home from work where so many times I was pushed into the wrong train because taking the subway in Manhattan at rush hour requires a tremendous amount of know-how which, obviously, I didn't have. I also remember clearly that one of the people who was very kind to me at Macy's was a young woman who was black and it didn't take very long for people to take me aside and tell me that I had to understand that friendships with blacks were not the road I should take and I should be extremely careful. Here I was, landed in the country where everybody was supposedly equal, and I learned my first lesson.

Did I mention that my name became Claire when I first started at Macy's? People asked me what my name was and when I said Zezette, they just never had heard anything like that and someone, I don't remember who it was, baptized me, so to speak, with the name Claire. So, I became Claire, which in many ways is an ironic coincidence. I worked every day. There are many, many stories I recall from that first year. For instance, I learned that you could give blood and would be paid for it. And so, inasmuch as I was very short of money, I decided to give blood on a Thursday morning, because Thursdays I worked in the evening. I went up to, I don't remember where . . . Herald Square, maybe, to give blood. It was very cold outside. I gave blood, everything went fine, and then, in order to pass the last hour before I was supposed to go to work, I went into Woolworth's, where it was very hot. Within two minutes I had fainted and found myself on the floor at Woolworth's.

Marjorie: Tell me about learning English. You speak French so beautifully, I am curious to know about your relationship to English.

Zezette: I started to speak English little by little. I joined the Dutch Club in New York where I met some people and formed some friendships. I started to feel more at ease. When the six months passed that I had agreed to try, I felt very strongly that I had not learned enough of the language. I was very determined, so I decided not to go back, and to stay on here for an indefinite amount of time. At the School of Foreign Born, I met Sven Larsen, who later became my husband. Sven was Danish, or is Danish—blond, blue eyes, very handsome, not Jewish. As a matter of fact, he looked very, very Germanic. We married, I think it was the end of 1951. I would have to look to confirm that. It was very soon after the marriage that I realized what I had done: I had married because I was lonely, not because I loved Sven. That marriage ended in 1956 with Sven calling me a dirty Jew and I had to place an assault and battery charge on him because he hit me. So I left. I just turned around and left and never came back. I have no idea where he is, what he is, or whether he is still alive. All I know is I never took anything with me. I just left.

Marjorie: And it was then that you moved to New Jersey?

Zezette: There are obviously many stories about my life in New York and the move to New Jersey; getting tired of stuffing envelopes and entering the field of social work in the United States; going to Rutgers University to get my American degree; becoming supervisor in a child care agency; foster care and adoption; leaving the United States in 1968 to return to Europe to see if the grass was greener there; being disappointed again and moving to Israel, where I lived for one year and learned Hebrew. Finally, I came back to the United States. It took me years to discover that the grass is not greener on the other side of the fence and that wherever you go, you take yourself. You cannot leave yourself behind, and thus you take the pain and the memories with you. So, I came back to the United States and moved to Boston in 1970, where I still live.

At this point, we need to stop because I have to go to work. Yes, I still work. I think it's a leftover from my years in Auschwitz: "Working makes you free." I live with this, it is now almost four years since I retired from my profession, and I continuously take on jobs, consulting jobs, because I don't find satisfaction in sitting and relaxing and reading. I don't have enough peace in me to be able to do that. I need to be busy, to keep my mind going. I need to feel worthwhile and work; otherwise, I think I would die. So, I am starting a new job even though I am aware, at the back of my mind, that I don't have much time at the moment, but I will be able to do it and I will learn my lesson.

Marjorie: Zezette, I have wanted to ask you . . . Life is a collection of very privileged and special moments. Can you remember one such moment in your life?

Zezette: You are going to waste tape. It is hard to think of a big part of my life as privileged time. But my mind does immediately go back to my parents. And I think that the most vivid recollection is my marriage to Steve. I mean, that was a tremendous privilege. I know my mother was fun-loving and loved music. She sang and played the piano and just had the joie de vivre that she was allowed to have for that amount of time. Then, afterwards, there's that very somber, that very dark period until the meeting with Steve and then there is this feeling of happiness. Now, that is my immediate response.

Marjorie: You are a survivor of the Holocaust, and when we think of the Holocaust we think of a loss that can never be reclaimed because your house, your street, your life, are all gone. But do you remember . . . I mean, is it possible to remember some moments of happiness in your childhood or is everything blurred?

Zezette: It is very, very difficult to remember a happy moment. I think that when I talk about my mother, for instance, the clearest memory to me is the fact that, like a typical teenager, I used to walk the streets of Brussels because it was Brussels, and I would walk in front of my mother, not next to her, because I did not want people to know she was my mother . . . She would have liked to put her arm around me, and I did not want her arm around . . . I have terrible guilt feelings about that. So when I say nostalgia, I would like to have had happy days with them. I am sure I did [laughs], but they are completely blurred in my mind. The other pronounced recollection that I have is that . . . both my father and my mother were very loving people and I have a very clear image of going to school and having . . . having her hang out of the window to wave at me and I waved at her until we could not see each other anymore. But the waving also means parting and I am not . . . I am not sure of what the connections are between those losses. So, that's a very vivid picture. And . . . and maybe you are right. I am sure there were very, very happy moments because . . . because they were very good people, they were loving people. But everything that I remember is, has something do to with separation, walking separately from her, waving good-bye to her . . . It's all related to the loss and I know it and I cannot remember anything else.

Marjorie: What has it been like to live in the U.S.? Are you comfortable here?

Zezette: I was nearly twenty-two when I came to this country and I think that . . . I know that for . . . at least thirty-five years I never spoke of my Jewish identity. I did not want people to ask me questions. I have a big scar on my arm because I had the tattooed number removed. For me it was safer not to speak of being Jewish . . . All the time I inwardly was extremely happy at the freedom which allowed me to celebrate holidays, Jewish holidays. I have always felt very much of a stranger. I always felt that I could not talk because people could not understand and I did not want people to feel guilty or sorry for me. But I have lived, I have lived very much, trying to be very superficial about things. Keeping my . . . the life of an ostrich. I don't know if I have been . . . Sometimes I feel guilty when I am happy.

Marjorie: Yes . . .

Zezette: I have now dredged this up again and put it back into perspective. But I think I pretty much would have spent my life working hard, running, rushing . . . looking forward to going back to Europe because I have gone back, go back religiously . . . I went back for the fourth time to Auschwitz in August, this past August. I had a terrible time coming back to [the United States]. Terrible, terrible. And even though I had this wonderful husband who wanted to help me, I . . . I just could not be happy. I felt it was being disloyal . . . to the people who were dead. I could never live again in . . . in Belgium. As a matter of fact, my voyages there are never longer than a week because then I feel . . . almost paranoid. No, there's too much . . . too much history there for me . . . Too many nightmares that . . . that I do not want to . . . to look at. I think that . . . I think that as a European Jew, having lived through the war years in Europe, I think that going back is not possible. I mean, it's part of . . . my heart would like to go back, would love to go back, and then when I physically get there . . . I want to run back from where I came from. I don't know where home is anymore. I don't know. I am not sure.

Marjorie: How you feel about the English language? In what language do you dream, do you love, do you feel?

Zezette: I love to speak French! I love it . . . I count in French. I think that is true of most foreigners, you count in your own language. I love having the opportunity to speak French. I love plays on words and I can do them. I mean, in French. I think I have a pretty good sense of humor in French. I don't have a great sense of humor in English . . . I guess I don't know . . . It's pretty strange. I know that I become alive when I speak in French.

Marjorie: Do you think that maybe language is home? That maybe you are home in a language rather than in a place? You feel that the French language has fewer memories of pain?

Zezette: I think that's part of it. I don't associate the language with pain . . . no I don't. I associate the land with pain. The people, but not the language. And so I feel very good using it.

Marjorie: So you arrived in the United States and it's like the stories . . . you do not speak a word of English. Who picked you up? Who took care of you? Here is this twenty-one-year-old girl . . .

Zezette: With a Master's degree in her pocket from the Rotterdam School of Social Work! Kind enough people picked me up, my sponsors. I stayed with them for a while and they helped me find a room in . . . in New York. They also helped me find a job . . . at Macy's . . . I stuffed envelopes at Macy's for a long time [laughs]. I don't know, it's maybe because it is around Thanksgiving, the thought comes to me . . . I was earning very little money, obviously and I had no money. One of the frustrating things is that I would eat . . . eat at the cafeteria on Thirty-fourth Street. What was frightening was that because I did not speak English I would point to all the things that I wanted and always got more than I really wanted which meant that the bill was more than I could spend for the day . . . So, the first Thanksgiving I was in the United States and I understood that . . . I had been in the United States for eight months and I had no friends. I lived in a room in Kew Garden. I understood that the employees who wanted to work on Thanksgiving would be paid double time and also get breakfast . . . The Thanksgiving Day parade would take place. I had no idea what that was all about! But I did know that double pay appealed and . . . breakfast appealed very much and plus, I had nothing else to do. So I signed up and got to my place of work on Thanksgiving morning. First of all, breakfast was coffee and doughnuts which was . . . a trauma because I had visions of a really hearty breakfast, you know. But that's what it was. And then, they put a big clown hat on my head (I have pictures of it!) and I had to walk Fifth Avenue, down Fifth Avenue, in the Macy's parade, as a clown. And it was . . . it was a very frightening experience for me, so frightening that it remains a very vivid, very sharp memory.

Marjorie: This type of experience—the breakfast and the parade—allowed you to distance yourself from America?

Zezette: I think I stopped thinking. I think that when I said to you before that I have lived a lot of my life as an ostrich, I think this statement is very, very, very true. I am very afraid to think.

Marjorie: Can you ever get used to being in America? What country do you call "home"?

Zezette: I don't have an American flag. I think I am much more European than American and yet I have lived most of my life in America. I think, I definitely still . . . my house looks European. There is something European about my house. I love my home, my house. That's not very American. Oh, yes, the way I dress, the way I eat, the way I set the table, it's all very European. All the things I would like to do, like sit with my friends in cafés and talk, the freedom of . . . of . . . what? . . . Let me put it this . . . This Puritan kind of thinking that exists here is something that is not at all part of my background. And so, I guess the answer is I feel much more European than I feel American.

Marjorie: Do you think that the Jewish immigrants that came to America from Eastern and Central Europe have a place that they can return to? Could you begin to live again in Brussels?

Zezette: No, no. I think there is something in this country that makes us strangers. I think that's due to the fact that we live long distances from each other and that nobody drops by. I remember the first time I came to this country and I was working at Macy's and hardly spoke any English and people would say to me at the end of the day, "See you later." I would go home and prepare the teacups and get ready because they had said, "See you later," which to me meant they were coming to visit. The human touch, being able to hold a hand, to touch one another in whatever way you want, that is missing in America.

Marjorie: Have you found it easier to be Jewish here?

Zezette: I, don't . . . I can't even put into words what it means to be a Jew for me, because I don't believe in God anymore. I don't. God, God is good. How, how can it be? If that is so, then how could this have happened?

Marjorie: Do you feel that you can enjoy life now? That you can be happy?

Zezette: I am starting to realize this and I am starting to be able to say this. I am sad and angry that I had to reach my age to be able to feel. I want to take my time and do things! That's what I want to do. I want to go back to where we lived, where I was born. I want to . . . where we were hidden, or where my parents were hidden. There are people there now . . . I don't even remember their names. I wish my brother would talk because maybe he does remember them. Steve took me to see the convent once. There was one sister from the time when I was there. The others were all dead. The place had changed tremendously. The sister did not recognize me. Apparently they had three or four Jewish kids hidden there. I don't know what happened to the others. It's interesting because I think I have put it to rest, that period of being hidden. It's not something I keep thinking about.

Marjorie: So you have made peace with that?

Zezette: Yes.

Marjorie: Maybe because, amidst all the horror, it was a happy time . . . they were good people.

Zezette: Oh, of course!

Marjorie: I was very intrigued by the fact that you chose to spend so many years in silence and other people have chosen to speak. How important is it, do you think, for you to remember the past, to remember the history, the Holocaust? Are you very obsessed with memory?

Zezette: Not at all. Not at all. As a matter of fact, I make it my business *not* to remember, not to speak. At the same time, I think that there is also, now that I have more peace in my life, there is also something that says that in order to have less inner turmoil, in order to really be able to enjoy life, which is very difficult for me, very difficult (you know, I wear two things around my neck, one says "chaim," which means life, and the other one is a worry bird because I worry all the time), I think that in order to be able to feel good things and relax and experience peace, one has to feel it inwardly too. I think . . . I think that by keeping everything inside it is going to be very difficult for me to ever, ever find inner peace. I don't know if I ever will, but I am trying to learn, and at this age, it's about time that I do, try to learn to say a few more sentences every time I speak. Sometimes I can and sometimes I cannot. But I know I am not . . . I am obsessed with not wanting to remember.

Marjorie: Even though you tried not to talk about your Jewish background or to practice the rituals of your faith, have you experienced anti-Semitism in America?

Zezette: I am sure I have experienced anti-Semitism. There is no doubt in my mind about that. They see me as a Jew and again, I don't know how I (or they) feel about that.

Marjorie: Last time we talked about the dangers of being a bystander. With your experience, with Auschwitz, what can you tell us about the dangers of indifference as a human being, as a Jew? How much have you thought about all of this?

Zezette: How much have I thought about it? I think about it every day. One cannot let things happen. One has to participate, one has to react, one has to defend. There's this wonderful poem by Pastor Niemöller.[8] I don't remember the name, but it is a very important poem because it says it all. People, people in general . . . I mean generalization is wrong, but most people are very indifferent and very comfortable. I hesitate when I say most people, because very few of my friends are. But sometimes, you know, the people that were not in the war, that were not there at that time want to know who was good among so much evil? Who was there for you or for others? What do you think happened to people, like you said, surrounded with so much darkness? What did it take for people to be good? I don't remember one person being good. I mean that's a . . . it's so much easier to talk about the present and see how many people write to their congressmen . . . People are trying to take a political stand on what's going on in Bosnia. There are those who read the paper, close the paper, and go about their business. How many . . . how many people have had a discussion on what is going on in public schools here, in the city of Boston? Or is it something we don't talk about because my child goes to private school so I don't have to worry . . .

One of the things I am most looking forward to is having more time to think and talk and be involved with people. I think that there is a whole world out there that we have to take care of. And that, it really is so much easier not to, and to close your eyes. But that is so dangerous . . .

I only have one purpose. That is to hope that kids . . . My purpose in talking to you is very different than my purpose when talking to high school students, obviously. But my only purpose in talking to young people is to try to make them realize the insanity of condemning a people for the mere fact that they are

Jewish, just the same as condemning blacks because they are black. It just does not make sense. Or condemning Puerto Ricans for being Puerto Rican. It's stereotyping and it makes no sense. It's dangerous. But anyway . . . we should not be talking about the Holocaust. We should be talking about other things.

Marjorie: I would like to talk a little about your friendships here. Are they very different from the ones back in Belgium?

Zezette: Friendships are . . . are very different here. [Laughs.] When I am in Europe, and again, when I talk about Europe it's Holland or Belgium or France, and I walk with my arm on the shoulder of my friends or we hold hands, that's the most natural thing in the world. Here, it would be looked at as something . . . That has been a mind-blowing experience for me because just four or five weeks ago, a couple of months ago, when Steve and I were in Europe, we spent much time with loads of different friends of mine, we held hands or we walked arm in arm. That is part of what I am used to. And we really deeply care for each other. I think distances in this country, well first of all there is the whole Puritan kind of, one just does not do that! One does not hold hands with another woman.

Marjorie: Yes. Do you think, even though we live in a place known for its democracy, that we have too many rules?

Zezette: We certainly do. One does not do that. I don't know if distance is a criteria, but I know for instance the person I call my best friend here, because I feel the most comfortable with her . . . we laugh together . . . Although our relationship is very different from my European relationships, I am deeply fond of her. She just recently moved out of Newton to downtown Boston. She is coming over tonight and I have not seen her in months!

In Europe I would sit at a café with friends, that's the most important thing I could be doing. I don't have to rush away to go and make money. It's not necessary. I enjoy them. I enjoy having my glass of wine with them. That's what . . . Here there is no more enjoyment of the moment, of the present. This business of rushing and doing and having to call this one and that one and meeting for this and that . . . I am also realizing that Europe, at least the countries I know, may not be the same as I remember, and maybe there is more . . . more programming and rushing, but I don't think that friendships have changed. At least, I know that because I go back all the time and I see it. So it's just . . . it's just different.

Marjorie: What has been the hardest thing about living in America? What has been the most wonderful thing?

Zezette: [Sighs.] Well, the great . . . let me begin with the great thing. I started as a person working at Macy's stuffing envelopes, and I eventually became the president of a company, through very hard work. And that's . . . that's great.

Marjorie: It is the American dream. It happened to you?

Zezette: Yes. It happened. When I think about it, you know, I am proud for two seconds and then . . . you know, then I forget about it. But, it has been a very good thing, in my mind, to have been able to do this. The worst thing . . . missing Europe. I miss Europe. I miss my way of life in Europe, the quality of life. I really miss, what the French call ambiance, the hominess. It's just this something that when . . . It's interesting. I can recreate it in my home. There is a fire burning in the fireplace, and there are all kinds of good things to eat and I have some friends here. I look around and I think, "Isn't this cozy?" I find it very un-American. It's just very un-American.

I can adjust very quickly in Europe, very quickly. I mean, it's like I have lived there my whole life. I'm suddenly used to small cars and I think . . . I think we almost have schizophrenic personalities. You know, we can adjust wherever we are. I do, anyway.

Marjorie: What city would you like to sleep in and dream in forever?

Zezette: Paris. Because I love it. I love the beauty of its buildings. I love the people. I love the cafés. I love the life. I love croissants! That's silly! But that is where I would want to be, Paris.

Marjorie: When you go to Europe, do you remember what you have here or does it feel like you never really lived in America?

Zezette: It's more like I never lived in America.

Marjorie: What books did you read as a child? Do you read the same books now? I mean, are those authors still dear to you now that you have grown up?

Zezette: I barely remember when I was a little girl . . . There is no way that I would . . . Then there was a whole period of my life when I did not read. I did not have any books. After that, I had learned a new language, so there is this space in my life. That is a very difficult question for me to answer.

Marjorie: Zezette, tell me what objects do you remember from your past, from your house, that were dear to you? Are any of these objects with you?

Zezette: I think I only have one. I only have one because . . . everything else was destroyed . . . taken. But, when I was hidden in the convent, I had a teddy bear. And that teddy bear is very, very precious to me. As a matter of fact, the fur of his face is completely . . . how do you say . . .

Marjorie: Faded?

Zezette: Faded, yes, from kissing the teddy bear. Going back to Magda—my friend from Belgium who just found us—it was very important finding her, or rather her finding us. I would like to talk to my brother about our youth. I want to remember happy moments . . . times with our parents . . . I mean, I am just talking and realizing things that I haven't . . . I want to remember happy things, good things. I only remember our parents as wonderful people. But, I need to . . . to say these words and not just have the facts. And Magda told me . . . She told me that she had fallen from a streetcar. I did not remember that. And she remembers my mother going to see her at the hospital, almost every other day. I don't remember that. So these are things . . . you know . . . We didn't have enough time together.

Marjorie: What hope do you give people?

Zezette: Well, I tell you, last week was an inspiration for me. Yes. Seeing Steve teach German, young teachers, and seeing the intensity of interest in the history of their grandparents. German teachers. And the depth of their discomfort with the subject matter . . . but the thirst to know about it was there. Today, in the mail, came a book for Steve. It's in German. It's also going to be published in English. It's not a book. It's a thick pamphlet . . . very thick, probably 150 pages. It is beautifully done. It contains all the German monuments commemorating the era between 1940 and 1945, the destruction of the Jews. I mean, the country is filled with monuments.

Marjorie: I want to ask one last question. If you were to begin a letter to your brother, and your brother . . . represents so many people who don't want to remember. What would you say? How would you begin this letter?

Zezette: I probably would say, "How can I make you not feel guilty about what happened to me? You are not responsible. I want to remember . . . and I want to . . . I want to honor our parents with you. I don't want to silence their existence." That is what I would say.

ELENA OTTOLENGHI NIGHTINGALE

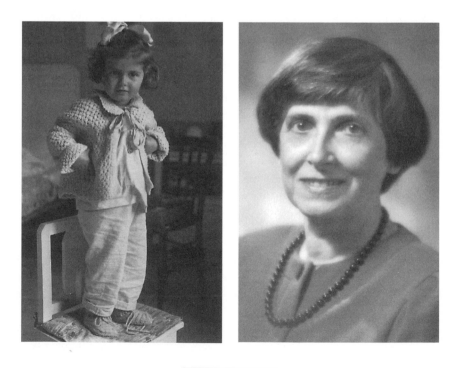

November 1, 1932	Born in Livorno, Italy
Fall 1938	Anti-Semitic laws passed; barred from public schools
November 9, 1939	Leaves Livorno by train, with parents and sisters, for Genova, Italy; then boards the "Conte di Savoia" and sails to America
November 23, 1939	Arrives in New York City on Thanksgiving Day and travels to Princeton, New Jersey, where sponsor lives and has an apartment for the family
1940	Paternal grandfather, Umberto Ottolenghi, dies in Livorno
1940	Moves to New York City, Somerville, New Jersey, and Providence, Rhode Island, as father changed jobs after nine months of unemployment
June 1946	Returns to Florence, Italy, to look for relatives. Livorno had been bombed flat
January 1947	Returns to Providence, then moves to New York
Spring 1947	Maternal grandmother, Clara Luisada Levi, dies in Florence after surviving hiding for eighteen months and a stroke
June 1953	Returns to Italy to visit family
1954	Bachelor's degree from Barnard College, *summa cum laude*
1954–1956	Attends Columbia University College of Physicians and Surgeons
1956–1961	Attends Rockefeller Institute on special fellowship; doctorate in microbial genetics
1961	Post-doctoral fellow in medicine at New York University
1964	Medical degree
August 1964	Returns to Italy for sister Gianna's wedding
1964	Instructor in medicine at New York University
July 1, 1965	Marries Dr. Stuart L. Nightingale, then returns to Italy to introduce husband to family
1965–1970	Assistant professor of microbiology at Cornell University Medical College
February 1966	Paternal grandmother, Ida Cingoli Ottolenghi, dies in Livorno
April 28, 1966	Daughter Elizabeth Sara born in New York City
June 6, 1967	Mother, Elisa Levi Ottolenghi, dies after a six-month illness
March 2, 1968	Daughter Marisa Ottolenghi born in New York City
June 1970	Moves to Baltimore, Maryland; faculty, along with Stuart, at Johns Hopkins University

1972	Returns to Italy to visit family; visits often after that
June 1973	Moves to McLean, Virginia. Fellowship in pediatrics and genetics at Georgetown University. Starts genetics clinic with a senior pediatrician
September 1974	Awarded fellowship in science policy at National Academy of Sciences
October 1974	Father, Dr. Mario L. Ottolenghi, dies in New York City
1976	Starts Division on Health Promotion and Disease Prevention at the Institute of Medicine of National Academy of Sciences. Remains until 1983
June 1978	Moves to Bethesda, Maryland
1980–1984	Visiting associate professor in social medicine and health policy, Harvard University; lecturer 1984–1995
1981–1988	Participant and then chair of the American Association for the Advancement of Science (AAAS) Committee on Scientific Freedom and Responsibility, human rights subcommittee
1983–present	Adjunct professor of pediatrics, Georgetown University
1983–1994	Special advisor to the president and senior program officer, Carnegie Corporation of New York
1985	Edited, with E. Stover, *The Breaking of Bodies and Minds: Torture, Psychiatric Abuse, and the Health Professions* (W. H. Freeman and Co.)
1985	Human rights mission to Chile with the AAAS
1987	Edited, with S. B. Meister, *Prenatal Screening, Policies, and Values: The Example of Neural Tube Defects* (Harvard University Press)
1989	Human rights mission to South Africa with the AAAS
1990	Coauthored, with M. Goodman, *Before Birth: Prenatal Testing for Genetic Disease* (Harvard University Press)
1993	Edited, with A. C. Peterson and S. G. Millstein, *Promoting the Health of Adolescents: New Directions for the Twenty-First Century* (Oxford University Press)
July 1993	Moved to Chevy Chase, Maryland
1994	Human rights mission to Trieste
1995–present	Back at National Academy of Sciences as a scholar in residence
1994–present	Adjunct professor of pediatrics, George Washington University

The Fasci di Combattimento (the Fighting Leagues founded by Benito Mussolini on March 23, 1919, in Milan) initiated the attempt of the Italian right wing to transform Italy into a fascist nation. Soon transformed into the Partito Nazionale Fascista (PNF), Mussolini's party consolidated the radical right in the political sphere. King Victor Emmanuel III, threatened with a Fascist march on Rome in 1922, allowed Mussolini to form a coalition government. But by 1926, Mussolini had declared the PNF the only legal political party in Italy.

During the 1920s, Italian Jews remained largely unaffected by the Fascist regime. The PNF, focusing its efforts on building a powerful Italian state, had not developed an anti-Semitic agenda. In fact, the party had 7,300 Jewish members in 1933. Italian Jews were largely assimilated, with nearly 50 percent of married Jews having non-Jewish spouses by 1938.

Fascist Italy flexed its industrial muscle in the mid-1930s by invading Ethiopia and sending weaponry to General Franco's Fascist army during the Spanish Civil War. The Rome-Berlin Axis of late October 1936 cemented an Italian alliance with Germany, and Italy followed Germany in withdrawing from the League of Nations the following year. Drawing closer to Germany, Mussolini instigated racial discrimination laws in Italy in 1938.[1] By the time Hitler invaded Poland on September 1, 1939, Italy's official position was one of nonbelligerence. It was during this time that Elena Ottolenghi Nightingale and her family left Italy for the United States. It was not until June 10, 1940, that Mussolini declared war on Great Britain and France.

In the early years of the war, the Italian government made little effort to round up Italian Jews and many successfully hid (or were hidden) from the authorities. However, during the German occupation of northern Italy (1943–1945), Germans and their Italian collaborators increased their efforts and almost eight thousand Italian Jews were deported to concentration camps and murdered. By war's end, the Jewish population of Italy was reduced to twenty-eight thousand, from its prewar number of approximately thirty-six thousand.

The first lecture I heard by Elena Nightingale was at Tufts Medical School in Boston. A longtime activist, she spoke on human rights for women and children. At that time I was pregnant with Sonia Helena, and Elena very tenderly advised me on how to take care of my daughter right after she was born. She also urged me to take care of myself. From that moment on, I loved that woman of extraordinary strength and spiritual beauty, a beauty reflected in her Mediterranean face and deep-set eyes. We have been friends for over ten years. On one level we are sisters in the fight for human rights, and in other ways, Elena Nightingale, at the age of sixty-four, could be my mother. We have a mother-daughter relationship, except that sometimes she speaks to me as a mother, sometimes as a daughter.

Our conversation took place at the offices of the National Research Council in Washington, D.C. While we talked, she showed me some photographs of her childhood. I expected black-and-white images, yellowed sepia photographs, worn by years of handling. Instead she showed me perfect blue postcards of Livorno. My eyes fixed on the promenade, and I could see myself there, strolling with my grandmothers, as if Elena's memories were twined with my own. She paused as she looked at the photographs, remembering her mother's sweet scent. Elena, gentle and soft-spoken, looked tired. Her tiredness, unrelated to her age, was linked to something more sacred: the fatigue that results from a life poured out for the benefit of others. I felt honored to be in the presence of a woman who has dedicated herself to memory, to justice, and to the dignity of all people. Elena believes this is her duty, and that there is nothing astonishing in her assumption that the medical profession should be socially responsible.

We left Elena's office and walked, arms interlocked, along the well-tended sidewalks of Georgetown. Here she returned to the Livorno promenade of her youth.

Marjorie: What was your childhood like in Italy?

Elena: I left Italy on November 9, 1939. I had turned seven years old on November 1. My memories go back to when I was about three years old, although now occasionally I get a flash of some images that may have taken place even earlier than that. My family was a middle-class family. We lived in Livorno, which the British call Leghorn, a seaport on the Tyrrhenian sea in Tuscany, in central Italy. The seacoast is beautiful there. There are, or there were, pine groves along the sea, and behind the pine groves you could see the mountains. The sea was clear and clean and there were so many fish and sea urchins and beautiful sea life. The town still houses the Naval Academy of the Italian government and often you would see the naval cadets walking up and down in their uniform, and all the girls (I was too young) eyeing them and trying to figure out which ones they wanted to approach.

The earliest years, from about 1935 or 1936, I remember as being very peaceful and happy. My mother was a teacher. My father, trained as a chemical engineer, was in charge of the Italian National Life Insurance Agency, which he had to take over from his father who was ill with heart disease. We lived near my father's parents, and their family. My father was the oldest of nine children. The youngest one died, at the age of one and a half, from what was probably meningitis, and this cast a shadow on my grandmother's life forever. My father, being the oldest son and the oldest child, was responsible for all of his younger siblings when his father became too ill to work. So I remember that he would go to the office in the morning, he had a tiny little Fiat called a *topolino* which means "little mouse," but in that tiny car he sat proudly next to the chauffeur, whom I remember very well because he was so good and kind to us children. And he would go off to work. He came home at dinner time, dinner being at 1 P.M., as was the custom then, and we would all eat together: my father, my mother, and at that time, my two sisters; a younger one was born in 1938.

After a rest, we often would all go to the beach together, not in a car, but in a horse-drawn carriage. The coachman would allow us children to hold the reins if we were good. After having had our dinner and siesta at home, we would spend the afternoon at the beach where we would meet many friends, a few Jewish, most Catholic. The Jewish community of Livorno was substantial by Italian standards, but still very small. We would play on the beach and we would swim, and I remember that we had a very small rowboat which my grandfather had given to my older sister, Paola, for her birthday. At that time, I was about three and she was five. We would row around in the shallow water and we had a wonderful time. Then we would go home and prepare for the afternoon walk, the promenade, where we would meet other people in the cafés and sit and have some ice cream or some chocolate and talk to people as they came by prior to going home to prepare for the evening meal.

Marjorie: Tell me about your family and your daily life.

Elena: I had two sisters at the time. My older sister, who was a year and a half older than I, and my younger sister, who was two and a half years younger. She is the one whose husband just died. Her name is Marcella. We had a good and peaceful life, surrounded by family and friends. We were not rich, but we had all the comforts. We lived in an apartment building. The apartment of my child-hood memories is very large, large enough for my sister (who got a bicycle on her fifth birthday) to ride the bicycle up and down the corridor.

We had two people who helped us in the house. One did general house-work and one took care of the children. I remember the latter very, very well. Her name was Lisetta, she came from the country, and everything for her was new: a flushing toilet, running water, elevator, everything surprised her. She was a wonderful, warm, and loving girl. She was sixteen when she came to work for us. The village she came from had no Jews. She had never known any Jews. And so the first request she had was to bathe my younger sister, so that she could see for herself whether Jewish children indeed had tails. To her delight, we did not. When my father came home in the evening, we all had supper and then, after the children were tucked in bed, we would recite the Shema.[2] Then, my parents would go out for the evening. My mother was always nicely dressed and smelled so good. She always had a smile on her face. Prior to going out, she would read to us, usually in French, so that we would learn French as we grew up. It was what people did in those days. I re-member very well the book she read to us most often—it was called *Les Mal-heures de Sofie*. It was about a little girl and all the naughty things that she did. My parents would then kiss us good night and go out for the evening. I am not sure where they went, but they were happy. That period of our lives never returned.

45

Marjorie: Tell me more about your family.

Elena: My older sister and I shared a room. We were friends, very different in personality, but we got along very well. We always had aunts and uncles who came to visit, my father's siblings. He had two brothers and five sisters, and most lived at home at that point. My grandmother, my father's mother, was an extraordinary lady. Having borne nine children she had become very heavy and spent most of her life in an armchair, reading all the newspapers she could find and talking to us as if we were adults. She respected us, and she respected our opinions, even at a tender age. Her oldest daughter, Emma, was really the one who raised the rest of her children. My grandmother was a liberal and an intellectual. But, it did not keep her from falling, at first, for the ideas of the Fascist government. She was a great admirer of Giuseppe Mazzini,[3] who was the heart and soul of the unification of Italy. Mazzini was a friend of a relative of ours, Sara Natan, and he actually died in her home. My grandmother idolized Mazzini and all the liberal (what they then called Republican) ideas that he stood for. But they were mixed with nationalism and it was that nationalism that was the side that eventually she had to reject.

Back in my own family's apartment we had a life that by today's standards was extremely comfortable. We did not have to go out for things, they came to us. The baker's boy would deliver fresh bread twice a day, so that it would be warm and crusty for each meal. The dressmaker came, took measurements, and made our clothes. There was an old lady who came, *la trinaia*, whose job was to put lace collars and trimmings on our clothes. The laundress came and took our clothes away, and brought them back clean, fresh-smelling, and neatly ironed. The shopping and marketing was done each morning early by our maid. The meals were delicious and fresh. We had no refrigerator, we had a little box in which we would put a cube of ice delivered by the ice man each day for the small piece of butter and the small perishables that we had. But most of the food was bought and consumed the same day. Even though we were very young, as was the custom in Italy at meal times, we were allowed to have a spot of wine in our water. The water, by itself, tasted pretty foul. We also were allowed to have coffee and milk for breakfast, mostly milk with a little coffee. But the milk was not pasteurized, and had to be brought to a boil three times and the skin removed before we could drink it. It did not taste very good, and the coffee and sugar helped. These days, in the United States, to give children as young as one a taste of wine and a taste of coffee would be viewed as child abuse. I don't think we were abused.

Marjorie: What was the world of each of your parents like?

46

Elena: My father's father, who was ill most of the time, was also devoted to us and the source of constant surprises and treasures. Every time he came by, he had little gifts for us in his pockets. I remember particularly one day when we were in the country for the summer, that to surprise us he hung gifts on a pear tree, and then said: "See what the pear tree has borne overnight!" And we were absolutely thrilled. All of this is what I remember. I remember our friends. I remember the toys we had: a beautiful toy house, a small bicycle which my sister and I both learned to ride at the same time. We learned to swim also very, very young. I think I learned to walk and swim at about the same time. It was a time of, in my memory, good times, family times and times with friends.

My mother's family was very different. She was raised in Florence, a much more sophisticated city. The Florentine spirit, although it is difficult to generalize, of course, was quite different from that of Livorno. I remember that the people from Florence had quite a sharp and sarcastic edge. I remember their laughing a great deal in their conversations. And I remember my mother's mother, sister, brother, and sister-in-law very, very vividly. My grandmother on my mother's side, Clara, was the antithesis of my paternal grandmother. She was thin and beautiful and very quiet. She would come and stay with us very often, and she played the piano so beautifully. She never emerged from her bedroom unless she was completely dressed and coiffed, with her beautiful hair (still dark at the age of seventy) piled high on her head, a velvet ribbon with a brooch or a cameo around her neck, and smelling of lavender, her room in perfect order. She was calm and she was quiet. She spoke to us and read to us. She was close to us, but in such a different way. She had a sad life. Her husband had been thrown out of the house by my grandmother's brothers because he gambled. So from the time my mother was a very young toddler, she had no father and her uncles were the ones who made the decisions about her life and that of her sister and brother. I think this situation made the whole family rather bitter.

My aunt, my mother's younger sister, was like a second mother to us. We loved her very much. When she came to stay she played with us, she took care of us, she loved us as if we were her own, and I have memories of her that will never fade. I loved her very, very dearly, and leaving her when we came to America was perhaps the greatest grief of that whole adventure. My uncle, my mother's brother, was a quirky fellow. He was intelligent, and trained as what I guess in the United States would have been called, not an accountant, but a lawyer who did financial work. He had a wife who was not Jewish. She had been his secretary. The rest of the family, unfortunately, was not very welcoming to her because she came from a very much less educated background and she was always striving to be accepted as an equal by the rest of the family. She was kind in her own way, but very touchy and very easily offended. So I do not remember, in the early years, having much to do with her.

Marjorie: What was your religious life like?

Elena: Our family was not a very observant family. We had our synagogue, which was of the Spanish-Portuguese rite. Many of our ancestors came from Spain and Portugal after the Inquisition. But we did not attend services often. The women were separated from the men and had to go upstairs and sit behind a grill. The women always chatted and made a lot of noise and did not pay much attention to what went on below. The men conducted the service. I remember that on High Holy Days, at the end of Yom Kippur service, we were all permitted to go down and to stand by our father, who put his tallis around us and we were all given the blessing as a family. We did celebrate the High Holy Days, but I do not recall going to services any time in between. We went to services for Rosh Hashanah and Yom Kippur.[4] My parents fasted for Yom Kippur. We all went to my father's parents' home for Passover seder, which was a very long affair with the foods more characteristic of Italy than of the Ashkenazi tradition familiar to American Jews. I remember the hard-boiled eggs and all the symbols of Passover, but the charoset was made with dates and almonds.[5] That part of it was good. I remember my parents breaking the fast on Yom Kippur with what was called stracciatella, which is really chicken broth with egg drop and parmesan cheese and a squeeze of lemon. It was delicious. But I do not remember that religion, aside from reciting the Shema and the High Holy Days celebration, played a very important part in our lives. Yet, we were very conscious of being Jewish and more so after the anti-Semitic laws were enforced. Some of our friends shunned us after the anti-Semitic laws were passed. Most of our friends made it a point to visit with us, to be extra solicitous, to come to see us, to include us in their activities, and to show that they were absolutely appalled by what was happening.

Marjorie: Elena, could you tell me how anti-Semitic laws began to appear? How did your family live through this period where laws were slowly being enacted to take away power and property from the Jews?

Elena: Nineteen thirty-eight was the year my youngest sister was born and also the year in which the anti-Semitic laws were passed. They were not enforced in full immediately, but things began to be bad. Prior to the passing of the laws, towards the end of 1937, my father, sensing what was happening in the rest of Europe, started to apply to other countries so we could leave Italy. We were turned down everywhere. After he died, I found among his papers an application to emigrate to Madagascar. Madagascar did not want us. My mother adamantly refused to go to France. She said France was not far enough. She said that if my father and she felt it was necessary to save their children, which she was not entirely convinced of, we had to go very far away. We had to put a whole ocean between Europe and ourselves. And in the end that is what happened. But I will get back to that a little bit later.

Marjorie: When did you begin to feel your Jewishness?

Elena: The Jewishness of our lives really came into focus for me after the anti-Semitic laws were passed. I turned six that year and was supposed to go to school. Of course, I could not go to public school because the law did not permit Jewish children to do so. The Jewish community of Livorno had its own tiny school and took in every Jewish child. My mother was the equivalent of a supervisor of the Jewish school. My sister was a year ahead of me and had started at the Jewish school even though the laws had not mandated it, because my mother felt it coming and did not want her to have to change school and be rejected by her Catholic peers. The morning was spent on academics. We wore black smocks with white collars and red bars on our sleeves to show what grade we were in. The smocks hid our clothes so that there would be no comparison of rich and poor. Many of the Jews in the community of Livorno were pretty poor, they were mendicants, street vendors, and the like. Some, like us, were professional, and a few were quite wealthy. But in that school, we were all the same.

Each morning we were lined up and given a tablespoon of cod liver oil, the same spoon for each child. Those who could brought a sugar cube or a piece of hard candy to remove the horrible taste. We were also examined for lice with a fine-toothed comb and those who had them were sent home to have their hair cut and shampooed. We then had our academics, which were very good. When we came to the United States, having gone only to first grade at the Jewish school of Livorno, I had completed the academic curriculum through third grade in the United States.

The afternoon was devoted to religious studies and Hebrew. As a child, the memories I have are those of attending the Jewish school, of the anti-Semitic persecutions, and, above all, of being Jewish. As I said, being Jewish became a reality because of the anti-Semitic persecutions. I was not that aware of it before. Our family was not very observant. But I feel the identity with my Jewishness is extremely strong. I am proud of being a Jew. In spite of the suffering, in spite of the persecutions, I am extremely grateful that I was born a Jew into a Jewish family that remained Jewish, that my beloved husband is Jewish, and that our daughter, Elizabeth, married a wonderful young man, Andrew Herrup, who is an American Jew, because we share some things culturally and historically that make life easier and closer for all of us.

Marjorie: Tell me about your departure.

Elena: My most vivid memory is that of my last birthday in Italy, November 1,

1939. My grandmother Clara celebrated that birthday with me every year that I can remember because her real birthday was October 28, which was the anniversary of Mussolini's March on Rome.[6] She was not a Fascist. She refused to have anything to do with those people, and she refused to have her birthday celebrated on the anniversary of the March on Rome. So she elected to celebrate her birthday on mine, and that was something that I treasured and I remembered.

On that particular year of 1939, we knew that we were going to leave in just a few days. So we had a birthday party and invited all our friends and instead of receiving gifts, we gave away all of our toys. The children promised to keep them safe until our return, which of course we did not know if it would ever take place. It was not the happiest of birthdays and it is etched in my mind as if it happened yesterday. I was able to take a few books with me, very thin books, and one little puzzle made up of wooden pieces which I kept for my entire childhood. That was it. Everything else went, and the goodbyes took place that day.

Marjorie: What was it like to be Jewish in Italy?

Elena: Being a Jew in Italy between 1938 and 1939 was not the same as Poland or Germany. We were not mistreated that badly, although we could not go to school with the other children and we had to go to the public school on Sunday morning to take the state exams (we had to go on Sunday so we would not contaminate the other children). The Fascists had drives to collect gold, and my mother and father had to give their gold as well, including their wedding bands! They were put in an enormous pile in the square and collected and taken away. There were Fascist marches down the street and sometimes we Jews had to join them in our little uniforms. I do not remember that with a particularly bad feeling; it was a fact of life.

I remember once going to a crowded café with my mother, and a German (not in uniform) could not find a seat. The town was small; everyone knew we were Jewish, and he came over and he said to my mother, "Get up, you Jewish pig, and give me your table." My mother said something to him, I do not remember what, but he did not punish us and we left. Aside from small incidents like that, the worst memories are that our Lisetta, our baby-sitter whom we loved so much, and our housekeeper had to leave. First the housekeeper. Then we were given an exemption, for what reason I do not know, and were allowed to keep Lisetta for a while longer. Then she too had to leave and we all cried. No Christians were allowed to work for Jews.

When my father lost his job, it was a tremendously difficult time because not only we, but his parents and several of his brothers and sisters depended on his income. There were so many things we were not allowed, I cannot even detail them. I do remember that in the Jewish school, in my first grade, children left, teachers left; I had six different teachers in one year. The deportations to the concentration camps had not started, but people were trying to leave and the anti-Fascists were being persecuted, tortured, and murdered, as were the parents of one of the children in my school that I remember very well. It was a sad time. I remember my mother crying and arguing with my father about what we should do. She was reluctant to leave. She did not want to leave the only home she knew, and her mother and brother and sister. My father was also reluctant to leave, but he insisted that it was a choice we had to make, and that he wanted to save his children's lives if only someone would take us in. And eventually the United States did, through a series of very strange circumstances.

My mother had a cousin who was married to a wealthy man who had a number of brothers and cousins and relatives in the city of Turin. One of them was a professor of mathematics, a brilliant man, who was invited by Albert Einstein to go to the Institute for Advanced Studies at Princeton, which he did. He in turn brought my mother's cousin and the other wealthy relatives by signing an affidavit and depositing money in a bank in the United States that would support the entire family for two years. Those were the requirements to be eligible for a visa in those days. This family had money in a bank in England, was able to transfer funds to the United States, and eventually signed an affidavit for us as well—for all six of us. So it was really because of Albert Einstein that we ended up getting a visa to enter the United States.

Marjorie: That is extraordinary. What was it like going to the consulate?

Elena: I remember going to the American Consulate in Naples where we were examined and questioned by the consulate's officers. We were examined by a doctor, we were all told to take our clothes off. I was seven by that time, and rather modest, and so were my sisters, and I remember saying, "Fine. But not my underwear, that does not go." And the doctor at the consulate smiled and allowed us to keep our underwear on, lined us up in a row and examined us, and we all passed. But then the consul said to my father, "Six visas is a lot. Perhaps we could arrange four, but six is too many." My father, I recall, and perhaps he told me and I was not in the room, it's hard to remember exactly, but the fact is that he said to the consul, "Look at my four children." And there we were lined up, the oldest eight, the youngest a year and a half, standing on her own. And he said, "You choose. Which two of my daughters should I leave behind to meet certain death?" The consul relented and gave us six visas, and we were able to leave.

Marjorie: Elena, in all of our conversations, you have often talked about departure, about leaving your world and your life. Can you elaborate and tell us a little more about the intensity of those moments?

Elena: The departure from Italy was the saddest moment of my childhood. We traveled to Genoa to board the ship. My aunt Giulia, my mother's sister, came with us to see us off. It was an enormous, beautiful ship, the *Conte di Savoia,* or Count of Savoy. It was one of the two newest luxury liners of the Italian company, the other called the *Rex,* or King. We went on board having had all kinds of shots required by the American government so that we would not arrive ill; vaccinations, this, that, and the other thing. My aunt on shore (and perhaps there were others, I only remember her), was in tears as we all were, as she waved good-bye. The ship pulled out, and my youngest sister, who was one and a half, kept saying, "Zia Giulia, zia Giulia, zia Giulia," and she wanted to jump overboard and swim to be reunited with her second mother.

The ship left and we were really, really sad. My mother became ill because some of the inoculations she received had festered and made boils. For most of the journey she was unable to take care of us because she had a high fever and was quite ill. The ship stopped in several places. The last dangerous stop was Gibraltar; the British were not sure that they would let this ship through. We were there for several hours—anxious hours—and finally we were through the Straits of Gibraltar and out to sea, hopefully out to freedom.

It was November and the weather was stormy. The crossing took fourteen days as I recall (perhaps twelve, I'm not sure). Most of the people on board were refugees like us. There was a little French girl, Catherine. We played with her a great deal. We learned some French, she learned some Italian. There was a lady who wrote poetry. Her name was Mrs. Schwartz; she was Italian and she entertained us. There was a doctor, Castiglioni, who was a medical historian of some note. He too told us stories and entertained us. But it was all very difficult because my mother was ill. My father, in the old-fashioned tradition, had no experience in caring for young children, especially the youngest one, and so it came to the two oldest (ages eight and seven) to care for the two youngest (ages five and one and a half). I vividly remember chasing my little sister, trying to keep her from jumping overboard to go for a swim. It was a long journey and we were very afraid of what would happen when we arrived if my mother was still ill. Would they send her back? Would they allow her to disembark?

Marjorie: When did you catch your first glimpse of the United States? What did you feel?

Elena: We arrived in New York City on Thanksgiving Day of 1939. There were not many longshoremen because it was a holiday. The wait was interminable while they unloaded our baggage, little as it was. We were allowed to take one hundred dollars per person out of Italy and some personal belongings. My father had identification tags made of heavy gold on a heavy gold chain, hoping that he would be able to sell them and have a little bit of extra cash. He had also saved a very valuable stamp (he was a stamp collector), hidden amongst some papers, hoping that he'd be able to sell that. That was not to be. The stamp was found and confiscated. The gold chains remained with us. The time on the pier in New York seemed endless. The customs agents looked through all of our possessions. They slashed a rag doll that my youngest sister had, looking for jewelry or other valuables, and she burst into tears. They looked through the pages of the books we had brought, and finally an inspector came over and took my father and me aside and took us to another area, leaving my mother (who had been dosed with aspirin and been told to behave as if she were very healthy) alone with the other three.

The reason we were taken aside was that both my father and I wore glasses. The health inspector was looking for trachoma. If we had trachoma, an infectious disease of the eye, we would not be allowed to stay; we would be deported. We spoke no English, we did not understand why we were taken away, and I was petrified. I was petrified at being separated from my mother and my sisters, but I was also scared at the thought that I might have to spend the rest of my life, whatever it was, alone with my father, who up to that time (though a kind man) had been a distant and rather forbidding presence, and I was afraid of him. We thought we might be sent to Ellis Island and from there back to Italy. Instead we were examined, passed the examination, and were returned to the rest of the family. By that time, my mother was hysterical, thinking we had been taken away forever.

Marjorie: Did anyone come to meet you when you arrived?

Elena: Finally the people who had come to meet us, our cousins, were able to approach and greet us. We were also greeted by a Jewish organization that met refugees. They spoke to us in Yiddish, which we did not understand, and they implied that we were impostors. We were from Italy and therefore we were probably Catholic. We spoke no Yiddish; how could we be Jewish? That ended our relationship with that organization. My mother's cousin who had come to meet us took us to her home, which was on Central Park West, and from her windows we saw the Thanksgiving Day parade. What a welcome to the United States of America! We thought the whole country was a huge playground created for the benefit of entertaining little children. We had never seen floats and balloons of that size. We had never seen buildings of that height. Our breath was absolutely taken away. All I knew about America, and maybe my older sister was more sophisticated, was what we had seen in some Shirley Temple films, and we had also seen the film about the Dionne quintuplets. We knew the Dionnes lived in Canada, but we thought perhaps we might get to meet Shirley Temple. We had also heard that the streets were paved with gold; what a disappointment that was!

But we were not prepared for New York City, we were not prepared for being immersed in the English language. My mother had tried to get us a tutor in English the last few weeks we were in Italy. She was a very nice British lady with the longest, thinnest feet I had ever seen on a human being. But all that I ever learned from her was, "Pussy cat, pussy cat where have you been? I've been to London to visit the queen." That did not turn out to be of tremendous help.

Marjorie: What do you remember about those first days in the United States?

Elena: My first memories of living in the United States were of the drive from New York City to Princeton, New Jersey, where we had to live because that's where our sponsors were. I remember seeing for the first time in my life people who now are called African American, but in those days were called Negroes. It was an incredibly different experience for me and for my sisters. We did not know what to make of these people who were walking along the street in large numbers (because we drove through Harlem for some reason), and who looked very different from anyone we had ever seen. I also remember arriving in Princeton and being taken to our new home, the top floor of a two-story house. It was a house, American-style wood clapboard. I had never seen anything like it. It was adequate in size, but very, very cold. It was the end of November; we had never experienced such cold. We had brought with us some clothing, a few books, and some personal possessions, and that was all. We had a total of six hundred dollars. My father's valuable stamp had been confiscated, but we still had our gold chains with our names around our necks which we wore all the time, and which in due course my father was able to sell for some extra cash. My mother had purchased a few items of clothing for us in Italy. They were the most expensive she could find, since we could not take much money. The clothes were large, so they would last a long time. The older three girls had been outfitted in rabbit-fur coats and blue velvet leggings. We were the laughingstock of our school. In addition to not speaking English and being new in the middle of a term and looking different, we felt isolated and alone and miserable. The windows of the bedroom that I shared with my two sisters looked out over a cemetery. I wrote a letter to my grandmother Clara shortly after we arrived, and my mother said, "Try to be as cheerful as you can." So this is what I wrote—I still remember: "Dearest Nonna, we are in a place that is very different and very wonderful. It is cold and wintry, but when I look out the window, even in this cold and wintry weather, there are flowers all around." After the war, my grandmother could no longer speak, but she had kept that letter.

We missed our friends, we missed our family. The possessions were not that important, although now we had so much less than we had in Italy. But that did not seem to matter at all. What mattered was the isolation and the distance from everything we had known and loved and from the people who were so close to us in our very, very closely knit family. In school, I was placed in second grade because I was seven years old. It was a progressive school. There were no other foreign children in my class and I withdrew into myself. Even after I learned to understand English, I would not speak to anyone. We were given workbooks to fill out, which I did in the first week or so because I had covered all that work and so much more in my one year at the Jewish school in Italy. After that I brought my Italian books from home and I sat there and read. Nobody spoke with me, and I spoke with no one.

Marjorie: This reminds me of my experience in Georgia, where there were very few foreign children, and where being a foreigner was so difficult.

Elena: Ours was a strange classroom. I was used to a classroom which was very structured and very orderly and where everyone wore black smocks. Here children wore anything they wanted; they ran around the room; there were guinea pigs and rabbits in cages in the room. To me it did not seem like a school, but more like a really chaotic playground. Much to my amazement, at the end of the first grading period I received top grades in everything except in English in which I received a D because I refused to speak. Shortly after that, I saw my second grade teacher walking up the path to our house. I was petrified. In Italy if a teacher came to the house it meant trouble, but very big trouble. I hid under the bed. The teacher, Miss Dorothy Henry, spoke with my mother. I could hear them speak but I did not dare come out. My mother's English was practically nonexistent, so the conversation was mostly Miss Henry speaking to my mother and my mother not answering. Finally my mother came into the bedroom and dragged me out, partly because she did not know what I had done, and partly to act as translator since she knew that, even though I refused to speak, I did understand English by this time. When I came out, fearful and angry, Miss Henry said to me, "I am here to find out why you are so quiet and to help your family to learn English." She was kind, she was sweet, and she and my mother struck up an agreement. Once a week she would come for dinner, and in exchange for an Italian meal she would teach us all English. We kept in touch with Miss Henry for many years and she became a wonderful friend.

Nonetheless, the year we spent in Princeton was not a happy one. In fact, I do not remember my childhood in the United States as being particularly happy. The war broke out, we became enemy aliens even though we were Jewish refugees. We moved a great deal. At first my father could not find a job. He did not speak the language, and he was considered to be an enemy. Before the United States entered the war in 1941, the Depression was still prevalent and jobs were scarce. Every morning we children would help him translate the want ads in the *New York Times* and he would set out to find a job. Every evening he would come back without a job. It was an experience I will never forget.

My father, who had been the patriarch of our family, in control, intelligent, organized, who had saved our lives, was reduced to begging for a job and to relying on the kindness of strangers. It was a very humiliating and depressing experience.

Marjorie: And what did your mother do?

Elena: My mother found a little bit of work baby-sitting, particularly when she was able to travel to New York, taking the train, going into the city, and baby-sitting for the children of refugees who wanted a mature baby-sitter who would speak to the children in Italian and French, both of which my mother knew well. She would take them to Central Park in the freezing cold and come back at the end of the day exhausted. Evenings were spent doing piecework. My mother brought back boxes of hats and bows, and we would pin the bows on the hats for a penny apiece. It was new poverty, but it was not the poverty that was the problem. The problem was the war; and being considered the enemy; and being foreigners; and being dislocated and not belonging; and having no friends. Finally, my father found a job, and as he moved from a very low-paying job to a better one and a better one and a better one, we kept moving.

Marjorie: What were you like at this time in your life?

Elena: I was a shy child to start with and was convinced that I was hideous because I had to wear glasses. I was very nearsighted and got my first glasses at the age of five. In those days, in Italy, little girls did not wear glasses and the kids made fun of me. But without them I could not see. I overheard comments and I was convinced that I was too ugly for anyone to like me. Looking at photographs years later, I really was not that ugly a child, but the glasses did distort my face. How wonderful it is that things are no longer like that.

Marjorie: Was your experience with anti-Semitism in the United States different from that in Italy? I was startled and intrigued to hear you say that you were considered an "enemy alien."

Elena: In the United States we experienced anti-Semitism in an overt way that we had never experienced in our hometown in Italy. Although Jews were persecuted periodically in Italy in previous centuries, in this century, prior to Fascism, there was no problem.

Let me backtrack and talk for a second about the relationship between Fascism and anti-Semitism. At the beginning, Fascism in Italy had nothing to do with Jews. It was a nationalist movement and many, many Jews joined the Fascist party, including my father's mother. She was a Liberal, a Republican, a patriot, who loved her country and she thought that the Fascists could do away with the corruption and poverty, and bring the country to a level of development that matched the United States and other countries. How wrong she was! Anti-Semitism in Italy really began with the passage of the laws in 1938, under pressure from the Germans. The anti-Semitic movement in Italy originated and was pushed by the Germans and the Nazis. The persecutions, the deportations, and the torture only occurred after Mussolini had to abdicate power and Badoglio took over [in 1943]. Mussolini was set up in a puppet government in Saló. The Allies had landed and they were pushing the Nazis further north up the Italian boot. That's when the atrocities began in earnest. But, as I said, at the beginning, Fascism and anti-Semitism were not really linked. By the end it was the same as in Germany, although the main and very important difference was that the Italian people by and large in those days were not anti-Semitic.

Many of them, so many, helped to save Jews. My mother's sister and brother and sister-in-law and mother, the four of them, were hidden by twenty-seven different families and organizations over an eighteen-month period in the city of Florence. They were hidden by nuns, they were hidden by the hospitals for the mentally ill where they made believe that they were mentally ill, and they were warned in time that the Nazis were going to kill everyone in the institution and they moved on. They were hidden by individual families who put their own lives at risk. They were given food, although at one point the food ran out for everybody as the Nazis pillaged and destroyed and there was no food left, and for several days they went without anything. One day they had one split pea left, which they each took turns sucking on and passed on to the next person. The rats had been eaten, the cats had been eaten, the dogs had been eaten. It was a very, very horrible time, but the Jews were protected to some extent, more than in any other country in Europe except perhaps Denmark or Holland. It is also that the Italian military, the army, not the Fascists (the Blackshirts) but the regular army was not convinced about anti-Semitism and they did not carry out the atrocities and tortures in the camps that were established in Italy prior to deportation to Germany and Poland. In fact, in countries where the Italians were in command for a while, the Jews were protected. This happened in Croatia, Southern France, and Greece, but eventually, when the Nazis came in, the deportations were completed. Most of the Italian army and the Italian people did not have their hearts in the anti-Semitic persecutions.

Marjorie: What about your experiences with anti-Semitism in the U.S.?

Elena: In Princeton we did not meet much with anti-Semitism per se, but we met with hostility against foreigners in general. Later, during one of our moves (we lived in New York City; I was in third grade at that time) we lived on 113th Street and Amsterdam in a basement apartment in a building with a fire station, the fire engines going all night. Our window, the only one, connected to a fire escape. It was not a great place, it was very small. I shared a bed with my younger sister. My father worked in Hackensack, New Jersey. When he came home for weekends, I had to sleep in the crib with the baby so the other two girls could share the bed. It was not exactly an easy life, but I do not remember that part as being that difficult, although I do remember standing in line for day-old bread and for broken cookies which were very cheap. And I remember going to the grocery store with my mother to see what we could buy that had the lowest price and the largest size. Some of those items were very surprising—like pumpkins—we had no idea what they were or what to do with them.

But back to the anti-Semitism. I was in third grade. One day, a boy in my class started chasing me around the class calling me a dirty Jew. The teacher called us both to her desk and said to the boy, "This girl is from Italy. Before you start calling her names, you better find out the facts." She did not mind his calling someone a dirty Jew. She just thought that he had called the wrong person one.

Then we moved to Somerville, New Jersey, a small town with very few Jews. In fact, I think there was only one other Jewish family aside from us, and then there was a rabbi in the next town over who would come by sometimes, and who had a daughter about our age. We had rented the top half of a house that was owned by an Irish policeman and an Italo-American elementary school teacher. They were very friendly at first. One day, the rabbi's daughter came to visit. The landlady came stomping up the stairs and she said, "I do not want any Jewish feet walking on the floor over my head." My mother said to her, "That's unfortunate, because all day, every day, you have six sets of Jewish feet over your head." The woman was appalled. Again, she thought since we were Italian we could not be Jewish.

From then on, she and her husband started a campaign of persecution and she tried to get us evicted. But since there was a war going on, and you could not evict people without cause, she failed. She declared to the authorities that my father had drunken parties. When my father had a laboratory accident (he worked in a chemical laboratory) and spilled sulfuric acid on himself, and was bedridden with extensive burns, she called his employer and said that my father was out all day and was not ill at all. The employer sent someone to the house and saw that my father was bedridden, unable to walk. Every morning when she left for work, she turned off the heat, even though my mother and my youngest sister, who was then a toddler, were at home. The landlady would not allow us to use the front door, so we had to use the side door. And she parked her car so that we had to squeeze between prickly bushes and the car in order to get to the door. In other words, she made life as difficult for us as she could, but she could not evict us. It was a relief to leave there and to move on to the next place.

Elena Ottolenghi Nightingale

It is strange that we were treated worse as Jews in the United States than we had been in Italy, but that's the way it was. Years later, in 1970, we experienced anti-Semitism in Baltimore, Maryland, when my husband and I, both on the faculty of Johns Hopkins, and our little girls, moved into a restricted area. We did not know it was restricted. The Realtor again thought that since I was of Italian origin, I must be Catholic. And shortly after we moved there, in order to repay the kindness of our neighbors, who were members of the medical school faculty at Johns Hopkins, we invited two couples to dinner. During the predinner conversation they said how nice it was that our neighborhood had such nice people in it, and they went on to say, "Well, we had one family who did not fit in, but we got rid of them pretty quickly." It turned out that this family was also on the faculty of the medical school and they were Jewish. The only way they were able to force them to move was by painting swastikas on their car windows and burning crosses on their lawn. We told these couples that we were Jews and never spoke to them again.

Marjorie: What was the process of life and acculturation for you and your family like? Did you adapt completely, or did you leave parts of yourselves behind in Livorno?

Elena: My parents never assimilated, particularly my mother. My father a little more so. Our family home was a small enclave of Italy of the late 1930s. My parents' expectations of what we could and could not do remained the same, they were not affected by the world around us. So we lived in two worlds. Our Italian, old-fashioned home, and America. It was stressful and it was difficult, but it gave us an opportunity to know two worlds, two ways of living, two ways of looking at everything. In a way, it allowed me to see the world through more mature eyes. I find in retrospect that it was an enriching experience and that it contributed to my understanding of different cultures and to being able to take what is good about them and accept that with joy. Within our family we had to speak Italian. If we spoke English at the dinner table we would not be allowed to eat. At the time I thought it was pretty harsh, but now I am so grateful because even though I came to America at the age of seven, now, in my mid-sixties, I am still completely bilingual, even though I have no one left with whom to converse in Italian except when I go to Italy to visit my family, which is becoming harder and harder to do because of my poor health.

Marjorie: Elena, can you tell me what it has meant to you to live with two languages?

Elena: Having two languages meant having two cultures. My mother was a teacher of Italian literature and language so I learned a lot from her too. My father was a chemical engineer and from him I learned about science and how to look at things objectively, how to do critical analysis. They were wonderful parents in some ways, but as far as discipline goes they were, as I said, Italians of the late 1930s. So, when we arrived at dating age, my father would sit in the living room of our apartment and wait until we came home. If we were late, he would berate the young man and us equally. Also, he had to meet the young man prior to our being able to go out. He had to know where we were going, how long we were staying there, and what we were doing. I did not date very much. It was too difficult, and I was too shy, not to mention that I went to girls' schools throughout elementary and high school, even through college. I did not really date or become interested in boys, believe it or not, until I was in medical school, at which point I was able to interact with young men both in a work setting and in a social setting. And that's when I finally became an adult.

It is difficult to tell all of this in chronological order. I know I am going back and forth, but I guess that is the only way to retell one's life.

My sisters and I became half "acculturated." We adopted some of the American ways. We had to in order to survive. When we were not in our own home or if our parents were not present, we spoke English to each other. We were still very attached to Italy and to our relatives in Italy. During the four years of war since we had left, we did not receive any news. Every evening my father would turn on the radio and we would have to be absolutely quiet while he listened to Gabriel Heatter tell us the news of the world.[7]

Marjorie: How did you feel during the war years? What awareness did you have of the war?

Elena: We heard about the bombings in our home town, how our home town was razed to the ground and about some of the atrocities that were going on in Europe, and we had no way of finding out if our family was safe. The atmosphere in our home, as you can imagine, was not cheerful. Nonetheless, my father worked hard. We went to school. My sisters made friends more easily than I, but they would allow me to join them sometimes. I was pretty much alone. I liked to read, I liked to think, I liked being by myself.

The war years also were difficult because my mother became more and more upset over the situation and over not knowing what had happened to her family in Italy. She was pretty high-strung and nervous, and we had to treat her very delicately. It ended up that as we grew older, we took care of her more than she took care of us and we also took care of each other. We were very closely attached to our parents. They would not allow us to go away to college—that was not the way things were done. A girl left home only to be married. I rebelled and moved out when I went to medical school. I had lived at home all through college, but I could not deal with the crowded apartment, having no quiet place to study when I was in medical school on a scholarship. So I took out a loan and moved out. My father never forgave me. It was a difficult time also because my two younger sisters apparently suffered more than my older sister and I. I guess they had fewer memories of the old Italy and the family. But they suffered due to the atmosphere at home, the strains between the inside and the outside worlds. Their problems are an entirely different story, which affected our lives very deeply.

Marjorie: Do you feel you have adapted to the American culture?

Elena: I now feel that I have one foot in each culture. I admire the American way of life in some respects: the freedom, the democracy, the ability to express yourself, the opportunities to work hard and get somewhere. I do not admire the lack of closeness in the family, I do not admire the self-centeredness, the "me first" attitude, the need for self-gratification and personal happiness above all else, the lack of tolerance for working out problems in personal relationships. I admire and stick to the Italian way of family life, which I believe is very important: eating meals together, which I insisted upon with my husband and two daughters. Even though my husband is American, he went along with it, even having breakfast together when our children were at home. Breakfast and dinner were family occasions, and it has paid off. Our children are grown up, but they are close to us, and they are wonderful adults. As far as acculturation goes, it went partway. As far as language, I have mentioned it, I am fully bilingual and I value it. However, my vocabulary in Italian is not that of a college graduate, it is more that of a young child. So I get along fine, but if I had to give a technical paper in Italian I would need help. Sometimes I dream in Italian. It's strange, sometimes I do sums in Italian in my head. It is even stranger that sometimes I dream in French, even though my French is very limited. My parents spoke to us in French when we were little, and in my dreams I speak it very well. Learning English was not hard. I just listened, and read. I read a lot and I listened a lot, and I did not speak much. I think it took me approximately three months to understand everything, and six months to be able to speak. It surprises me that there is so much argument now about bilingual education, because children learn so fast if you give them a chance.

Marjorie: How do you feel about your career and its impact on your life, and on the lives of your children?

Elena: My career as a doctor and as a scientist, now that is something that is very complicated. My father did not want me to be a doctor; he said that was no profession for a woman, and that even though realistically he truly could not afford it, on principle he would not help me pay for school. He did not help me with college either. I went through Barnard College on a full scholarship, having to maintain a B-plus average or I would lose the scholarship, and having to work after school in order to buy school supplies and books. I did not have time to socialize, but I learned a great deal. I was also given a prize when I graduated from college, a cash prize which enabled me to pay the tuition for my first year of medical school.

I wanted to be a doctor for a very practical reason: I wanted to be a doctor because I knew that the world was a difficult place and that wars were real and that they would recur. I thought that if I was a doctor, no matter where I lived, no matter where I was displaced, no matter what happened to my family, I would have a skill that I could use to help people. That was one reason I wanted to be a doctor. The other reason was that medicine was a skill that would enable me to be self-supporting.

I did not want to be dependent on anyone ever. I did not want someone to have to support me. I had seen how, on my father's side of the family and my mother's, one person had been sacrificed to help the family. A maiden aunt on each side helped raise the children, and helped to care for the parents, and did not have the freedom to choose a life of her own. I needed and wanted a life of my own, though I loved and was close to my family. And I was afraid because my mother was so dependent on us. I thought that unless I was able to earn my own living, since I doubted I would ever marry, I would end up depending on my family for financial support. I had always doubted I would marry because I felt so shy and so unattractive. I wanted to be able to support myself and to help other people and that is why I wanted to become a doctor. But it was not easy because I had to earn scholarships and shrug off prejudice. For example the Columbia University College of Physicians and Surgeons, which I attended from 1954 to 1956 had a quota for everything. After I had started there, one of the professors said that they were very happy to get my application because not only was I Summa cum Laude, but because I was female, Italian, foreign-born, Jewish, and a New York City resident I filled five of their quotas for that year. He added that if only I had had some Negro blood I would have been perfect!

I needed money urgently, and I was unhappy in that environment. Dr. Salomé Waelsch hired me to take care of her mouse colony, and she also suggested I apply to the new graduate school at the Rockefeller Institute for Medical Research. With her assistance I was given a full tuition-room-and-board fellowship while I studied for the Ph.D. degree. So I left medical school after two years. After earning a Ph.D. in microbial genetics I was awarded a post-doctoral fellowship with Dr. Colin M. MacLeod at New York University. He was a great scientist, one of the three who discovered that DNA is the genetic material. He helped me obtain a scholarship to finish medical school (which the dean at Columbia swore I would never do) and at the same time a grant so I could do my research. I would run from my laboratory to the wards of Bellevue Hospital, then back to the laboratory. It was on the wards of Bellevue that I met my future husband, Stuart Nightingale, because my name was next to his in the alphabet! What a gift Dr. MacLeod gave me when he encouraged me to return to medical school! I became a physician-scientist, and that is what I have been the rest of my life.

Marjorie: What is your primary field of research?

Elena: I have always focused in my research on public health and infectious diseases and on the needs of children, the health and developmental needs of children. Whether it was in research on children with cystic fibrosis or spina bifida, or whether it was on health policies for children, or whether it was in human rights. My Jewish identity shaped my ethical values in my profession very deeply. I knew what it was like to be persecuted, discriminated against, and poor, therefore I knew from personal experience that it was absolutely essential to respect and value the life of each and every human being, no matter who he or she was, no matter the age, the culture, the country of origin, the state of health, the state of the economic situation, or anything else. It is also the Jewish values that I was raised with and the experiences I had encountered that enabled me to work on human rights in my spare time. I have done this for twenty years and have tried to focus on encouraging members of the health professions and scientists to become active participants in the protection of human rights of all people in all countries including the United States of America.

Marjorie: Is there anything from your youth that you greatly value and feel you have lost?

Elena: I cannot think of anything. There was no object that was that important to me. We had toys, we had clothing, we had things, but there is really not one that I miss at all. Except perhaps my grandmother's piano. I have no idea where it ended up, but that too was an object. I do not value objects that much, perhaps because we left everything behind, perhaps because we moved so much and each time left so much behind and could not afford much. I feel so completely astonished that I have such a good quality of life now, that my husband and I have been able to earn a good quality of life. But if I were to leave everything behind today, as long as my loved ones were well, I would not care. I have this sort of irrational need to have a passport ready and up-to-date at any time so that I can leave, just in case. I have the irrational need to live not far from the sea, because that was our escape route. Now the air is, and we could live in the middle of the country, but I could never live in the Midwest, it's too far from either coast. There is something inside me that would make me very depressed if I could not be near the sea. Those are irrational things, but they are the result of my experiences.

Marjorie: In this book of conversations we are constantly dwelling on memories and the past. What do these mean to you? How do you stay in touch with your memories and your past?

Elena: I cannot stress how important those memories and remembrance are as part of my Jewish legacy. My grandmother, my mother's mother, was such a lady. She had such an influence on my very early years. I have mental images of her that are incised permanently in my mind as if she were in front of me right now. She was not an observant Jew either, except for what I mentioned earlier, but we were Jewish, we were part of the Jewish community. All marriages took place in the synagogue, and it was really a very important part of our lives. On my father's side, and my mother and father were second cousins, my great-grandfather was a rabbi in the city of Acqui in Piedmont.

My father's family migrated from Germany, from the town of Öetlingen in the fifteenth or sixteenth century, I am not absolutely certain. There were pogroms in Germany and the House of Savoy in Piedmont was welcoming Jews. Many Jews came at that time and settled in Acqui, Asti, and Turin. My family's name became Italianized from Öetlingen to Ottolenghi, and that is what my maiden name is—I neglected to say at the beginning that my full name is Elena Isabella Rachele Ottolenghi. I was named after my two great-grandmothers, Isabella and Rachele Tiring, who were sisters. My father's family is the one that came from Germany and settled in Acqui, and it is my father's grandfather who was a rabbi. My father's father Umberto Ottolenghi was a very observant Jew, but his wife, whose name was Ida Cingoli, was not. She rebelled against religion, so there was a compromise in the family: the Jewish ideals and the Jewish heritage and the Jewish history were retained and are precious. We attended the synagogue in Livorno which was bombed and destroyed completely. There is now a new one, but I remember the old one.

Marjorie: Has your vision of Judaism changed over the years?

Elena: It is strange that, until anti-Semitism, we had our traditions, we were Jews, but I did not feel as strongly about it as I have felt since. And now I feel very strongly about the history of my family as Jews, including the migration from Germany. The Tiring sisters whom I mentioned migrated to Livorno from Constantinople because their father wanted them to marry Jews, and there were not enough eligible young Jewish men at the time in Constantinople. My mother's father, whose name was Eumene Levi, was the descendant of slaves brought to Rome after the destruction of the second temple, almost two thousand years ago. So our Jewish roots go back a long way. There are many stories. My father and mother were both born in Rome and lived there the first few years of their lives. There had been a rash of kidnappings of Jewish boys by the Catholic church and the boys were taken away to be raised as Catholics. One member of our family had been kidnapped, a little boy, and it was after that the entire family, my mother's family and my father's family, moved north. My mother's family moved to Florence, and my father's to Livorno.

It turned out that this little boy who was kidnapped and raised as a Catholic became a bishop, a very important person. The family found him again, years later, and on September 11, 1930, in the synagogue of the city of Florence, my parents Mario Lazzaro Ottolenghi and Elisa Vittoria Luisada Levi were married. In the synagogue, at the service, the Catholic bishop was in attendance to congratulate his relatives, the bride and groom.

My mother's side of the family (Luisada is a Spanish name) came to Italy after the Inquisition in Spain and Portugal. We have relatives with Spanish names still: Lopez, Peña, and so on, and Luisada as I mentioned. Certain members of my family were very much aware of the kind of freedom that existed in the United States and what it meant to have the emancipation of the slaves. And one of my relatives who was born in the late 1860s was therefore named Abramo Lincoln Luisada.

There are many other stories, but one I would like to tell now, even though it is out of order. When we lived in Italy, before the war, we had a pediatrician whose name was Professor Funaro, a wonderful man. He was also pediatrician to the royal family. He was the best pediatrician in all of Italy, and he was Jewish. The royal family offered him special dispensation from the anti-Semitic laws if he would remain as the pediatrician to the grandchildren of the king, Victor Emmanuel III. Professor Funaro refused. He did not trust the king, he did not trust that the protection would last, and he did not want to have anything more to do with the royal family. He had a portrait of the family in his office and he turned it around to face the wall. He was able to leave, as we were, at the end of 1939. We found him again in New York. He tried three, four, five, six times to take the examination to be a practicing physician in the United States. He kept passing the medical part and failing the English exam. The medical part was in English, how could that be? There was no way. Professor Funaro was never able to obtain a medical license; however, he took care of us when we were in the United States, even traveling far to where we lived because we could not afford a doctor, and he was the best. But he could not prescribe medications, so he had to find someone who would. He is one of my heroes.

Marjorie: Elena, it is wonderful to hear your stories and see the positive influence people like Professor Funaro had on your life. Tell me, what has become of your sisters and family?

Elena: Of my three sisters, Paola is the oldest, then I am next, then Marcella, and then finally Gianna. Two of them, the oldest and the youngest, Paola and Gianna, returned to Italy after college to do graduate work. Paola was on a Fulbright and Gianna from the Language School at Middlebury College. They met people in Italy whom they married and they have established their homes and their families in Italy. Marcella, the one after me, two and a half years younger, married an American Jew, a teacher. My brother-in-law Maury died just two weeks ago. They were a part of the Jewish community of Flushing, New York, where they lived. My sisters in Italy did not marry Jews. My older sister, Paola, married someone who is not a religious person at all and their children have not been raised in any religion, but my sister remembers her Jewish heritage and goes to Livorno to celebrate the High Holy Days with my father's remaining sisters who still live there and with the one Jewish cousin who is left.

My sister Gianna, who lives in Florence, married a Catholic who is not very observant himself, but his parents were, so she has raised her children Catholic, although neither of them practices very much. The times we visited them, when our children were young, I was very uncomfortable because there was a crucifix on the wall and a crèche at Christmastime. I'm glad those do not appear any more. We visited Italy several times after we were married when we had young children, to introduce our children to their relatives in Italy. And when our two daughters Elizabeth and Marisa were each fifteen, we sent them to spend the summer with their Italian relatives and in exchange their cousins came to the United States so they would also have a taste of being bicultural. Both my daughters are fully bilingual. Elizabeth, our older daughter, more than the younger one, Marisa, because she spent her junior year in college abroad, in Florence. So the acculturation is mixed, and it has gone into the next generation.

Marjorie: Did you return to Italy after the war? What had happened to your family?

Elena: In 1946, as soon as my father could gather the funds and obtain permission (you must remember that we were not citizens of the United States. We had come as refugees with the intention of returning to Italy after the war), we obtained what they called reentry permits valid for six months, and we obtained passage on what was a troop ship going to Europe to pick up war brides, and we went back to Italy to look for our relatives and to make the decision as to where to settle. We landed in Genoa and took something that resembled a bus, a beat-up old vehicle. There was very little gasoline in immediate postwar Italy. It was a long, long ride from Genoa to Florence and we saw the devastation of the war, partly due to the Allied bombings, partly to the mines that had been placed by the Nazis as they retreated north. The mines blew up everything in sight and continued to kill for many years. There was rubble everywhere. People were poor, rummaging through rubble for the remnants of something that was useful.

We finally arrived in Florence and found our relatives. Of our large family, three cousins had been deported and killed. Everyone else had survived. However my mother's mother had suffered a massive stroke and could not speak. She looked at us all. I think she knew who we were. She died a few months later. My father's father had died at the very beginning of the war, before the atrocities began, and my grandmother was grateful that he had been spared what the others went through. We found my father's mother and one of my father's sisters in a convent in Florence where the nuns had taken them in for shelter, since they owned nothing.

We found all of our relatives scattered here and there, and heard their stories which I will never forget. Several of them made their way into Switzerland walking over the Alps, led by a smuggler who was paid a large sum. One of these refugees was my father's mother who was in her sixties at the time and quite heavy and unused to walking, but she made it. They were arrested by the SS in the train station in Florence, but fortunately there was an air raid and the SS officer went to a shelter. My grandmother and two aunts who were traveling together ran out into the street. They were able to reach Milan by train, and then the smuggler took them the rest of the way. At the Swiss border, the guards tried to turn them back. They could hear the police dogs barking and the shooting behind them. My grandmother had hidden a brooch that the guard liked, and so with that bribe he let them in. But he said, "We do not want any more Jews in Switzerland."

They were treated rather roughly in the camps, but not tortured. They were put to work, all of them, to earn their keep. We now know that Swiss Jews paid for those same expenses. They slept on straw pallets, their food was minimal, but that is another story entirely.

My Aunt Lea tells this story in a diary she kept during her confinement in a refugee camp in Switzerland. The diary speaks of the indignities imposed on her, but also of the hope for the future. When finally I read it a few years ago it touched me deeply. Half of my aunt's diary is addressed to her fiancé and the need to know what happened to him and whether he was safe. In the camp, my aunt writes, children were fed separately from adults, and one of the Swiss matrons would time by a clock how much time they had to eat and would force-feed them if they were too slow. One of my little cousins kept vomiting because he was force-fed. Another one of my aunts was pregnant when she arrived in Switzerland. Her husband arrived separately, but was there in the same camp. When she gave birth he was not allowed to visit her because men and women were kept separately. These were the kinds of things that happened, that were certainly far removed from what happened in the

Nazi concentration and extermination camps, but I cannot say that the Swiss welcomed and treated the Jewish refugees well.

One of my uncles, my father's sister's husband, was captured by the Nazis twice. Once he was placed before a firing squad. The bullet missed him, he fell down as if dead, and before they collected the bodies he got up and walked away. Another time, he was able to kill the guard and escape. He was a school teacher, a mild-mannered man. He is still alive, a kind and gentle soul. That is their story, but it has become part of my life as well.

Marjorie: How did you become involved in the human rights area?

Elena: It took me many, many years before I was able to work directly in human rights. I don't know whether it was because I was suppressing it since it was too painful or whether my social awareness had really not matured enough. It was so time consuming to get an education, to establish a professional identity, to have a family, that I didn't have a single moment to think about other things. But that is no excuse because you can always make the time if it is something that is important and uppermost in your mind. Working on behalf of human rights with people all over the world really became a mission for me. I feel sometimes in retrospect that I wasted a lot of time, that I should have been more aware and more active earlier in life. But I just wasn't. On the other hand, it's better to have started late than not to have done it at all.

I became an activist in human rights about twenty years ago when the American Association for the Advancement of Science invited me to serve on their Committee on Scientific Freedom and Responsibility, which had a subcommittee on human rights and which needed a physician. At that time there were many cases of physicians who were detained or who disappeared, and also of physicians who participated in torture and other human rights abuses. The doctors were mostly in Latin America or in the Soviet Union. As part of this work I collaborated with Eric Stover on a book, *The Breaking of Bodies and Minds: Torture, Psychiatric Abuse, and the Health Professions*. I think that this book has perhaps been more useful than any other work I have done. And I am indebted to Eric because without his collaboration I would not have been able to understand the situations he had witnessed firsthand.

I have also worked a long time on the rights of children, first with Amnesty International, U.S.A., now with Human Rights Watch and other groups. I work still to raise the rights of children higher on the agenda of human rights and relevant professional organizations because children are innocent victims of what adults do and they do not have their own independent voice. They are victims more than once; they themselves are often personally victimized, as happened in Pinochet's Chile or apartheid South Africa, and more recently in other places such as Rwanda or Bosnia where children were raped and tortured in other ways. They are victims also when their parents are tortured or disappear. Even if one parent remains, the impact of losing a parent is grave. The remaining parent may not be able to provide security, attention, and nurturing to the children while grieving and searching for the disappeared. Children are victimized by living in a world of uncertainty and fear, which can affect their entire lives adversely.

Closer to home, social policies here in the United States do not always keep the best interests of the child as a top priority, because children are not viewed as a national treasure and an investment in the future as they should be. It is for such reasons that I am deeply committed to working for the rights of children everywhere, including here.

I remember very vividly what it felt like to be a child. It was not the happiest part of my life, at least not after the age of seven when we left Italy. But that is nothing compared to when I try to imagine what so many children must have felt as they went through unspeakable experiences and survived, or prior to execution. It is too real, and I cannot deal with it emotionally. Marjorie, it is something that hurts too deeply to begin to describe, but it reinforces my special interest in the rights of children.

Marjorie: Was it very hard for you because you were trying to establish your career and be a mother at the same time?

Elena: Every moment of every day was occupied with keeping my head above water. I was teaching in medical school, doing research, and raising young children with a husband who was very, very busy, even though he was very helpful when he was at home. And I was very busy with my parents, both of whom were very ill. My mother died when my older daughter was only one year old. She died after an illness which lasted six months. It was a very agonizing experience for me. My father died seven years later. He had a heart attack right after my mother died and his condition was delicate.

So I helped as much as I could to care for my parents. Two of my sisters were in Europe and could not help very much. There were two of us in New York who shared the burden. It was a very big burden and emotionally draining as well. This was at the same time that I was trying to establish a career and my family.

In retrospect, it was all at the time when the human rights movement was most active in the United States, the late 1960s. I regret not being more active at that time in that movement because I should have been. I should have been more aware. I read the newspapers. I knew what was happening, but I did not get involved directly. I did not take an active part. I wish I had, but that is something I cannot correct now.

Marjorie: What was for you the most poignant experience you have had as a human rights activist and as a physician?

Elena: I think perhaps the one experience that remains with me most vividly is my visit to Chile in 1985, when I went into a prison in Santiago to visit some political prisoners. It was amazing how easy it was to go into a prison. We had been told just to line up at the time that the visitors were allowed to go in and not to bring anything with us—no possessions except for our passports.

So I did that and they took my passport and patted me down to see if I had weapons or anything else. They asked for the name of the person I was visiting and I gave them the name of a woman who was a political prisoner there. I went in with a colleague, Eric Stover, who had the name of another person. We just walked into this big room during visiting hours and these women were there. Some of them had their children with them. I spoke with several of them. I understand Spanish, but I don't speak it very well and I did not take any notes because I did not want to arouse the guards' suspicions. But what they said was vividly memorable.

There was one woman who had been taken prisoner because her husband was Bulgarian and had gone home to visit his parents. At that time, anyone suspected of having any dealings with any Communist country was an immediate enemy. This woman was Chilean, but her husband was from Bulgaria, a Communist country at the time. So he was arrested in a different place. She was arrested and ended up at the San Miguel prison in Santiago. She told me what had happened to her.

She was rather fragile mentally to start with and they knew that, the people who arrested her. Before she was actually made a known prisoner, with a name and a number, she was detained without charge or trial in a secret place. She was shown a film of her parents being executed. Again and again and again and again for hours at a time. She was forced to keep her eyes open and watch. These were not actual executions, they were sham executions. Her parents were alive and well, but the point of this psychological torture was to break her will and get her to release the names of people she knew and whom her husband knew, who might have Communist sympathies.

Instead, she became psychotic, completely psychotic. When that happened, they put her in the San Miguel prison, where she was a known prisoner with a number and so forth. Her mind came and went, though. She had no treatment, nothing. No psychiatrist saw her, no doctor saw her, and she was in terrible shape.

One of her coprisoners was standing nearby and I spoke with her also. She had been arrested, too, for suspicion of having acted or spoken against the government, which she had not. But she had two very young children and since she had no one to take care of the children, they put them in prison with her. I don't exactly remember their ages, but they were both under four years of age. She told me how hard it was to keep these children in prison.

This was a prison that was not just for political prisoners. It also housed convicted murderers, thieves, and other criminals. One of the ways of torturing political prisoners was to put them in prison with felons and criminals and to have the separation of the cells between the women and the men so thin that the men could come through anytime. In fact, the guards aided the felons so they could rape the female prisoners. These women were constantly being terrorized. The woman I spoke to had kept her children there for a full year and a half. She could not subject them anymore to observing that kind of violence, or the lack of nutrition and hygiene in prison. She gave them up and she did not know where the guards or the people in charge had taken her children. She did not know who had them or whether she would ever see them again. I don't think I will ever forget that.

Marjorie: Do you think citizens and civilians are taking human rights more seriously now? You said that you wished you had been more active in the 1960s. Do you think we are becoming a saner society?

Elena: In some respects yes, in some, no. I think the creation of Amnesty International,[8] more than thirty years ago, has helped to make ordinary citizens aware of the violations of human rights around the world and has created a grassroots movement which includes many young people, at the high school and even elementary school level, who are willing to take time to write letters on behalf of prisoners of conscience in other countries, whom they will never see or know. But they feel that it helps for them to write these letters and the letters do help. There is no question about it. So there are thousands of people in the United States—I think the membership of Amnesty International worldwide is in the millions—and I think that the organization, which is basically a grassroots citizens organization that speaks out on behalf of human rights, has helped to raise awareness.

On the other hand, it is much more difficult in some ways to be a human rights activist now, because the lines are not as clearly drawn as they were when there was a cold war going on. The kinds of human rights violations being committed are different. There are prisoners of conscience who are imprisoned, tortured, and murdered, and prisoners of conscience are still important. But there were millions of people whose human rights were violated through genocide, like in Rwanda and Cambodia, and violations in African nations, such as under apartheid in South Africa. There are violations in Southeast Asia, in China. The victims are very, very large numbers of civilians, more than three quarters of them are women and children who are not in prison, but who are being preyed upon by either political insurgencies, ethnic cleansing (as in the former Yugoslavia), frank genocide, mass movements of refugees, confinement of many millions of people in refugee camps that are substandard and provide no protection from violence.

I don't think that the general public is sufficiently informed about these atrocities. With more education there would be more commitment. By and large, most young people have a streak of altruism in them until it is destroyed. It is important to take advantage of this altruism, but if they are ignorant of what is going on, young people cannot act on behalf of human rights. That is why education about human rights is so crucially important. It also sensitizes people to respect all human beings.

Marjorie: Why are you so passionate about human rights? Does it stem from your childhood? From your experience as a Jew?

Elena: I think so. How could it not? I was young and impressionable and entered my teen years during the Second World War. I saw with my own eyes the devastation of the war in Italy after the Second World War and heard the stories (even though I was not there) of the people, the Jewish people, who had been hiding for two years, never seeing the sun . . . children I knew who had rickets because they had never been outside of the basement for two years . . . people who had starved to death while hiding . . . people who had been tortured . . . people who had been through unspeakable experiences. It left a mark and since my home and family were in Europe and those I knew who were suffering were mostly Jewish people, I was much more sensitive to that group. But it does not mean that I did not care about others, such as the Koreans or Chinese, who were horribly treated during that war.

Marjorie: Do you feel that Italy is still very much your home? Or is the U.S. your home now?

Elena: That is a very difficult question to answer. In some ways both are home and in some ways neither is home. At times, I feel like a permanently displaced person because part of me is rooted in an Italian-Jewish tradition that no longer exists because Italy has changed so much. But I do remember the way it was and my experiences many years ago.

At the same time, I grew up and had all my education here. I built my professional life and my family in the United States. And, it was the United States which, despite its anti-Semitism, saved our lives and allowed me, who had no money, to have a quality education and to have a career and be able to support myself and marry and have a wonderful family of my own. These are things that I appreciate. I appreciate the freedom in the United States, although there is that freedom in Italy now—to be able to speak out about anything without the risk of being arrested. I still feel that it is extremely important to have the right to criticize the president, even to his face, if I feel that is what I want to do. So . . . I guess I have lived most of my life in the United States, but part of my life, even though I was physically in the United States, was emotionally across the ocean.

When I am in Italy and people criticize America, I defend it. When I am in America and people criticize Italians, I defend them. There are good points and bad points about both. I appreciate the good ones and despair at the bad ones. So, I don't know . . . I think I have enough influence from my Italian-Jewish background that I am not *really* American. But, I have enough influence from my American upbringing to know I am not *really* Italian. I cannot see myself working in Italy because it is so difficult now to get ahead professionally. Unemployment is high. You can only get ahead if you know someone who knows someone. Here it is based much more on merit. It is a huge difference, and a really important one. And yet, I appreciate the strength of the family, a closeness in Italy and an ability to enjoy life and to laugh that seem to exist less here. This, in Italy, is something I value very much.

Marjorie: Has it been very painful to be from nowhere or to be from both places at once?

Elena: It has been painful, but it has given me strength. I think sometimes, when you go through painful experiences, they make you wiser and stronger than if you have been protected your whole life. In fact, that is one thing I worried about with my own children—that they would not learn to deal with major problems. Certainly, they had the problems of doing well in school and getting into a good college and peer relationships . . . but I am grateful they did not have to confront serious problems. I wonder, if at some point they have a serious crisis, I hope that my husband and I have done enough to give them the inner strength to deal with it.

Marjorie: When you arrived in the United States, you were a young girl. Do you have an image of this country that has remained with you? I always had this image that gold grew in America and even now when I see things that shine . . . something like that?

Elena: Well, you know, the myth that in America the streets are paved with gold . . . it was really a metaphor for the wealth that was here for everyone to take if you worked hard enough. But my image of America when I was little was that it was so big; that everything was big and the distances were so vast.

The way of life was so advanced, technologically and in every way from what I had left. There was a whole generation lag in Italy from the way things were done there and here at the beginning of the 1940s. The transportation, the way of life, the medical care . . . it all seemed so efficient and mechanized and impersonal. At the same time, I admired it and was intimidated by it.

Then there was the vast number of people. When we lived in New York, I had never imagined a place that big with buildings that high and with so many people on the sidewalks. Being surrounded by so many people who were strangers, who did not smile at you or say hello . . . In Italy if you see someone on the street you acknowledge each other and say hello. Here that was scary. I was quite intimidated, really, by the whole experience.

Marjorie: Do you still feel intimidated now? Have you gotten used to it?

Elena: I have gotten used to it, but I don't like large crowds. I am afraid of large crowds in a sense. Maybe it's because of the mass demonstrations. When a fascist government wants to show power, a demonstration is organized. People come and they shout and scream and clap. So I have never liked places that have very large crowds. I find large crowds distasteful and at times scary, even if it's a large crowd at a ball game or an amusement park. I try to avoid those and I don't know if it is because of early memories or because I don't like a lot of people in one place. I feel the danger of masses of people.

Marjorie: You have traveled throughout the world. What country is the most special to you?

Elena: Well, my travels have been limited to the former Soviet Union and several European countries, a couple of places in Africa and south of the border into Mexico and Chile. I don't know which country to choose. There are different ones for different reasons. I was really taken by the physical beauty of Norway, but somewhat taken aback by the coldness of the people I encountered and the climate. I did not see the beauty of South Africa because I was there on a human rights mission, but I saw one little bit on a drive to the Cape of Good Hope because driving in a car was the only place I could talk to this person without fear of being overheard. I saw ostriches and baboons running around. It was amazing. But I don't know that I would want to spend a lot of time in that country, even now.

I think really of all the countries where I have been, my favorite is still Italy. If I had to choose a place to retire in comfort, I would retire in Italy. But my family is American, so I won't do that. I am happy with my family here in America.

Marjorie: When I say good-bye to Elena, I begin to think that true conversation is not just a casual interchange but rather quite the opposite: it is an inquiry, an investigation, an eternal search for humanity. I have realized that conversation is an enterprise similar to writing, that both occupy a time during which the open and sometimes secret zones of the word must be preserved. Where everything can be said and not said. Is this not the place occupied by spoken memories?

SUSAN BENDOR

February 5, 1937	Born in Budapest, Hungary
May 1944–January 1945	Family in hiding in Budapest
December 25, 1948	Leaves Hungary with parents and brother for Vienna, Austria. Attends Hebrew school for refugee children operated by the American Joint Distribution Committee
January 1951	Moves to Zurich, Switzerland. As a foreigner, cannot attend public school
June 21, 1951	Emigrates to Montreal, Canada, with parents and brother. High school instruction was in English, but study of French compulsory
December 10, 1951	Maternal grandmother dies in Budapest
1953	Lives in Israel at two different kibbutzim with friends from Zionist organization in Vienna
1957	Bachelor's degree in mathematics and physics with awards at Bishop's University, Lennoxville, Quebec, Canada
1957–1958	Heidelberg University in Germany; studies psychology and sociology with World University Service Fellowship. Works in Paris as an au pair during school holidays
Fall 1958–1959	Montreal, Canada; market research assistant at Canadian National Railways
November 29, 1959	Marries Edgar in Montreal and moves to Long Island, New York, for his job
1960	Moves to Great Neck, New York
1962	Master's degree in social work at Adelphi University
February 11, 1965	Daughter Jane is born
1966	Edgar's parents, also Holocaust survivors, move to Great Neck
September 21, 1966	Daughter Cathy is born
1968–present	Variety of social work positions including associate director of social service at Montefiore Medical Center and director of social work, Molloy College
1981	Brother dies of complications from juvenile diabetes in Ottawa, Canada, at the age of forty-five, on the thirth-sixth anniversary of their liberation from German occupation
1986	Doctorate in social welfare from City University of New York

1988–present	Associate professor at Wurzweiler School of Social Work, Yeshiva University
May 7, 1989	Father dies suddenly in Montreal
1992	Visits Hungary with Cathy
1996	Journeys to Budapest with the aunt who had been in hiding with her family. Visits grandmother's grave
April 8, 1997	Mother dies suddenly in Montreal

At the close of World War I, Hungary rescinded its oath to the Hapsburg monarch in Vienna and set out to create a government independent of Austria. Political turmoil ensued for the next two decades, with clashes within and outside parliament between right-wing parties and Communists. By the mid-1930s, Hungary strengthened its economic ties with Germany and signed a series of agreements with Italy and Austria to cooperate in matters of trade and export. These economic ties brought Hungary in line with the Axis governments ideologically as the thirties progressed.

On March 1, 1935, Ferenc Szálasi, a former military officer, formed the Party of the National Will, which espoused fascist principles. This group merged with the Hungarian National Socialist Party in August 1938 to form the formidable Arrow Cross party. This newly strengthened political right wing made a series of militaristic gestures, which included passing a universal conscription law for all citizens between the ages of fourteen and seventy and expanding Hungary's borders to include southern Slovakia, southern Ruthenia, and northeastern Transylvania. Although the government had an official policy of "armed neutrality" at the start of World War I, it nonetheless passed its first anti-Jewish legislation in the spring of 1939, mandating the expulsion of Jewish government workers and the limitation of Jews in business professions. It also developed an emigration program for Hungarian Jews.

Poland's division between Germany and the Soviet Union following the German invasion on September 1, 1939, left Hungary in a precarious geopolitical position. By mid-1940, the Hungarian government, under immense pressure from Germany, introduced and enforced more extensive anti-Semitic legislation. Later that year, Hungary entered the war on the side of the Axis powers. In the early years of the war, the Hungarian government remained ambivalent about its alliance with Germany and attempted to protect its Jews against deportation. However, the powerful pro-German Arrow Cross party and its followers essentially undermined these efforts. When Germany occupied Hungary in the spring of 1944, the Arrow Cross and Budapest police began to organize the deportation of 450,000 Hungarian Jews to concentration camps in Poland. It was to escape this deportation that Susan Bendor and her family hid in a Budapest cellar for eight months. By the end of 1944, Hungarian Communists seized control of the government, renounced all ties to Germany, and declared war against the Axis powers. Early in 1945, the Hungarian Red Army seized control of Budapest, forcing German troops to evacuate Hungary by the spring. The tragedy of the annihilation of Hungarian Jewry is heightened by the fact that most of the 565,000 Jews who were killed between 1941 and 1945 within Hungary's concentration camps actually died in the final months of the war.

Susan first introduced herself to me in a letter in which she described how two German soldiers—who guarded a factory that manufactured uniforms for the Gestapo—had secured that cellar for her own, and several other, Jewish families. She was also writing to Yad Vashem in order to honor these men.[1] In December 1997, I finally met Susan face to face in New York, a city electrified by the multiplicity of languages. We met, kissed, and embraced like good friends reunited after a long absence. She was slender and graceful, perhaps due in part to the many years she studied ballet in Budapest. Her deep bright eyes revealed an extraordinary capacity for observation, an ability to see beyond the surface of events. She viewed herself as a skilled detective, always on the lookout for danger. I smiled, knowing exactly what she meant.

She spoke of her beautiful city of Budapest, of strolls along the Danube, and of her mother's love of open spaces. I kept thinking of what it must have been like in that stuffy cellar filled with rancid odors in a besieged and fearful wartime city. I asked Susan what she did to fill those long hours and she told me that she could not remember, that she would like to, but that so far she has not been able. She was seven when she was trapped in the cellar, and what she did remember was the intensity of that year. Subsequent years in Hungary dimmed by comparison. This is why it was difficult for her to answer my questions about her life in America—this period, too, lacked the vividness of her prewar Budapest childhood and the eight months in the cellar. She remembered the enforced silence of the cellar, and told me that in the cellar, silence itself became a way of existing, a way of staying alive. Then one day, suddenly, on a ski trip to Vermont with her family, she heard people yelling wildly all over the slope, and she wanted to do the same thing. As the sun went down and night approached, she left her family and went alone to yell on the mountainside. She said it was one of the most memorable days of her life. She felt liberated.

These are the things that have marked Susan's life, the once small child who lived in silence in a Budapest cellar, who has learned about open spaces and is able to yell at a mountainside.

Marjorie: How was your life affected by the Second World War?

Susan: The war plays an enormous role in my early memories. One of the earliest ones involves my giving up my pacifier. I must have been three or four in 1940 or '41. My father was away in labor camp and I missed him very much.[2] My mother, knowing that he was to come home for one day's leave, told me that if I acted like a big girl and gave up my pacifier, my father would come home. I did give up my pacifier with great reluctance, but then he had to leave again. I was inconsolable since I now had neither my pacifier, nor my father. My brother, who was only two years older than me, was always the soother in the family. He sat on my bed for hours and offered me one of his precious toys, I don't remember which one, if I would stop crying. Eventually I did.

I also remember having my first haircut, and my mother picking up some of the gold hair from the floor in order to send a lock of it to my father in labor camp. When my own daughters had their first haircuts, I automatically saved their hair and put it away in a box, as if I too had to send it to someone we all loved, though my husband fortunately was at home and did not have to miss the big milestones in our children's lives the way my father did. My mother's attempts to keep him actively involved, directly or indirectly, had a profound effect on me.

Marjorie: Are all your memories distressing, or are there happy recollections, too?

Susan: There were also happier memories. My grandmother lived with us in our large apartment in Budapest and my married but childless aunt was actively involved in every aspect of our lives. When my mother took my juvenile diabetic brother for tests, or to hospitals, my aunt took wonderful care of me. Until the war, I remember that there was always somebody close by to play with, someone who loved us and always had time for us. We played lots of card games both before and after the war, and going to the theater was a fairly frequent event, with my mother, aunt, and grandmother taking my brother and me. My father was usually too busy working in his textile store, both before and after the war, to join us.

Early childhood activities also included taking piano lessons from a teacher who came to the house, whom I hated, and taking ballet lessons from age four or five on, which I loved, three times a week at the opera ballet master's private ballet school. My mother was convinced that it would make me into a graceful child, which I suspect it did for a while. I was good at ballet and the teacher, Mr. Nadasi, was very fond of me. He is one of the first heroes of my life. The year in ballet school ended with a semiprofessional performance in the opera house. As one of the members of the youngest group of children, we were to be the Little Dolls whom the Matchgirl sees coming to life through the window, as she freezes to death on the street. I practiced along with everyone else and had my measurements taken for a costume along with everyone else. But when the beautiful taffeta dresses were delivered to our classes for everyone to try on, there was none for me. By then, Jews were not allowed to participate in public events. I did what any small child would do, which was to cry bitterly. This time I was again inconsolable. My mother and aunt tried to explain to me that it was not because I was bad, or a worse dancer than the others, but because we were Jewish. I was too small to understand that and kept crying, and did not want to go back to ballet classes. A few nights later, I heard my mother and aunt whispering outside of the room I shared with my brother. They had told Mr. Nadasi why I would not come back to class and he decided that, "If one child cannot dance, there will be no performance." These words resound in my ear as if I heard them yesterday. In the next few days, there was a flurry of activity. The seamstress took new measurements from me and miraculously delivered a blue dress for me. Everyone else's was pink, but, by this time, there was no more pink material left to be bought. Each night repeated whispering between my mother and aunt went on outside our room. My name would have to be changed on the program from "Blum," so obviously a Jewish name, to "Virag," a Hungarian name, so that my Jewishness would not be noticed. The little Jewess stood out in her blue dress, yet Mr. Nadasi took the risk of disobeying the law in order to make one little Jewish child happy, and resist the injustice of the ban against public performance by Jews. His dictum, "If one child cannot dance, there will be no performance," has profoundly shaped the kind of person I have become. Mr. Nadasi remained my favorite person in the world until we left Hungary.

Marjorie: What else do you remember of your early childhood?

Susan: Other early memories include going to the circus and zoo, which I loved, and going to the country, to Lake Balaton, where my father had built a small but beautiful villa named after me: it was "Zsuzsa Villa." Like most prewar memories, my early recollections are inexorably mixed with later, less happy memories of wartime. This villa was the one we went to on the day the Germans invaded Hungary, on March 19, 1944. My father, convinced that Budapest would be bombed to ruins, thought we would be safe in the country, and ordered my mother, from his labor camp, to take us to the country, my grandmother and aunt included. The day we left, German soldiers were everywhere, in what seemed to me to be the thousands, and the air was filled with fear and danger. We stayed in the country only a few weeks in March. It was dreary and lonely. None of my parents' friends or other people were around, and for food, we bought three chickens, both for eggs and for meat. Then my first understanding of deportation came one sudden day. My mother and aunt realized that deportations were to begin in the countryside rather than in cities, because it was easier to round up Jews where they were most conspicuous, and least numerous. My brother and I were told one day that we were leaving our Balaton villa the next day. We were given new names, and practiced day and night what we were to say if someone approached us on the train. My father was sending two men for us, and they would take us back to Budapest as if we were their families. My brother and I were terrified, afraid that we might forget our new names and give our real ones. We also did not want to leave the chickens behind. We had gotten attached to them and had named them, as our companions. The train ride back to Budapest was terrifying.

Marjorie: What was happening to the rest of your family?

Susan: I learned sometime later that my paternal grandmother, aunt, and two cousins who were in a more Orthodox part of the country were deported to Auschwitz the day after the Friday we returned to Budapest. My father had also sent someone for them, but my grandmother refused to allow the family to get onto the train because it was too close to Shabbos [the sabbath]. They were deported Saturday morning and never came back. My father never forgave himself for not acting faster, or for sending them to the country in the first place. His grief about his mother, sister, and nieces permeated much of our postwar life. My mother and I put the names of those lost family members on the headstone of my father's grave after he died in Montreal in 1989 so that at least there should be a record that they lived at all, and so that my father could at last rest in peace, symbolically united with them. My own negative feelings towards rigid Jewish Orthodoxy can be traced back to the loss of my paternal grandmother, aunt, and cousins. To this day I cannot understand how my grandmother could risk her own and her family's lives, rather than risk disobeying the command of not traveling on Shabbos.

Marjorie: How did it seem to be living through those times?

Susan: Once we got back to Budapest, life deteriorated rapidly. Our house was designated as a Jewish house, with a big yellow star on it, so we did not have to move to the ghetto, but four strangers, people who used to work for my father, moved into our small two-bedroom apartment. Every day there were new laws and prohibitions against Jews. Jews could no longer own telephones, radios, or go to school or to work in their old jobs. My brother and I had to wear a yellow star on every garment we owned, as did my mother, aunt, grandmother, and every other Jew we knew. It was a risk to go onto the street because you never knew if someone from the Gestapo would stop you, find something wrong with you, and shoot you on the spot or take you to the Danube to shoot you. My mother and aunt tried to protect us from much of this knowledge but we now lived in a very crowded apartment and the talk of the grownups dominated the apartment. My brother and I were not allowed out to play, and we could no longer engage in our usual activities. We also witnessed when officials, I do not know who, came to our apartment to take our telephone and our radio, which was my mother's lifeline. My mother was totally preoccupied with developing new avenues for escape. They ranged from standing in line for most of a day at the Swedish Embassy to obtain a precious Wallenberg-inspired visa,[3] to spending all our money on building an annex to the house of a farmer which we never occupied. Another plan involved giving all of us an insulin shot so we would go into diabetic shock and the Germans would mistake us for dead and leave us behind. After they supposedly left, Mr. Klein, our kind, elderly neighbor who was too old to be taken to labor camp, was supposed to come and give us grape sugar to bring us out of shock. It was not until many years later that I realized the fallacy of this plan: Mr. Klein would have been deported, too, so would not have been around to raise our blood sugar levels to bring us out of insulin shock. As a child, the only thing I disliked about this plan was the prospect of getting a shot, which I hated as a child. Otherwise, I felt greatly comforted by the fact that my mother would find a way to save us and keep us from being deported. If one plan did not work—if, for example, we could not get one of the few Swedish visas—I was sure that my mother would come up with another. My mother, a very beautiful, shy woman who only had an eighth-grade education, was both inspired and relentless in her commitment to save her children. She began hoarding insulin in 1939, when my brother was first diagnosed with juvenile diabetes. She kept much of the insulin in a red leather bag which never left her arm. When we went into hiding in May of 1944, that red bag saved my brother's life.

Marjorie: What was it like right before you went into hiding?

Susan: Before going into hiding, the air raids, which repeatedly forced us to go into the cellar of the apartment building and to spend evenings without lights in the apartment, were the most memorable and disturbing events to my brother and me, since the notion that you might die or be hurt was ever present. Here, my Jewish faith was very helpful. In April of 1944, there was a particularly bad air raid in the midst of a Passover service which we were conducting in the dark. My father had escaped from labor camp in order to bury his father and he was conducting the service when we had to go down to the cellar. The grownups were very worried because judging from the sirens, they knew that this was a particularly serious attack. My brother and I knew that we were not going to die. We had not yet opened the door for the prophet Elijah, so we knew we would have to go back upstairs in order to finish the service. "You cannot die before you let Elijah in, and before Father reads you the Chad Gadya," said my brother.[4] This was very reassuring, and even now, as an adult, I get very upset if someone in my Reform temple tries to change the order of prayers. It is very important to me that the service should proceed exactly as it is written, just as it did during that memorable Passover service.

Marjorie: Do you have clear memories of the moment you went into hiding?

Susan: The day we went into hiding was definitely the most traumatic day of my life as a child. Wuchte, the tall German officer who headed the German uniform factory to which my aunt was assigned to work, came to get us, to take us to the hiding place in his car. My brother and I were told to be very quiet and very good. My father had escaped from labor camp a few days earlier in order to bury his father. He was the only child still in Hungary. As the son of Orthodox parents, he did not shave in honor of his father's death. When Wuchte came, he told my mother that he could not take my father because his beard would attract attention. My brother and I cried bitterly. We had just gotten him back, and we did not want to lose him again. Wuchte ordered my father to shave quickly and my mother begged us to stop crying and making noise. We went downstairs to wait in the tiny car. Soon after, my father came down to the gate of the apartment building where we lived, holding a handkerchief to his face. He had been in such a hurry that he cut himself badly. Wuchte said that he still could not take him because the bloody handkerchief would be so likely to attract attention. My brother and I (we were nine and seven then) said that we wanted to stay, too, because we could not leave him behind. By this time, my mother was crying, too. Most of the communication was nonverbal, since I cannot remember anyone speaking German except my father. I remember feeling terrified, afraid to leave and afraid to stay. Finally Wuchte walked across the street to get my father, so it would look as if he were arresting him. My mother begged us not to make a peep. We didn't. We were so relieved that my father was in the car with us, that we would have kept quiet forever.

Once we were in the cellar of the apartment building, Nagymezo utca 6, which housed the uniform factory which Wuchte directed, to which my aunt had been assigned to work (to contribute to the war effort), my memory bank only contains certain highlights. They are vivid memories of specific events, and sources of fights between the adults, rather than a proper history. There were two other families with children and one deaf and dumb couple there in hiding with us. The families had two children: one girl, Eva, who must have been about eight—she was closer to my brother's age than to mine—and the other, a very beautiful girl named Baby, who was a teenager.

Marjorie: Do you remember your hiding place clearly?

Susan: The cellar was dark and had a sickening, sweet, stale odor. The only light came from a candle which I believe resembled a yahrzeit candle.[5] I have no memory of how we killed time for eight long months as children. We must have played some word games and some storytelling, because we were not allowed to make noise and there was not enough light to play or to read. The fights between the adults were mostly about access to the light and the need for the four men to take turns at night going up onto the street with the pail we used for a bathroom, and emptying that pail onto the street.

Marjorie: What was all this like for your mother?

Susan: My mother always got into trouble for taking too much time at the light. She carried a red leather bag day and night, tied to her wrist, which contained my brother's insulin and the needle paraphernalia. When we went into hiding, my mother had put all of the insulin she had been hoarding since my brother had been diagnosed with juvenile diabetes in 1939 at age four, into her red bag. It also contained a tiny jar of face cream she had brought with her into hiding. My mother was an incredibly beautiful and appearance-conscious woman until the day she died, just recently. The other mothers did not mind her using the light to give my brother his insulin shot, but they did get mad when she put her cream on. I remember for a long time being scared that the women would get into a physical fight over it. I often worried that maybe my mother really had no right to worry over her face cream. At the same time, I desperately wanted her to have the chance to use it. Not only was my mother's beauty something we were all proud of, but there was also something reassuring about your mother worrying about looking pretty. You know that you are not going to die if your mother is willing to have such a big argument about looking good for the future. It was so dark in the cellar that nobody paid much attention to how you looked today. The arguments between the fathers were even more scary because we as children knew that whoever had a turn that night might never come back if he got caught. And if he were caught, that would be the end of all of us. As children, we were not allowed to take sides or to participate in the adults' fights. In retrospect, that was a brilliant decision on the parents' part.

Marjorie: You often speak of your brother. This experience must have affected how the two of you got along.

Susan: For us as children, this was a time when much empathy developed among us. Eva, the girl closest to my brother's age, had to have all of her hair shaved off one night because she had lice. My brother and I were forbidden to play with her. Eva cried bitterly and her mother hit her for crying because noise threatened all of us. No one outside was allowed to hear that anyone was living down here. By now, the superintendent of the building had been paid off. I only realized that after the war was over. But the adults had pooled all their money in order to buy his silence and cooperation. By the time Eva had to have her hair cut off, we also had an additional person in the cellar with us: Martin, Wuchte's aide, who was a young soldier with acne on his face. I have no idea how old he was. I only remember his very friendly face, his bad skin, and his kindness to us as children. He tried to comfort Eva as best he could. I remember feeling terribly sorry for her. I did not like her very much—she competed with me for my brother's time and attention—but I felt so badly that she had to be nearly bald. I had no idea what lice were except that they must be awful. Both my brother and I were terrified that our hair would be cut off, too. We kept imagining that things were crawling in our hair, but said nothing when our mother subjected us to the daily hair inspection.

I don't remember how long we were not allowed to play with Eva, but I do know that no one else's hair had to be cut off, though we remained afraid for a long time. We all slept very close to each other, a bit like they do now in big homeless shelters, so contagion was a very serious concern.

Marjorie: Was obtaining food a problem?

Susan: I do remember dreaming about food a lot. We ate a lot of sauerkraut, since the adults found a huge barrel fermenting in the cellar. There were a couple of times when my mother and I, as the least Jewish-looking people of the whole cellar, had to go out during the evening to make arrangements to get the elderly gentleman who used to work for my father to bring us more food. Those trips were terrifying because my mother always rehearsed with me what we would say if anyone stopped us, and although I had a very good memory, I was always afraid that I would make a mistake and get everyone in trouble. The worst eating experience was when the elderly gentleman, whom I adored as a child, told my mother that he would soon be able to bring us some horse meat. My mother agreed without any hesitation because she knew that we were barely eating any protein. When we went back and I told my brother that we would be eating horse meat, we almost went into shock from the ambivalence. On one hand, we knew many of the horses that were pulling wagons and carriages on our street. The thought of eating one of them was unbearable; it felt like cannibalism. On the other hand, we were dying to eat something solid, something that you could actually chew and sink your teeth into. When the horse meat actually arrived, all the children were agonizing together. To eat or not to eat, that was the question, not that our parents would give us much choice, but our inner battles were considerable. In the end, we all gave in and ate the very sweet-tasting and unbearably sweet-smelling horse meat. The experience was both horrifying and gratifying. It was wonderful to eat something solid and filling, but we kept wondering which horse we were eating. I have never overcome a fear of horses since then, almost as if I am still expecting them to retaliate one day for the travesty we committed during the war. When a horse nearly ran my mother down outside a swimming pool in Vienna more than five years later, I was still sure that this was punishment.

Marjorie: What happened as the weeks and months went by?

Susan: The worst was yet to come. By now, we had spent so many months in the cellar that we were prone to colds and coughs, and the adults felt that we desperately needed some fresh air. They worked out a system by which every few weeks, someone else could sleep in the superintendent's apartment for one night in order to get some fresh air. To protect us from possible searches, Martin would sleep upstairs with the person whose turn it was. It was my family's turn one night, and when I felt too feverish and too sick to go upstairs, my mother reluctantly gave up our turn, thinking that the commotion and tension of the overnight move would be too much for me. She nevertheless wanted to run upstairs, to get an egg which she had already put in the super's kitchen in anticipation of cooking it for us. My aunt yelled at her not to run up "just for a stupid egg" and my mother reluctantly settled down. Not too long after, I have no sense of the time, the apartment building under which we were hiding was hit by a bomb and most of the house caved in. The super was killed and most of the people who were upstairs in his apartment were badly injured. Those of us left in the cellar knew that something terrible had happened because we heard the hit and the whole cellar shook. Everyone was afraid to move. Then after a very long time, some of the wounded came down. Our beautiful teenage girl, Baby, came down with a huge bandage on her head, her face was terribly burned. We did not see how bad the damage was until much later when the bandages came off. Martin was also badly injured on his head and he did not come back until the war was nearly ended because he was able to go to a military hospital.

My father, who went upstairs some time after the bomb fell, to see if he could help, came down shouting: "There is no God, there is no God!" (I did not remember this episode of his shouting until I went back to Hungary in 1989, and saw the now rebuilt apartment house and cellar.) My father was raving against God because the deaf and dumb man was now blind, as a result of the damage caused by the bomb. He and his wife had also been sleeping at the super's that night. All I can remember are the terribly conflicted feelings I had as a child, relief that we were not the ones that got hurt, and tremendous guilt for surviving unscathed, and for being the reason that other people, especially Baby, had taken our turn at the super's that night. If I had not felt ill, we would have been up there, too. And if my mother had been stubborn enough to go upstairs for our egg, she would have been killed or injured, too. My lifelong sense of vulnerability and danger, especially when it affects my own children, probably stems from this traumatic incident. Our empathy as children developed even further. We were devastated for Baby, who hated her bandages and hated who she had become. The mood for the rest of our stay in the cellar was somber and filled with even more apprehension than before. There was no overt recrimination among the adults, only sadness. I asked my aunt recently what happened to the deaf and dumb and now blind man after the war. My aunt is an incredibly caring, generous human being and I thought that she would have stayed in touch. She told me that she did stay in touch for a while and she knew that the young woman eventually had to institutionalize her husband because she could not take care of him alone. I suspect I must have repressed some of this information until recently. My aunt also explained to me that all of us as families drifted apart and maintained absolutely no contact, not because we were indifferent to each other, but because the conditions in the cellar were so crowded and so tense that people never wanted to see each other again after it was over, nor did they want to be reminded of the bad times they shared.

Marjorie: What happened towards the end of the war?

Susan: In January 1945, word began to spread that our life would soon change. No one talked to us children, but because we lived in such close quarters, without even eavesdropping we could hear much of the conversation even if we did not always understand it. The Russians were advancing and the Germans were retreating. To us this meant that Wuchte and Martin would leave. This was not only frightening, it was unbelievably sad. We had become totally dependent on their protection and good will and trusted them fully. Once they left, we would be at the mercy of roaming Hungarian fascists, individuals and groups who were determined to kill and loot until their last breath.

In fact, after Wuchte and Martin left, we all kept hearing, or imagining, steps coming down the cellar stairs. No one actually came until the Russians arrived. By now word about the Russians was bad, too. There were stories of rape and wanton destruction. We children did not understand what rape meant, but we asked questions when we saw the women make themselves deliberately ugly by tying ridiculous things into their hair and rubbing dirt on their faces. They explained that they did not want the Russian soldiers to like them. This puzzled us. Lo and behold, one day soon after January 18, when we were liberated according to the record, two very young Russian soldiers came down into the cellar, their machine guns held close to their chests. Our parents were terrified. I think we, as children, saw their arrival in part as a welcome change from the horrendous boredom, and we may also have been burnt out from being afraid so much. Suddenly one soldier put his arm around my brother, the other around me, in a friendly, playful way. They looked so young, they must have been adolescents. I will never forget the look of terror on my mother's face. My brother and I looked at the young soldiers' friendly faces and we truly did not understand why she was so upset. They were smiling broadly at us. We had seen very few smiles during the war. And to our wonderful surprise, the two soldiers pulled out a huge loaf of white bread from their bag, broke it in half and gave my brother and me one half each. It was one of the most delicious moments of my life. The bread was soft, it smelled fresh, and we could not wait to bite into it. We shared it with everyone, of course, chunk by chunk. The soldiers left after a while without any incident. We gathered from the grownups' comments later that the Russians had seen so many of their own families and children killed during the war that they were happy to see children who reminded them of home. Our parents were still not fully trusting yet, but the decision was made to venture up from the cellar and to see what was left of our house.

Marjorie: What was it like to go back home again?

Susan: The trip back to our apartment building took a very long time, although the distance was not far. We had to step very carefully for fear of mines and explosives, and my mother had my eyes and my brother's eyes covered. She had her arms around the two of us, one hand covering each of our faces. She did not want us to see all the dead bodies of people and animals on the streets. My brother and I objected, but not too forcefully. We literally trusted her with our lives and had grown accustomed to listening to adults without protestation while in the cellar. I do not remember whether my aunt and my maternal grandmother, who were both in hiding with us, also walked back to our apartment, or whether they came later. What I do remember is that when my parents said we had arrived, we looked at our old building and one corner of it, the corner in which we had lived, was in ruins. The building had been hit by a bomb, mortars, or other explosives—we did not know. We all began a frantic search in the rubble. My brother and I were looking for toys, like starving children looking for a scrap of food. The months before we went into hiding, I had a birthday, and I received a beautiful doll dressed in blue with a white fur hat and a white muff. That doll was my pride and joy but I only had a short time to enjoy it. I wanted desperately to find it. My parents searched for what was important to them. Toys and books were matters of life and death for my brother and me after the long months in the cellar. After what seemed like an eternity, we found a soiled white muff belonging to my doll. I did not care that it was soiled. I just wanted the rest of her. She was nowhere to be found. When my grandmother arrived, we had to stop the search, not because it was unimportant, but because she thought we needed to start rebuilding the semblance of our old life. We eventually moved into one of the apartments in the building that had not been damaged. My father spent considerable time trying to locate Wuchte and Martin, without success. He wanted to tell the authorities who captured them how wonderful they had been to us, that they had saved our lives. Every Russian soldier and officer he went to told him that no German prisoners were taken during the retreat. In the fierce battle of the Russian occupation of Hungary, the retreating German troops were wiped out.

My parents did not tell us this until later, when they were particularly saddened by the fact that since Wuchte and Martin never told us their last names, in order to protect their families in case we were caught, my parents were not even able to write to their families and thank them in whatever way we could for what the two soldiers had done for us. This is one of the pieces of unfinished business in my life. Both my brother and I have incorporated Wuchte and Martin as role models in our lives, and we have both spent both our professional and personal lives dedicated to helping others in need.

Marjorie: Susan, I wonder if we could talk a little about the postwar period. How did you feel about all that was happening then?

Susan: Reconstructing our lives after the war ended took a long time. Food was still hard to come by, and the early weeks were spent searching for food. Later, my parents became concerned about sending us to school again. Since so many Jewish children and teachers died, it wasn't until almost the next winter that the old Jewish elementary school that we had attended before the war reopened. The ground rules were that those who were fortunate enough to have wood for heating, and food for eating, had to take turns bringing wood and food to school. I remember hating to walk so many long blocks carrying a big plate of bread and butter and jam for everyone in my class. My brother, as the stronger male, carried the wood logs when we had them. They were used to heat the school.

Marjorie: Are your memories of the postwar period as vivid as the ones of the time in hiding?

Susan: I do not have a clear sense of time or events after the war. I remember events, like the day my father brought home a big, golden, delicious apple; it felt as if the war had been won again. It tasted miraculously wonderful. I remember when my maternal uncle came home from prisoner of war camp in Russia. We were all incredibly happy to see him alive. My brother and I loved him. He came back as a very tired and physically broken-down man, and he slept wherever he sat down. My brother and I could not believe that a human being could sleep so much and we wanted him to play with us. We used to put keys in his mouth to see if he would wake up. He rarely did. But he, too, moved in with us, and although our apartment was crowded, there was none of the tension and fear we experienced while we were in hiding. But my most precious postwar memory involves my brother. We were liberated by the Russians on January 18, and my birthday was on February 5, my brother's on February 6. He was two years older. There were still no stores open, and no toys to be found, but my brother knew that I desperately wanted a present. He came home from somewhere on the morning of my birthday with what to me was a beautiful necklace, big colorful beads, which I promptly hugged and hung around my neck. I even went to sleep wearing it. Sometime during the night, I woke up to noise in the room. My brother was whispering to my mother and aunt. He had apparently borrowed this necklace from two elderly ladies, an aunt and her niece who lived two doors away from us, and he promised to give it back to them. He wanted to make me happy. Now he had to try to pry the necklace off my neck while I was asleep. I remember lying in the dark not being sure what to do. I loved the necklace and did not want to give it up. It was the first playful, colorful, nonessential object I had seen in nearly a year, and God knew when I would get something else. At the same time, even though I was only eight years old that day, I sensed, without fully comprehending it, how very much my brother loved me, if he even dared to approach those two ladies who were not known for their friendliness, never mind ask them to loan something as a gift for me. I do not know how long it took before I decided to loosen my grip on the necklace—it could have been minutes or hours—but I knew I could not let him get into trouble with those two ladies. That warm sense of being loved so much, and having such a caring older brother gave me a sense of security that has been one of the biggest, most lasting gifts in my life, even if I had to give back the necklace on February 5, 1945.

My brother died of complications from juvenile diabetes at age forty-five, two weeks before his forty-sixth birthday. He lived in Ottawa, but we remained close throughout our lives. Fortunately, I did have the chance to tell him over the years how much that postwar birthday gift has meant to me. I have been blessed with a wonderful husband and two terrific children whom I treasure, yet no birthday gift has ever matched the real and symbolic significance of the borrowed necklace.

The day after my eighth birthday in Budapest, my uncle made me a doll from a potato, to try to cheer me up and make up for the present that had to be returned. I thought the doll was pathetic, but I felt his love, too, and so I behaved as if the ridiculous potato was the most fascinating doll I had ever seen. What really mattered was to be surrounded by people who loved you.

Marjorie: What was it like to leave Hungary? Was it difficult to leave Budapest?

Susan: We stayed in Budapest after our liberation on January 18, 1945, for three more years. My father rebuilt his business and by then the Nazi threat was followed by the Communist threat. It was clear that the Russians who liberated us in Hungary were helping to establish a regime in which Jews would again be persecuted, this time because they were businessmen or intellectuals.

Without involving anyone else in the decision, my father concluded that we must leave and arranged for a false passport under the guise of taking my brother to Vienna for better treatment for his juvenile diabetes. Because the passports were illegal, and by 1948 when we left, foreign travel was not permitted, my brother and I were not told about leaving until the evening before we left, and we were not allowed to say goodbye to my grandmother, my aunt, and my uncle who lived in the apartment building with us. My father was afraid that we would cry and they would cry, attracting too much attention. (We learned never to attract attention during the war.) Even my mother was not allowed to say goodbye to her own mother, and this grief and sense of betrayal was never resolved for my mother, who never again saw her mother, who died of breast cancer three years after we left. The experience of "sneaking out" in the early morning to get on a train to Vienna was a terrible way to start a new life, especially since we could not say goodbye to anyone or shed the tears that we felt about leaving very beloved relatives who survived the war with us, and leaving a life that to us as children had just begun to resemble normalcy. We were going to school regularly, had friends, and a busy, nonfrightened routine in our lives.

We left Budapest on Christmas day, 1948. We stayed in Vienna from December of 1948 until January of 1951. My father's plan was to go to Israel to join his brother, the only surviving member of his family of origin. But since Israel was in its first year of independence, he and my mother were worried about their ability to secure my brother's insulin supply without trouble. My father left us in Vienna for about two months while he went to Israel to check things out. He came back, reluctantly convinced that we could not immigrate there as yet. The situation was too warlike, too tense, without guarantees for the insulin supply my brother needed for his juvenile diabetes. The plan then was for us to wait until conditions in Israel got better. The wait stretched into two years.

Marjorie: What did you do while you were waiting?

Susan: My brother and I went to a refugee school. Every child there was a displaced person on the way to someplace else, mostly to Israel. Hence the language of instruction was Hebrew. We had to speak German on the streets and in the shops, but at school we spoke Hebrew. At school we did not feel like outsiders; in fact, we were very happy. We joined a Zionist organization, Hashomer Hazair, which became the center of my life and my brother's. It brought us a huge circle of friends, most of them displaced people like us, with some native-born Austrians added. The only times I felt like a stranger were when we had to go shopping, speak to our landlord, or go to ballet classes, which I resumed in the second year of our stay. Both my brother and I were embarrassed by our mother's inability to speak German. It made every trip to the grocery store a mini-nightmare. We lived in rented apartments, but we could cook and I remember the first trip to the local grocery store when my mother had to act out what an onion is, since none were visible, and she wanted to buy some. In retrospect, she was incredibly creative and good-humored in acting out the crying onion that was peeling layers off itself, but at the time, I wanted to die of embarrassment when I saw the grocery clerks smirk among themselves.

In the second year, my parents took us out of the refugee school, since they did not think we were learning enough, and sent us to regular Austrian school. That was not only hard, but it also made me feel like a stupid alien. I was way behind the others in an all-boy school, and trying to fake my virtually nonexistent German was both stressful and humiliating. Our wonderful social life at the Hashomer Hazair, which included Israeli folk dancing and singing several nights a week, made everything else bearable and gave us a wonderful sense of community. Then one day that, too, came to an abrupt halt. Vienna was still occupied by the four Allied powers with jeeps staffed by American, Russian, French, and British soldiers visible every few minutes, so that you could never quite forget the war that was. In 1950, after the Korean War broke out, my father, fearing that this could become World War III, decided that remaining in an occupied city was too unsafe, and Israel was still not safe enough for us. So he decided that we should

Susan Bendor

go to Switzerland and wait for better Israeli conditions there. In January 1951, the four of us left Vienna for Zurich. This time we had some warning and were allowed to say an unbearably painful farewell to our friends at Hashomer Hazair, many of whom were going on to Israel shortly.

Marjorie: How did you feel about this abrupt departure?

Susan: I felt betrayed by my parents and arrived at the pension in Zurich where we were to spend the next six months of our lives, hating it in advance. I was just a few weeks short of my fourteenth birthday, feeling more and more critical of my parents and more and more distant from them. The six months in Zurich were terrible indeed. The small pension, or boarding house, where we stayed was rather lovely, and the food was terrific. However, my brother (sixteen) and I (fourteen) did not belong in a pension which was occupied by business people without a single other young person in sight. The Swiss, in their inimical, inhospitable fashion, did not allow us to go to school. Finally, out of desperate boredom, I took a typing course at a private business school which willingly accepted our money without asking questions or looking at papers or report cards. My brother was sent off to a boarding school for three months because my parents were more worried about his lack of schooling since he was a boy. As far as I can remember, I spent most of my time writing letters to my friends in Vienna and waiting for their mail to arrive. There was no place for me to make any Swiss friends, and there was no one I encountered in our six months there who made me feel welcome. To this day I hate the Swiss with a passion.

Chronologically, our next move was to Canada. The conditions in Israel were not improving fast enough for my mother to feel that my brother's health would be safe if we went there, and it became clear to my father that even though, yet again, he was doing well in his textile business, our life in Switzerland was bad for the family. He had to find an alternative. An old friend who lived in Canada was willing to sponsor us for a visa. In June 1951, we sailed from Liverpool to Montreal.

Marjorie: Was it a great disappointment not to be going to Israel? How did you feel about this journey?

Susan: Only my father was optimistic about the trip. For my mother and my brother and me, it meant moving farther and farther away from my beloved grandmother, whom we had already abandoned, although we still desperately missed her, and also farther and farther away from the immigration to Israel for which we so longed. It also meant having to learn yet another language, which turned out to be two: English and French, and trying to make new friends and succeed in school in yet another foreign land with foreign customs. I arrived there determined to be miserable and so I was, for the first couple of years. I developed some thyroid problems which I suspect were psychosomatic in origin. I also lost a lot of weight and threw myself wholeheartedly into schoolwork, since the principal of St. Urban High School, who was a Jew, accepted us conditionally, without any proper report cards, with the understanding that my brother and I would work hard, and if we did not learn both English and French by December of our first year, we would be sent back to a lower grade, below the one we belonged in agewise.

Marjorie: What was it like to be a foreigner there? It must have been hard to adapt.

Susan: In terms of belonging, I felt as if I came from a different planet. At fourteen and a half, I was still dressed in a girlish European style, while my classmates were young women with makeup, grownup clothes, and completely different preoccupations from mine. They also ate food that was different: they lived on tuna fish and peanut butter, things I never heard of, while they laughed at my Hungarian sandwiches which contained sliced chicken, fried veal, and green pepper in everything. Green peppers were my favorite food in Hungary, but in Montreal, I began to be ashamed of them and hated eating them at school since my classmates did not even know what they were and certainly never saw anyone eating them voluntarily. At age fourteen, these trivial things matter a lot. I was fortunate to have one teacher who took a serious interest in me and gave me a tremendous amount of support, not only raising my self-esteem but stopping others from teasing me about being different. In school, one classmate befriended me and after we graduated, even invited me to her wedding, an act for which I will be forever grateful. She made me feel that I was not a total freak in high school. There was an episode in high school when, not speaking English, I was diagnosed as having an IQ of sixty-five. Only my father's faith in me, and his willingness to challenge the school, prevented them from scarring me for life. But the experience added to my determination to prove that I was just as good as the others, and I studied like a demon, getting excellent grades on tests and graduating with two prizes. That drive to prove academically what I can do stayed with me for life. Outside of school, we settled into a fairly social and comfortable routine. We made many new friends, all of whom were European refugees like we were. Thanks to my brother's leadership, we established our own community, our own sense of belonging. After the months in the cellar, and the months in the repressed, restrictive Swiss boarding house, being able to laugh again, to make noise, and to behave like adolescents, was a terrific experience.

In 1954, after graduating from high school, I took probably the biggest risk of my adolescent life. I did not want to go to McGill University, where my brother was, because it was too big for me. I would have gotten lost. So, on my own, I initiated contact with a small Anglican college I discovered through a newspaper ad, Bishop's University, one hundred miles from Montreal. They accepted me, with a scholarship, after an interview and after seeing my transcript. They had never had a foreigner in this very British, very upper-class school before, and for the three years I was there, there was only one other Jewish student there. The university, affiliated with Oxford, was tiny, even by Canadian standards—we had a total of three hundred students—and I was treated wonderfully. Most of my teachers invited me to their homes, and although divinity was a required subject, the divinity teachers made sure that I did not feel I had to go to any classes on Jewish holidays, and for Passover, they arranged for me to have a seder in the nearest big town, which had a decent-size Jewish population. During the first two years of my stay, I still felt like a stranger and that I was different: different in dress, thought, behavior, values, and priorities. This was made particularly difficult when, during my second week in school, my father had to declare bankruptcy, and he made a very serious suicide attempt. My brother and I rallied around my mother and father, and the petty concerns of college life suddenly seemed very insignificant. For the first year and a half of school, I commuted home by train almost every weekend. My mother, who depended on my father financially and in most other respects, had to find a way to live and support my brother and me while my father underwent repeated hospitalizations for severe depression. My brother and I had to grow up awfully fast, and we did. We became the spokespeople for the family, since my mother's English was still minimal. She only learned English after both of us left home eventually: my brother for graduate school, and I for marriage.

By my third and final year at school, life had settled down into some kind of routine. I became more active in campus life. In 1956, during the Suez crisis and the Hungarian Revolution, I invited two prestigious speakers to the campus as my commitment not to let my fellow students and the faculty just sit by obliviously while wars were going on elsewhere. The campus had never had a political speaker before, but the guests were well received and my initiative was supported. I continued to get very good grades, had a boyfriend, and played the lead in the main college play, a French comedy, *To Be Enchanted*. Winning that lead, and doing well in it was probably the highlight of my youth. I think I felt that I had finally arrived. I could do something well on "their terms." I would no longer be the object of anyone's pity or sarcasm. I went from the role of loser, or of the hidden invisible child, to the very visible center of a play, in a role that others coveted. Until then, I was probably the one who did the coveting of the confidence, sophistication, and carefree existence that other students appeared to possess. When, during graduation, I found out that in addition to academic awards, I won one of the five Golden Mitre awards, given by fellow students to those whom they felt had contributed most to the life of the university, I was deliriously happy, feeling more accepted and valued by others than I have ever felt in my life. It was a long way from the little girl who had to wear a yellow star.

MATILDE SALGANICOFF

1930	Born in Buenos Aires, Argentina
1948	Obtains elementary school teaching certificate
1952	Bachelor's degree in education
1957	Marries León (Leibe), Doctor in Sciences, National University of Buenos Aires, biochemist
1961	Daughter, Alina, born
1963	Masters in psychology at National University of Buenos Aires
1964	Son, Marcos, born; settles in Philadelphia, Pennsylvania
1965	First job in U.S.A. as psychology intern
1966	Bilingual psychologist at St. Christopher's Hospital for Children
1967	Begins coursework toward doctorate from Temple University
1968	León obtains permanent residency in the United States
1968	Father dies in Buenos Aires; buys first home in Philadelphia
1971	Alina and Marcos attend secular Jewish school
1973	Stops visiting Buenos Aires because of political unrest there
1974	Opens private practice as a therapist. Faculty appointment at Hahnemann University
1976	Mother dies in Buenos Aires
1977	Matilde and family become United States citizens
1978	Doctorate in education from Temple University
1983	Political situation in Argentina improves; resumes visits
1984	Fellowship at Wharton School; founds the first Seminar for Women in Family Business, which she then runs privately until 1995
1985	Consultant to family-owned business
1990	Appointed to faculty at Widener University psychology department

Argentina has received more Jewish refugees this century than any other nation with the exception of Palestine. Between 1933 and 1945, approximately forty thousand Jews of all nationalities emigrated to Argentina, increasing the Jewish population there by 73 percent; nonetheless, Jews constituted only 2.2 percent of Argentina's total population in 1949.

Jews in Argentina had many opportunities for upward mobility. The public schools and university system provided them with the education necessary to enter banking, finance, and an assortment of industries. Jewish writers and poets established a new intelligentsia in Argentine society. Cosmopolitan Buenos Aires was especially nurturing of Jewish culture. In the mid-1930s, almost half the adult population of Buenos Aires had been born outside Argentina, making the capital accommodating to foreigners.

Argentine nationalism in the 1930s left Jews at a disadvantage. The government used the term *criollo* to designate the true Argentine as someone of European/Hispanic descent—Jewish immigrants, naturally, did not fit this description. At the same time, the Catholic church ignited a major resurgence of power by restoring Catholic religious education in public schools. Fearful of Jewish presence in universities, banks, and the crucial grain industry, the Argentine government passed a series of discriminatory laws that included the prohibition of Yiddish in public meetings and the dismissal of Jews from professions ranging from medicine to academia. Several synagogues were bombed and immigration policies became much more restrictive.

Argentina's fascist youth group, the Partido Social Argentino, was formed in 1938. A reactionary organization based on the German youth Nazi model, the PSA's members marched in the Jewish quarter of Buenos Aires in 1939 demanding the implementation of the Nazi anti-Jewish policy in Argentina. When Jewish citizens tried to defend themselves by fighting back, they were immediately arrested by police.

Historians still dispute the extent and effect of fascism in Argentina during the 1930s and 1940s. Because Nazism ideologically challenged both Argentine nationalism and the Catholic church, it never gained the wholehearted support of most Argentines. The concurrent rise of Argentine and German anti-Semitism, however, reflected Argentina's close historical and cultural ties with Europe.

In 1946 Juan Domingo Perón, a military officer, won the extremely close presidential race. His presidency was one of extremes; he was popular with both the conservatives and the labor unions, with the military and the bourgeoisie, with the right and the left. His wife Eva ("Evita") achieved great visibility as a role model for women. Despite his close ties with the Axis powers during the war and his creation of asylum for former Nazis, Perón was able to count progressive Jews among his supporters.

The Peronista government had engendered a new bourgeois nationalism, but the mid-1950s and early 1960s saw tremendous changes politically and economically. Evita died of cancer in 1952 and President Perón was forced out of power in 1955, returning the nation to military control under General Eduardo Lonardi. In exile, Perón became a mythical figure for the populace. The nation, devoid of its patron saint, fragmented as class struggles came to the fore and violent coups became the norm. The military governments were hostile to leftist academics, as evidenced by the brutal beatings of students by federal police at the University of Buenos Aires on July 29, 1966—thereafter called the "Night of the Long Sticks." Economic prosperity under these governments began to spiral downward quickly, and five thousand Jews emigrated from Argentina between 1955 and 1959. Most headed to Israel, Venezuela, Mexico, and Spain.

Anti-Semitism became more visible as Jews were dismissed from government positions and other distinguished institutions. The infamous Triple A (Alianza Anticomunista

Argentina) was formed in the early 1970s by federal police and headed by the Minister of Social Welfare, José López Rega, in an effort to quell fighting between extremist guerilla factions; this organization, dedicated to the purging of subversive elements, often resorted to kidnappings, secret executions, and indiscriminate violence. The Peronista government fell to a military junta under General Rafael Videla on March 24, 1976. Initially called the Gentleman's Coup, the new military regime sponsored organized extermination of political enemies that was labeled the Dirty War. Argentina's Jews suffered tremendously as thousands of innocent civilians disappeared, becoming *desaparecidos*. It is now estimated that between nine thousand and thirty thousand Argentine citizens disappeared during the seven years of systematic extermination, and Jews—who account for less than 2 percent of the Argentine population—numbered 10 percent among the *desaparecidos*. One dramatic response to this terror was the formation of the Mothers of the Plaza de Mayo in 1977. It was begun spontaneously by a group of fourteen mothers who had gathered in the main square of Buenos Aires, the Plaza de Mayo, to demand information about the whereabouts of their children, and it evolved into one of the most influential human rights organizations of this century.

With the election of Raúl Alfonsín in 1983 came a promise of change. Military leaders who had previously terrorized the population were tried in civil court in 1985. Inflation reached 700 percent, one of the world's highest rates, and Alfonsín reacted with the institution of PAN, the Programa Alimentario Nacional, which aimed to remedy the malnutrition that plagued the country's poor. Carlos Menem, a Peronista, took office in 1989 with the slogan, "Follow me, I will not fail you." Under his government, state-run corporations such as the telephone company and the national airline were privatized, followed by the privatization of the oil state monopoly. These changes deepened the divide between the classes, and by 1990 conditions reached that of social crisis.

Matilde Salganicoff often refers to these recent upheavals in Argentine politics; she left Buenos Aires for Philadelphia in 1964 with her husband and children. Her husband, a scientist, had a year-long post at the University of Pennsylvania. Planning to stay a short time, she brought only two suitcases. She has lived in the United States for over thirty years, earning a doctorate, and practicing as a family counselor, women's therapist, and consultant to a family-owned business.

I first met Matilde on a rainy day in Philadelphia in the spring of 1992. We were attending a colloquium on solidarity with the Mothers of the Plaza de Mayo. She looked like one of my aunts, who were always present at family gatherings, eager to gossip about people falling in and out of love, about birthdays and deaths. When Matilde sat down at this very different family gathering, she swept back her silver, rain-colored hair, and her hazel eyes scanned the immense hall. I recognized myself in her. I could tell that she was Jewish and that she had traveled here from some other country. I read my poems about the Mothers of the Plaza de Mayo, women who loom in my memory as skeletal figures, crossing rain-wet fields, shedding masks of solitude to protest the absence of their dead children.

Afterward, Matilde and I embraced. We talked as though we were two old friends.

Suddenly Matilde asked me, "Do you feel transparent?" I looked at her in astonishment. "Yes," she continued, "I feel transparent, as if we did not exist, as if no one could see us." I thought of my first years in North America: when I had just arrived in Georgia and was trying to learn English; when my mother's grief poured forth in an empty house; when everything was a dark palpitation of mists and memories of times gone by. I thought about how invisible I felt at the university. Even though people greeted me, they excluded me from clubs, from stories, from gossip, and from official positions on committees. I was welcomed as a token Latina or Jew. "Yes, Matilde," I said, "I have felt transparent."

"Come over to my house," I kept saying to Matilde. We Latin Americans have a long tradition of welcoming people into our homes. Matilde invited me to her house, too, in the heart of Philadelphia. When I arrived, she greeted me warmly. She showed me her wedding album, which revealed a beautiful girl with delicate skin, short hair, and strong arms. I recognized myself in those Latin American photos of Sunday family gatherings, of families wearing Old World garments.

Matilde pulled out photos of her childhood, and her mother's spoons, and we began to converse.

Marjorie: Matilde, you are an educated and privileged woman who immigrated to the United States. Why did you immigrate?

Matilde: I didn't realize that I was immigrating when I came here on the 26th of December of 1964 from Buenos Aires. We arrived in New York. I came a week after my husband, I think. I arrived with Marcos, who was six months old, and Alina, who was three years old. I was thirty-three, and my husband, León—we call him Leibe—was forty. My husband is a scientist and we were coming to Philadelphia to the University of Pennsylvania, which was a center for research on computer applications for biomedical sciences. At that point we expected to be here just for a year. I had not wanted to come. I was not interested in traveling to the United States because in Argentina our attitude was that this country was tremendously imperialistic. The United States, since the beginning of this century, had constantly interfered with and oppressed the countries of Latin America. So we were prejudiced against, and very angry with, the United States and we felt contemptuous of it. Even today, many of my Argentine friends prefer to travel to Europe rather than come to the United States. At that point, I had no interest at all in coming to stay here.

Marjorie: What happened next? Why did you stay on?

Matilde: I entered with an immigration visa out of ignorance or destiny. I had a degree, the equivalent of a master's in clinical psychology. I thought I could work, so I applied for an immigrant visa, which was easy to do then. So I came in as an immigrant, and my children did, too, since they were on my passport. It was a lucky chance, because I had no idea of how important my immigrant visa would be for our future in the U.S. Then I had to find a job. I wanted to work, and I had to work because we were rebuilding the house that had been my mother-in-law's and we needed to send money. My husband had a fellowship from the Research Center of Argentina which paid us 432 dollars a month. It took me four months to find a job that also paid 400 dollars, as a psychologist. That gave us enough to pay for the house in Buenos Aires. We were going to go back in a year. By chance and luck, my first job was an internship, approved by the American Psychological Association. This made an incredible difference for my future. They hired me because they needed a living body. That was my only qualification for getting the job: blood was circulating in my veins. I could have spoken only Chinese without knowing a word of English and I still would have been hired. Because if they didn't have someone in that position right away, they were going to lose the funding for it. Right after we came, we lived in Philadelphia. When we left that first furnished apartment and moved, I bought our furniture at the Salvation Army. Little by little, I bought nicer things: posters, a rug, things I liked.

Marjorie: Why didn't you go back?

Matilde: My husband managed to get another fellowship for a second year. He was working on research on mitochondria. This second fellowship paid us better, almost nine thousand dollars, from some institution, so we moved to a better place. And so we stayed another year. By then it was 1966 and in Argentina the event known as the Night of the Big Sticks had happened. The military occupied the university and began to beat students and professors and practically invaded and occupied the university. At this point, my husband resigned his position at the university in solidarity with its faculty. León had been at the medical school as a scientific investigator. Later, when we wanted to go back, there was no laboratory space for him at the university in Buenos Aires.

Marjorie: So that year of research turned into the last thirty-three years of your life? It's like my own story. People always imagine that immigrants are farm workers or illegal maids, people who come to the United States for economic reasons. They rarely consider that well-off, educated people came here, too. What has it been like for you here?

Matilde: Well, I think it has been a real struggle. First, the fact of being completely unknown. Second, I came from the middle class and I was very poor here, at first. It was hard for me to get my first job because, who knew me? I was a psychologist, my English was poor, I spoke with a strong accent, and I had a professional background that was completely different. In addition, I expected to be going back to Argentina. That's what I wanted at that time. It wasn't that there weren't any job possibilities there, especially at first, though later on, my husband's job options disappeared. So I had gone down in social class, I had no help of any kind at home, and I didn't have my family here.

Marjorie: That's how my mother felt too. We came from a very secure situation in Chile where we had economic stability. I remember that some people in the Jewish community here told us we must have come to the U.S. to obtain greater material wealth. This affected us a lot, Matilde, but little by little we understood that this country's culture measures everything in economic terms. That was hard to get used to.

Matilde: Of course: you live in poorer and worse places. You don't have money. The first few months, we didn't have a car for transportation. We didn't have anything at all, nothing. We were totally poor. And in addition, something went wrong with the checks that came from Argentina and the university didn't realize this or the laboratory didn't realize this and four months went by when we didn't get a single penny. We got to a day at the end of the year, in December, when I had two dollars and León didn't have any money. And we were out of milk and bread.

Marjorie: What did you do?

Matilde: I told León it was impossible to go on this way. He went to the university and asked for a loan. He was very ashamed to do this.

Marjorie: You didn't have anything to eat?

Matilde: We didn't have anything. The university loaned him 100 dollars and then the lost four or five checks arrived, and soon afterward I began to work. It was a full-time job. We began to have a little money. But going back to your question, those were difficult times because of the loneliness, the physical work which was brutal, trying to pay attention to the children and the house while having to work full time. I did not have any moment for myself. Especially since I didn't have anyone to leave the children with. Day care centers did not exist in West Philadelphia then.

Matilde Salganicoff

Marjorie: And didn't you ever feel like just leaving?

Matilde: I don't know whether I really felt like leaving or not. That had a lot to do with how I saw my role as a wife, as a mother . . . We were able to move to an apartment that was a little better, but I don't think it ever even occurred to me to tell León that I didn't want to live in that neighborhood that was not good. He wanted to be near the university, but most of the houses there belonged to one woman, who charged as much rent as possible. She was a slum landlady. It was very difficult.

Marjorie: So, did you think of this country as the American Dream?

Matilde: No, not really. I did not have an American Dream. For me, it was very difficult and exhausting. León worked from eight in the morning until seven at night. He came back for an hour and then at eight at night he would go back to work sometimes until midnight, including Saturdays and Sundays. It was winter and I had never seen snow. We lived on the fourth floor and it was a very difficult experience for me, very hard.

Marjorie: Did you have friends?

Matilde: No. I didn't meet anyone at the beginning. I began to form ties to an American family and then to an Argentine one (people who were very kind to us) that went back soon after that. But in general I was very alone and without company. I was an educated woman who spoke English—with an accent, but I did speak it. Speaking English gave me some feeling of independence, and finally, after five years, I got a part-time job from 8:30 A.M. to 3:30 P.M., so I could be home early when the children returned from school.

Marjorie: When you knew that you were going to stay, did you begin to feel more reconciled to the place?

Matilde: When León obtained permanent residency five years after we arrived here, we bought a house. Before we bought it, he was offered a job in Washington. It would also have been possible to go to Yale, in Connecticut. But I didn't want to move because I didn't want to have to get to know another city, another neighborhood, another supermarket. I guess I liked Philadelphia. I didn't want to move again. Before he got his visa, he had been offered a job in Sweden. I didn't want him to accept it, either. I didn't want to have to deal with another country, another language. So we stayed on in Philadelphia. I don't know that I thought of it as permanent at that point, but it meant less change.

Marjorie: And did you like this country?

Matilde: I am very grateful to the United States. It seems a beautiful country to me, but I don't know whether I like it exactly. It's a good country despite its difficulties. We worked, and things went well for us. We didn't have to live through the Dirty War in Argentina. My children are practically assured of good futures. They are well educated. I am basically grateful. I felt very, very lonely at first. And now I'm a different person. Do you realize? I'm more detached now, more independent. But at first I suffered a great deal; I was very homesick and I wrote a lot of letters. In Argentina, I have a group of faithful friends who are very dear and close, who love me deeply and who are really happy to see me and be with me. And besides, the adult children of my friends are also my friends and love me and I love them. I grew and expanded my horizons not only because I lived abroad, but because I had very different experiences, I took great professional risks. I did things that seem unheard of to my Argentine friends. Besides, I am profoundedly feminist. They think that they are, but they are not. Some of the women think they are feminists because they do things. In reality, they have delegated the "feminine" role to another . . .

Marjorie: Woman?

Matilde: Employee. There are huge differences between us. I think I have a much wider perspective than they do. They may well think the opposite, but it's simply that I have been exposed to more, in a different country, and I have worked so intensely, and for such a long time I was navigating alone. But they probably have other visions and terrible experiences that I have not had. They survived the Dirty War and I wasn't there to live through it. So they have had other sufferings. That made us very different from each other, I think. But there is still a common base in the old affections that we felt for each other, an acceptance, history, a recognition of who the other person is. You can work in the U.S., live here, become established here, but in Argentina you are recognized in a way that is very different.

Marjorie: Yes: to be an immigrant means having to tell your story over again every day. It sounds as though you still don't know whether you like the United States. Does the American national anthem stir you?

Matilde: I feel indifferent about it.

Marjorie: Is there anything about this country and its symbols that moves you?

Matilde: Nothing.

Marjorie: And what about Latin America's national symbols?

Matilde: You mean like the flag and the national anthem?

Marjorie: Yes.

Matilde: They also seem to me . . . well, I recognize them, but I am indifferent to them.

Marjorie: The symbols of your country don't affect you?

Matilde: I remember bits of landscape, a song. A folk song. I like tangos. They seem beautiful and familiar to me. I like the landscapes. For years, I took my children to see Argentina. They've seen the North and the South. I felt that I needed to show them, because it is the country where they were born. I'm struck by how beautiful the countryside is, but not because it is Argentina. I used to be proud of Argentina and its landscapes. Now they seem beautiful to me, but it seems ridiculous to feel proud about it.

Marjorie: Tell me, Matilde, where do you feel as though you live? Which language do you relate to?

Matilde: To Spanish. I really enjoy language, being able to express myself in a beautiful and precise way. It seems splendid to me; I enjoy language, words, sentences. I am deeply moved by poetry, by things well said . . . I was reading some pages by Neruda about words and I wept because it is so beautifully expressed. It may be the equivalent of music for me because I don't have much access to music. I am tone deaf.

Marjorie: What language did your mother speak at home?

Matilde: She always spoke to me in Spanish, without an accent.

Marjorie: I'm surprised that as an immigrant she didn't have an accent.

Matilde: When she came from Russia, my mother was five or six years old, and my father, too. They didn't grow up with accents. No one would have suspected that the two of them were not born in Argentina.

Marjorie: What has it been like to shift into another language? Have you felt a great loss as you've had to shift into English and always been marked as foreign by your accent?

Matilde: Yes. I don't know whether it's a loss, because I've kept my Spanish, and I kept my children bilingual. It's only in Spanish that I have a real feel for fluidity, elegance, and the ease with which words flow. Speaking English is still an effort for me and I have to think about it. My English doesn't seem pretty to me, it doesn't sound musical.

Marjorie: Have you gotten used to English?

Matilde: I know how to listen closely in English, it is part of my profession, and it gives me great pleasure to hear it well spoken. I don't like to hear people speaking languages when they have accents. I enjoy hearing someone who is a native speaker because it sounds smooth and elegant, sweet and full.

Marjorie: Do you think that having an accent in this country has impaired you, made you different, made you feel more and more like a foreigner?

Matilde: I don't know that it has impaired me exactly, but it has made my life a little more difficult in general, especially when I've had to be with less educated people. Often, with them, I had to repeat what I say. I hate leaving messages on answering machines, because I think my accent makes me unintelligible. But it's an advantage to me professionally, for teaching and giving therapy, because people have to pay attention to what I say in order to understand me. It's not that I feel very uncomfortable with English or that I don't like the language. It's hard for me because I lack fluidity or real elegance of expression. I don't know, it just doesn't flow for me. However correct my English may be, I still have a very strong accent, no doubt about that. Is that what you asked about? I didn't acquire a country, I lost one.

Marjorie: Are you sure it is permanently lost? Doesn't the possibility of return always exist?

Matilde: I think that by now I have lost it, or I have lost the affection I had for it, and what I realize is that I lost it after the military pardons were granted, the pardons granted to the military and the police who had killed more than nine thousand citizens. I think I felt a cut like an amputation at first. But now I don't feel that way and I don't think that I'm just denying it. Philadelphia begins to feel familiar to me. I'd like to return to Argentina, but just to see friends; that I really do enjoy. And I think that there is an element there . . . a need to go back to Argentina, which may relate in some way to my having adapted, but I don't think so. I am very angry at Argentina and its terrible history, the Dirty War, all the denials, complicities, and pardons granted to murderers who are walking around free now. As I get older, I am angrier and even less forgiving. In the same way, when I went to Germany, I saw Nazis all over the place. When I see middle-aged people in Argentina, especially men, I wonder whether they were involved or if they were murderers themselves. Besides, there is a huge conspiracy of silence in general among the people. No one listens any longer to the Mothers of the Plaza de Mayo and the conspiracy of silence continues.

Marjorie: Why do you think this is happening, this denial of memory, which to us Jews seems so important?

Matilde: First, because it was so painful, and second, I think that fear and attachment to money and material possessions caused a great complicity of silence. That's why I call it a complicity of fear. I don't know whether I have any right to express myself this way and judge them; I don't know how I would have managed it. It may well be that fear would have made me act like them or even worse than them. It may well be that I can't forgive them because I never could have forgiven myself in that situation. I think that if I had lived in Argentina I would be totally destroyed or dead.

Marjorie: Tell me, what has it been like for you to be a psychologist in another language?

Matilde: Figuring out the culture and the systems here was even more difficult than the problems of language. It was really hard for me. It must have been difficult for you, too, to understand humor.

Marjorie: Here? Yes.

Matilde: It still seems a little difficult to me. I think it is even more of a problem for them to understand my sense of humor, which is more caustic. I have a *porteño* sense of humor.[1] I have a great sense of humor in Spanish, but not in English. I am very quick in Spanish, but I feel this is such a formal, structured society . . .

Marjorie: . . . and bureaucratic.

Matilde: Of course! Although it looks as though they are more casual in their way of dress, although they give you a lot of freedom, it is a very rigid free-dom, very structured, and that was very hard for me to understand. I had to transform myself into a "good girl" in the United States; I wasn't such a "good girl" in Argentina.

Marjorie: Did you have to change yourself to adjust to the system here?

Matilde: Yes. I think that all immigrants have gone through this kind of ad-justment with differing degrees of success. The ones who have adjusted the least are those who refused to learn the language.

Marjorie: What did you leave behind of your country? I remember that my mother brought Chilean earth, and wild flowers. And she wanted to tape-record the sound of the larks.

Matilde: For me it was an irreparable loss that I think I've now recovered from somewhat. I don't know what to tell you. It was a tremendous wrench. I had not wanted to come. My life was there. My parents and my friends were there. I felt myself to be profoundly Argentine and I did not want to stay in the United States. I stayed because there was no other option for my husband, and also because the situation in Argentina began to deteriorate. We had gone through that time of dictatorship before, and we did not want to go back under a military government. Do you understand? So we decided to stay on here. For me it was a tremendous loss. At first, I did not think of it as losing a country. I just felt foreign. Yes, but I don't know. I've never expressed it as hav-ing lost a country. It was as though the country was there and waiting for me, but I didn't get back there. I was the absent one. Now I have a totally different awareness of it.

Marjorie: What is this awareness like?

Matilde: Now I realize and feel that I have lost a country, but I don't feel that I have acquired one. I don't know where I live.

Marjorie: How did you feel when you came? Did you begin to define yourself as an immigrant?

Matilde: No, no. At first I felt like a tourist. And then I became curious. I vis-ited places, observed, and worked. It was a huge job to bring up the children, work, clean the house. I can't even begin to describe it. And then in 1977 I de-cided to take university courses. That was a colossal effort, but I did it.

Marjorie: When did that feeling of loss of your country happen?

Matilde: The loss of my country is much more recent. It has to do in part with my not having gone back to Argentina for twelve years.

Marjorie: Was that by your choice?

Matilde: Because of the Dirty War, I didn't want to go to Argentina. Because what was happening did not seem good, nor the denial on the part of Argentines. We have some friends who have come to our house and have denied the terrible things that were happening.

Marjorie: During the Dirty War were people denying the disappearance of people, like in Chile?

Matilde: Yes. And then I said, I can't go down there and just fight with everyone. I can't, and so I didn't go. When President Alfonsín was elected democratically, after the Dirty War was over, there was a program on the international news at eleven that night, showing the extraordinary events in the Plaza del Congreso. I saw that news bulletin, and I started to weep, and I said, "Now I am going to visit Argentina."

Marjorie: Did that make you return to your country: democracy, the awareness of a common future?

Matilde: That is what made me want to return for a visit. But once a constitutional government was in place, it was also very difficult for me to return since the denial was so massive; at that time "no one knew anything."

Marjorie: No one felt responsible for what had taken place?

Matilde: There was such total denial . . . A colleague at work would disappear and the rest just kept working along as though nothing had happened. I asked myself . . .

Marjorie: . . . if that were a little like what happened in Germany.

Matilde: Of course. It was fear. All you can think is that it was fear controlling people. It must happen in all countries and it might have happened to me, too.

Marjorie: At that point, did you feel yourself lucky to be outside and maybe even able to reconstitute your historical experience from the outside?

Matilde: Yes. I think that my family of origin made two very major historical decisions in this century. They both involved big emigrations for us. Both my parents, who were children and went to Argentina with their parents, escaped just before the Bolshevik war and thus avoided the two world wars.[2] And then later *we* came to the U.S.A. I think I would have died in the Dirty War.

Marjorie: Would they have killed you?

Matilde: Me, and my children, for sure. Or else, as León says, we might have escaped to another country.

Marjorie: What did you lose when you left your country?

Matilde: I think I gained more than I lost. But what did I lose? I was not with my parents when they died . . . My children did not have grandparents. I had no help and I had to work very hard here alone, bringing up the children and working. I lost being with my friends, especially my old friend Elena, sharing their stories and life events. They didn't know anything about my life, still don't know much about it. What I gained is that I grew a lot, my horizons expanded, I was much more useful here than in Argentina, and my children have opportunities they never would have had in Argentina. I made new friends.

Marjorie: What did you miss?

Matilde: The way of life and the language, family life, everything familiar and known. Here, everything was an exploration, everything was new. I couldn't understand the humor or the jokes. I still don't know how many things work. Do you realize? I know very little about the history of the U.S.A. I am just now beginning to educate myself. There I worked but could not accomplish much. Here I worked very hard and have accomplished a lot, I think.

Marjorie: So you feel that you owe a lot to this country?

Matilde: I think that this country offered me possibilities of doing things that Argentina could never have offered me professionally. And it may well be that coming to this country and seeing what could be done allowed me to think differently. I compare myself to people in Argentina and I'm very aware that they have no concept of "fighting city hall," of doing things differently, of philanthropy, of being a volunteer. It is the heritage of the terrible Spanish colonization.

Marjorie: Do you see this as a generous and charitable country?

Matilde: I think so. Of course, Argentines will help out a friend, but they are not going to "adopt" a school, for example; they aren't going to put benches in a park . . .

Marjorie: Do you see Americans as generous?

Matilde: I think they have a sense of civic conscience. Americans do things to help the community, but they do it in a generic way, not to help just an individual. If a school is improved, everyone will be better off. If the park has its benches painted, the neighborhood will look better. But someone goes out and paints the benches. See what I mean?

Marjorie: Did the act of leaving your country make you grow in unexpected ways?

Matilde: I think so, yes. Coming to this country where little things can be done . . . For example, the first thing that struck me, not negatively, but which seemed to me incredible, was the opposition to the Vietnam War. People began to have demonstrations. It seemed amazing that anyone would do that.

Marjorie: That is democracy . . .

Matilde: I didn't know that. They invited me and I . . . it seemed to me to be such a strange thing. For me to participate in a demonstration! People went to demonstrations . . . to oppose the government's decision to participate in a war. I was only familiar with Peronism and there were no demonstrations possible in that system. You couldn't oppose the government or the authorities in anything, or they would put you in jail. This country opened my eyes in two ways: the political world and the role of women. It's as though a veil were ripped off my eyes, literally. This complicated my life a lot because I began to change, to think in a different way, to function in a different way. I began to be aware of oppression. Before it was like seeing things, but not really seeing them. I hadn't seen anything.

Marjorie: Was your immigration very positive, then?

Matilde: It was very difficult but I grew enormously.

Marjorie: Tell me, Matilde, do you feel more Jewish or more Argentine?

Matilde: I never thought about myself as an Argentine Jew when I was growing up. It's interesting, because I knew I was Jewish and I did think of myself as
Argentine. I believe I felt more as an Argentinian.

Marjorie: Did you go to a public school?

Matilde: Yes. I went to the public school, normal school. I was there from second grade on (the normal school went from first grade and up, and included
elementary school and the five years of secondary school). It was all in the
same building, and in Buenos Aires there are eight normal schools, which give
teaching degrees.

Marjorie: What did you read? What books impressed you when you were
young?

Matilde: I remember the Grimm brothers' stories. My aunt Sara, my mother's
oldest sister, whom I loved a lot, gave the book to me when I was a little girl.
She was very affectionate. I took lots of books out of the normal school library. Every week I took out books and I read and read.

Marjorie: Were you fascinated by reading?

Matilde: Yes. My mother used to give me thirty *centavos* so I could buy a
sandwich, and I hoarded it. When I had saved up two-fifty I'd go to a bookstore near my house and buy a book of Spanish literature. I had an enormous
collection; I had to leave hundreds of books behind when I came to the United
States.

Marjorie: Did it matter to you that you were Jewish?

Matilde: Yes. There was no question about our being, and having been, Jews.
Culturally we were Jewish, but I never had a Jewish education. As far as I can
remember, my family did not observe the Jewish holidays. I assume we were
rather secular. I remember that the first time I went to the synagogue, I was already an adolescent. A cousin of mine who was older than me got married in

the Liberty Temple, which is a very elegant synagogue in Buenos Aires. The groom belonged to a rich family and they had a big party, and it was the first time in my life, at seventeen or eighteen, that I entered a synagogue. I didn't even know what a bar mitzvah was. I don't remember if the older people in my family had a Jewish education either. I don't know what happened. I did not even have a Jewish ceremony for my wedding (Leibe and I always agreed not to associate with synagogues or organized religion). But when I realized that Alina did not know that she was Jewish, when she was already six years old, I felt very ashamed. I looked for a secular Jewish school, the Folk Jewish Shula, and I registered my two children. Alina and Marcos attended it on Sunday mornings for several years.

Marjorie: Do you think your parents wanted to give you a Jewish education?

Matilde: They considered themselves to be profoundly Argentine. I haven't the slightest idea what sort of education they wanted to give us, but I did not get a Jewish education, nor did my brothers. I remember that my mother told me things. My father's family was from Odessa. They all came to Buenos Aires in 1905: two brothers and two sisters. And my mother's whole family, eight brothers and sisters, came too. The two oldest sisters had arrived first from Hamburg. But they were from a province called Ekaterineslav, and a little village named Dnieperpetrov. I think it is close to Kiev. The two oldest daughters had boyfriends in Russia who had come over to Argentina earlier. They worked, brought over the two girls and married, saved money, and brought over the rest of the family. My mother was one of the youngest, the next to the last. So she was part of the family that went to live in Pergamino.

Marjorie: Where is Pergamino? I've heard the name of the town.

Matilde: Pergamino is a town north of Buenos Aires in the country, near the Paraná River. My grandfather was a tailor. He supported his family by being a tailor. My mother told me that it seems my grandmother kept a kosher kitchen.

Marjorie: In Argentina?

Matilde: No, in Russia. She wanted to keep it in Pergamino, but the closest city with kosher food was Rosario, which was farther north, also on the Paraná River. But there was no refrigeration so that everything arrived spoiled, and my mother told me that my grandmother said, "To the devil with all this. I have to feed all these children." She began to buy food in the town. I think that

that's when the kosher kitchen of my mother's family disappeared. I don't know whether my father's family had kept a kosher kitchen.

Marjorie: Growing up in Argentina, didn't you ever feel foreign, different because you were Jewish?

Matilde: I never suffered from any direct anti-Semitism, but it was a profoundly anti-Semitic country. I was always in a Catholic situation, rather than Jewish. In school there were one or two other Jewish girls. In high school there were two of us, a girl named Vida and me. At that point, the military staged a coup d'etat. That was in 1943. Then there were a lot of different changes until finally they included religion in the school curriculum even though the school had been secular for years. So the few of us who were Jewish were taught what they called "morals." I think they wanted to teach ethics. Everyone else went to religion class. They were all Catholic girls. This was in a neighborhood of Buenos Aires where they were all daughters of the military. I never had much social interaction with them because I lived in a very separate circle, even geographically. I never had friends until I began secondary school. Before that, I thought that girls were boring and playing with dolls seemed absolutely idiotic to me. Later I began to have friends. I began with Vida. There was also another girl who was not Jewish, Nilda.

Marjorie: And then?

Matilde: Through Vida, I joined a Jewish young people's group and became a member of Hebraica, which was a cultural association, a very well known and very active club. I went to swim, and to go to lectures and courses. They were very progressive Jews, a lot of them socialists and leftists.

Marjorie: And there did you feel as though you were Jewish?

Matilde: I don't remember. I always knew that I was Jewish. But I didn't know what it meant to be Jewish. It's only now that I know I felt different and separate; I don't think I knew it then. That's very interesting, now that you ask me about it. It never occurred to me that the Gentile Catholic group was going to be my group. I didn't ask to be included and I was never offered inclusion. I went to that same normal school for ten years.

Marjorie: And you didn't have friends?

Matilde: No. I was very popular, smart, and happy. I always organized things, and I was a good student. I was accepted as an individual, but I was never accepted as a Jew, I suppose. I wasn't accepted as an insider in the group. I had another gentile friend, now that I think about it: Marta. Her father was in the military and she was a good friend of mine, a dear friend. When she moved, she invited me to visit her in Peru, because her father was named cultural attaché to Peru. My father didn't let me travel to Peru and I never forgave him for that because I wanted to visit Machu Picchu and all those things.[3] But now that I'm thinking about it, I remember that I had another Jewish friend. What was her name? Lula, I think, who had one foot that had been paralyzed, and there was another girl who has always obsessed me. I hope I'll see her again someday. She was not my friend. She was lovely, Lucy Lipschutz, a French refugee. She was tall and had big black eyes and long braids. I'll always be sorry that I didn't make an effort, that I didn't invite her over. I didn't understand that she was a refugee, an immigrant. I didn't know what that meant. This was at the elementary school. I was young, and then, what did I know . . . She had a French accent and later I always fantasized that I will see her again before I die, Lucy Lipschutz. She is fixed in my memory. I have photographs of each class, and there she is, beautiful, tall, languid.

Marjorie: Do you think that Argentines made you feel that you were Jewish?

Matilde: I think that I had repressed all that. I don't remember ever saying to myself, "These people are anti-Semitic and they are attacking me, belittling me here, in Argentina." I knew that it was not easy to be Jewish in Argentina.

Marjorie: So you knew that?

Matilde: I always knew that. In Argentina, it was not nice to be a Jew.

Marjorie: Did people tell you that?

Matilde: It's interesting. Tía Catalina, one of my aunts, who died two years ago at the age of ninety-two, was my father's youngest sister. Her daughters went to my normal school. I told you about that, the place where I went to primary and secondary school. My aunt told me that when I was about seven years old, I had told her how a girl from my school had called me a "shitty Jew." I don't remember this at all, but Aunt Catalina told me later that she was really enraged, furious. How could someone dare to say that to me? At the end of the summer, I went on a vacation trip with my mother to the South, where there is a saltwater lake. When we got back, I found out that I was going to go to another school, to Normal School number 6.

Marjorie: Why?

Matilde: My aunt Catalina had made up her mind that I, her niece, couldn't go back to that other school. I had to switch over to the school where her daughters went. She went to my old school, during the summer vacation, and she bribed the watchman to let her into the school office. She stole my file with all my information in it. She took this information and signed me up for Normal School number 6. She did all this on her own, without consulting my mother or me, no one. When I got back at the beginning of March, I began to study at the new school, which was twenty minutes from my house by streetcar. If this hadn't happened, I'd have kept going to the other school that ended with sixth grade.

Marjorie: Would you have stopped school after the sixth grade?

Matilde: No one would have thought much about it when I was twelve years old.

Marjorie: Wouldn't your mother have . . . ?

Matilde: No.

Marjorie: Because she wasn't educated herself?

Matilde: My mother read a lot, and my father was intelligent, but it never occurred to them that there was any reason for me to go to secondary school. My brother, yes; he is a dentist. But me, a woman, no. I had to fight a lot with my mother about this.

Marjorie: And your aunt wanted you to keep studying?

Matilde: My aunt . . . I don't know. I remember I had had a big discussion with my mother about paying for a preparatory course because it was a very demanding school and even though I was a good student, there was a tough entrance exam for the first year of high school and I had to study for it. I needed tutoring, like all the other students.

Marjorie: And what about the insults because you were Jewish, did they continue?

Matilde: Not at the normal school. I don't remember the elementary school insults—my aunt told me the story.

Marjorie: It's curious that you don't remember and that only as we keep conversing do some things begin to come out, as the act of recalling strains bits out of the past.

Matilde: She said that I told her that story. I think that's what mobilized her. She took it upon herself to make all those changes for me.

Marjorie: Matilde, how were you affected by the Second World War? What did you know about it? My mother always told me that little was said about it in the Chilean newspapers, that it was a distant experience. Nevertheless, there was a very strong pro-Hitler movement in Chile, and especially in Santiago.

Matilde: I remember that my mother knew that there were concentration camps. She felt deep hatred toward Hitler and the destruction. I remember that at noon the radio was always turned to the Radio El Mundo station with international news. The newscaster was a famous reporter, Carlos A. Taquini. At that hour, we were all gathered for lunch at home, the two boys and I, my father and my mother. We listened to the war news. My parents were not very strict, but they did not let us talk until after the war news had ended. The newspaper was delivered to my house at eight in the morning, and my mother would grab it and say, "What's happening in the war?" I remember that clearly.

Marjorie: Did you have family in Europe?

Matilde: No. The main members of both families had moved to America.

Marjorie: Did you feel any relationship with that war, in which hundreds of thousands of Jews were being killed?

Matilde: I don't remember. I recall that we were in favor of the Allies. I remember that a Victory Committee existed, there was one of those committees in every city. Sometimes we went over there with my mother, we packed up medical supplies that could be sent over through private organizations to the Allies. We went over in the evenings to do this. It was a committee that sent aid, that was not sponsored by the government. We never knew if the center would be open or not on any given evening, or if we could do anything there, because Perón kept closing it down. Perón declared war on the Nazis three days before they surrendered. You know, he received part of his military education in Germany. Perón was very pro-Nazi.

Marjorie: Even then, didn't you feel your Jewish connection?

Matilde: No. We knew the Nazis were doing terrible things. I was fourteen years old when the war ended. I may well have blocked out that period entirely. But I am sure that my mother never even imagined, nor would it have seemed possible to her (even more, it would have seemed horrible to her) that I could marry a man who was not Jewish, or that my brother might marry a woman who was not Jewish.

Marjorie: Wouldn't she have accepted it?

Matilde: She would have accepted it, but it would have been extremely painful for her. She wanted us to marry other Jews. I spent my time with Jewish people from adolescence on, through the Jewish associations. My first friends were Jewish.

Marjorie: Matilde, do you feel nostalgic when you speak of these friends?

Matilde: I don't know whether I have become hardened, but I no longer feel nostalgia about my first friends.

Marjorie: Matilde, what, then, do you feel when you think about your country, about your childhood, about your past?

Matilde: I changed so much. I moved beyond nostalgia, beyond wishing I were there . . . It's as though that doesn't matter to me anymore.

Marjorie: And there was a time when that mattered a lot to you?

Matilde: Tremendously. I dreamed and tried to remember things. I had visions of corners of Buenos Aires.

Marjorie: What did you remember the most, your house?

Matilde: What is interesting, now that I think about it, is that even though we had lived here for many years and even when we had bought a really pretty stone house that I liked a lot, I always had the feeling that it was a temporary residence. You know, like when you are in a hotel.

Marjorie: Did you feel that this was temporary?

Matilde: Yes, that it was not my permanent residence. I felt that I would be here just a while before returning . . . I don't know where to, Argentina I suppose. I still feel, in this present house, as though it is not my permanent residence. But I don't think that's to be found in Argentina, either. I don't know whether that idea of "homeland" is an elusive concept . . .

Marjorie: Where do you live now, Matilde? I remember that poem of yours where you get lost, forget the address, and never figure out what direction to take to get back.

Matilde: I don't know whether I have a real homeland any more.

Marjorie: A spiritual home . . .

Matilde: My kitchen is one place. My garden is another, at my beach house.

Marjorie: Is your garden your homeland?

Matilde: That is what you asked me in a letter. And I wrote a poem about it. Perhaps my garden is my homeland, but what happens is that it is my homeland on weekends. Do you know what might be my homeland? One of my dreams is to buy a little house in Philadelphia, near a park, with a back yard, where I can walk out the kitchen door and be in the garden. I don't want to have to get in the car and drive for an hour and a half to get to my garden. That would be a homeland for me. Can you imagine? To have a house with a garden right there. To have access to the garden every day, in winter and in summer.

Marjorie: And what is the possibility of that garden? When did this begin to matter to you, once you had left Argentina, or . . . ?

Matilde: No. This is a new thing. Not only do I not have a home . . . I don't know how to define it.

Marjorie: I will tell you a little about what other friends have said. Ruth needs Cuba to center herself. Zezette needs to return to Holland and see the places where she lived. What is it you need? It sounds as though you do not need to return.

Matilde: I already did all that.

Marjorie: How did you do that?

Matilde: Several years ago I went back to Argentina and I asked a friend to take me around to see all the houses I had lived in and all the schools I had gone to. I visited my parents' graves, also.

Marjorie: What sort of experience was this for you?

Matilde: The houses are in poor condition. The neighborhoods have become run down. Things have changed . . . I went to my parents' graves. My parents died while I was living here. I think that the death of my parents has a lot to do with my feeling independent of Argentina, because only after my father died did I give myself permission to buy a house in the United States.

Marjorie: Did you feel that it would be a temporary residence?

Matilde: Of course. At the beginning, I thought I was going to go back. Emotionally I had not separated myself from Argentina. It took twelve years before I applied for citizenship. I wanted to be able to vote but I waited for the Vietnam War to end before we became citizens because there was no way I was going to let Marcos be sent off to Vietnam. I was going to lock him up in a cellar for life, rather than let him go to Vietnam. All that seemed horrendous to me. As I was telling you, I was in Argentina and a friend went with me to the cemetery. I saw that my father's grave was falling apart, exposing his coffin, but it was marked with his portrait on it, and his name, because my mother had had it done. Next to it was my mother's grave, but it didn't have a name or anything on it. I knew that was her grave because they told me it was next to my father's.

Marjorie: Your mother's grave didn't have her name on it?

Matilde: Nothing. There was nothing on it. You couldn't tell whose grave it was. And I . . . I don't know how to tell you . . . I had an attack. It was as though I had been dreaming this and it didn't really exist, it couldn't be that my mother didn't have her name on her grave. Everything started spinning around and I was crying. No one could calm me down. They didn't know what to do with me. I think people can go crazy that way. I don't know how to explain it to you. The people who were supposed to care for the graves did not do it. Nor did they tell me when my father was dying; they just sent me a letter after he died. I was not there when my mother died, either. Later, I found out that my other brother was buried in a common grave. These are horror stories, that's what they are for me, horror stories.

Marjorie: Where is your brother now?

120

Matilde Salganicoff

Matilde: He is in a common grave. There is no way to get access to it.

Marjorie: And that made you feel even more distanced from your country?

Matilde: I think it influenced me a lot. I could not care for my parents when they were alive, and not when they are dead, either. The only thing I could do was to have the graves repaired and maintained. I think this is a frequent source of pain for emigrants. Recently, there was vandalism in the Jewish cemetery. I want to be cremated.

Marjorie: This story is very . . . It has a lot to do with the country, with its losses, with the camps and cemeteries where the corpses of the disappeared were buried, but you also make me think of the tombs of Jews that were desecrated during the Holocaust. They were tombs that recorded the history of people's lives. Is that what you felt with your parents and your brother?

Matilde: Now I am able to talk about this. For years I could not speak of it. I couldn't because it made me cry so. It is so horrible that my mother should not have had her name on her gravestone. It is as though she had not existed. It is as though I had not buried them. I don't know how to tell you.

Marjorie: Do you feel that your life has big holes in it?

Matilde: I don't know. I don't know—this certainly feels like a big hole.

Marjorie: Let's go back a little to how your life is here. What have these years been like, living in this country?

Matilde: Ever since I got to the United States, I think I have felt I am here temporarily, just passing through.

Marjorie: So that even after thirty-three years of living here, you feel transitory?

Matilde: At the beginning, I felt Argentine. Now I don't feel as though I am from anywhere.

Marjorie: Does it bother you, not feeling as though you are from somewhere?

Matilde: No. I think it is better not to be from anyplace.

Marjorie: At your age? Or for immigrants in general?

Matilde: I can't speak for everyone. For me, at this moment, in my daily living, I think that people shouldn't be from anywhere in particular. It's fine that I'm not from anywhere now. For whatever the reasons may have been, in my case because of my family, psychological reasons, political reasons . . . That's fine, it's a way to separate oneself.

Marjorie: From a homeland?

Matilde: From a homeland, from things. Right?

Marjorie: To be freer?

Matilde: I think so, yes.

Marjorie: What makes you happy, Matilde? When you think back over the past, what makes you happy? What moves you most deeply?

Matilde: The day Alina was born. That was the happiest day of my life. I am profoundly grateful for that. It was as though my life were perfect, as though my life had been transformed because Alina arrived. She was a marvelous baby. She taught me to be a mother. What else? When Marcos was born. Days when the sun shines, mornings when seeds are sprouting. That always seems miraculous to me. Something flowering. The beauty of nature gives me great happiness and it grieves me when it is not respected. Those are really irreparable errors. I think I'm fine, I am content.

Marjorie: What do you miss about Argentina?

Matilde: I miss having family nearby. My cousins had a tea for me in March. It had been years since I had seen them.

Marjorie: Your cousins?

Matilde: On my mother's side. They are simple people, good people. We got along well as children and they greeted me with such affection . . . they had a tea party for me.

Marjorie: Simple, sincere people? Did you feel emotional about being surrounded by cousins?

Matilde: Yes. It was a very emotional meeting. We couldn't stop crying. Each one came in and we gave each other a big hug and kissed and wept from happiness at seeing each other again. Even the second cousins came. I have some very elderly first cousins because there were nineteen years' difference between my mother's oldest sister and her youngest one, who are all dead now. I am one of the youngest cousins . . .

Marjorie: Haven't you wanted to return to that?

Matilde: Well . . .

Marjorie: Doesn't it give you a feeling of comfort to know that they are there?

Matilde: It brought me profound joy and I am very grateful for all they have done and I am going to stay in contact with them because there was so much, so very much affection between us. They had a tea party for me and they are not rich people. One offered her house, and we all went there, chattering away and recalling old times.

Marjorie: And has this happened in the United States?

Matilde: No, because there are no old times here to remember. What has happened is that when I came here, I became a person with no past history.

Marjorie: You don't have a history here? Tell me about that.

Matilde: I have thirty-three years of history in the United States, but it is my life history from age thirty-three on. I've created my history here, with new memories.

Marjorie: Do you think that you invented a history for yourself in order to survive?

Matilde: No, I don't think so. I did not invent a history. I created another life here, and I have people who care about me a lot, and of whom I am very fond, and some of them I really love.

Marjorie: What do you mean by living without a history, Matilde? How did you decide to define yourself here?

Matilde: People always asked me why I left Argentina, if I had relatives there, and if I traveled back often and what I was doing here. Everybody I met asked me all those things. So those were the things that I talked about.

Marjorie: I get annoyed when people ask me something and then say that the minute I open my mouth, they know where I'm from. In the United States you feel very defined by your accent.

Matilde: Well, that is my problem, too. It's the problem of the person with an accent, not of the person who listens to you. Why do people think they have a right to ask me? Because they do it affectionately or because they are interested? It's not an attack, it's curiosity, paying attention to your accent . . . I don't know why they have to ask. Why does this annoy me so?

Marjorie: It probably annoys you because . . .

Matilde: Because I have to keep repeating the story each time I'm asked.

Marjorie: And explain, because when I am in Chile, no one asks me where I am from, but anywhere else, they do ask, and that's why I'm happy in Chile.

Matilde: Since I've been away from Argentina for such a long time, I also have to explain myself there.

Marjorie: Not belonging to any one place is part of being an immigrant. You've always written about immigration and about being an immigrant. I'm interested in how you feel about this. Could you elaborate a little more about how you always feel in transit?

Matilde: It's like having no history, or not being visible. It's a way of not being, or of disappearing. That's why one has to keep explaining oneself in order to be visible.

Marjorie: Do you still feel as though you have to explain yourself? Is that part of what immigrating means?

Matilde: No. I'm not troubled by feeling invisible anymore, and, actually, I seek refuge in invisibility now. I don't need people to recognize me. If I'm invisible, I don't have to explain myself; I don't have to tell stories; I don't have to say who I am. It used to be painful, but now it's fine. I am comfortable. Now invisibility is the refuge that it was not before. Now invisibility is a pleasant house, it's like being in a glass house where you can see out, but others cannot see in. I define myself as a foreigner in two countries. For many people, I am only a foreigner here, not in my country. But I've gradually become a foreigner in Argentina. I don't know about your experience, or anyone else's. I've become more and more aware of this. I believe the pardons granted to the Dirty War assassins make me feel more of a foreigner in Argentina. Argentina can never recover if those pardons are not retracted, if the criminals are not punished. I don't know, maybe I am very vengeful . . .

Marjorie: No, it's that you can't forgive someone who has tortured another person. I feel that what I have left of Chile is my childhood, which is intact. But once I left it, there was nothing. Everything stopped existing. What do you see as the problems of a woman who emigrates?

Matilde: I think that there is a double problem for emigrant women, as women we define ourselves by our relationships and as emigrants we lament the loss of our relationships.

Marjorie: Tell me a little more about that.

Matilde: You see, I agree with Carol Gilligan,[4] who says that we women define ourselves by our relationships. I defined myself by the connections I had in Argentina, with my family and my friends, and then I lost those, and with that, part of my identity was lost, and I had to construct new relationships here. I lost the old ties because I came to the United States, but in reality, I didn't lose them totally because it's possible to reconnect with those we love.

Marjorie: I wonder if you don't have much more there than you think you do. Because if I didn't share your history, your culture, if we didn't have a life story in common, we wouldn't be able to have this conversation. Do you understand what I am saying?

Matilde: I don't know, it's something I have to think about.

(Translated from Spanish by Mary G. Berg)

RENATA BRAILOVSKY

March 19, 1931	Born in Breslau, Germany (now Poland)
1936–1938	Attends Jewish school in Breslau
November 8, 1938	Kristallnacht
February 1939	Father released from Buchenwald concentration camp
March 1939	Father goes to Czechoslovakia and obtains fraudulent visa for the family to Chile; father leaves Prague for Genoa and then Valparaíso, Chile
April 1939	Leaves Breslau with mother and brother for Genoa, then Valparaíso
May 1939	Family reunites in Santiago, Chile
June 1939	Attends English school
March 1943	Attends Liceo No. 1
March 1949–1953	Attends Instituto Pedagógico, Universidad de Chile, mención Filosofía
January 4, 1952	Marries David Brailovsky in Santiago, Chile
December 22, 1954	Daughter Isabel born
March 3, 1956	Daughter Sonia born
June 25, 1962	Mother, Rose Schnitzer, dies
June 26, 1962	Daughter Rose born
February 6, 1964	Father, Alfred Schnitzer, dies
September 1970	Moves to Buenos Aires, Argentina
October 1970	Moves to Mexico City, Mexico
November 1970	Moves to Mountainside, New Jersey, United States
November 1992	Settles in Newton, Massachusetts

Germany's democratic Weimar Republic was beset with difficulties from the moment it was established at the end of World War I. Undermined by the unpopularity of the punitive Treaty of Versailles, postwar inflation, internal dissension, and increasing pressure from the right, the Weimar republic survived until January 1933 when, following widespread Nazi electoral victories in the fall of 1932, Adolph Hitler was appointed chancellor of Germany. Hitler quickly moved to consolidate his power and that of the National Socialist German Workers' Party, the Nazi Party. The Nazis immediately began implementing legislation against the party's perceived enemies. Among them were the culturally assimilated, but politically marginal, Jews of Germany.

Anti-Semitic legislation increased in the mid-1930s. The term *Nichtarier*, or non-Aryan, was adopted on April 7, 1933, as a means of removing Jews from legal, municipal, medical, and media professions. The Nuremberg laws of September 1935 provided a definition of "Jew" by religion, by origin, and by family ties, and they essentially denied Jews citizenship. The aim of such legislation was the eventual declaration of the realm as Judenrein, or free from Jewry. During this period, about 250,000 German Jews (approximately 57 percent) fled to other European nations and South America. Renata Brailovsky and her family were among these German Jewish immigrants, arriving in Chile in 1939, when she was eight years old.

Like me, Renata lived in Chile as an adolescent and young adult. She emigrated with her husband to the United States in 1970, to escape the political turmoil in Chile. We met in my home on a snowy, mid-March day. I found Renata an eager and gifted storyteller. Her immense, deep green eyes, the color of rivers, animated her face as she spoke. Her eyes evoked the difficulties of her past, but also the joys of the present. Hers was a survivor's tale without resentment: Renata is a woman deeply grateful to be alive.

Marjorie: Renata, can you tell me about your journey to Chile?

Renata: I arrived in Chile in 1939 at the age of eight. We came with my mother, my brother, my aunt, and her daughter. We came on one of the last boats that left Italy for Valparaíso. My father had left before with his brother because he was in a concentration camp and was able to get out at that time, but he had to leave within forty-eight hours. He went with his brother to Czechoslovakia. Breslau, the town in Germany where I was born, is now part of Poland. But when I was born the region was called Silesia and it was in Germany. So, he went away to Czechoslovakia. Hitler was on his way to invade Czechoslovakia, and they managed to get visas the very morning Hitler marched into Czechoslovakia. My father and his brother fled to Italy. From Italy he took a boat to Valparaíso. He reached there about three months before us. The very interesting part is how we got a visa for Chile. While he was in Czechoslovakia, he tried to get a visa for anywhere in the world. There was no country that wanted to take Jews at the time but he got to know the janitor of the Chilean consulate who had stolen a stamp for visas. You had to pay him three thousand dollars per family to get a visa.

Marjorie: That was a fortune!

Renata: Yes! Three thousand dollars was a lot of money. It was a forged visa, after all. He had the stamp, but he signed it himself as the consul. So, we had these forged visas, signed by the janitor of the Chilean consulate. With these visas we arrived in Chile. I remember a very terrifying experience when we took the train from Germany to Italy.

Marjorie: With your mother?

Renata: With my mother and my brother, and my aunt and my cousin, who is two years older than I. My brother is four years older than me. I had my favorite doll with me because we could not take many things. Each one of us was allowed to take only one toy. So, I took my favorite doll. I remember customs coming . . . the Gestapo, before we left the train station . . . and they took away my doll and they cut the head off to see if there were any diamonds inside. To me, of course, it was like killing my doll! I was told immediately not to cry, not to make a fuss. I learned at a very young age to bite my lip and cry silently. The doll was fixed later on and I had my doll, but it was a terrible experience.

Marjorie: When you were telling me about your doll, your voice changed; you seemed to become that little girl, who was leaving everything behind. Was your escape very difficult?

Renata: At that time, you could still leave. I don't know if we bribed someone. I am really not sure. But I think that at that time you could still leave.

Marjorie: Yes, I think that is true because it was also the year that my grandmother, Helena, arrived in Valparaíso.

Renata: Before that, I can also remember another terrifying experience when they came to pick up my father. We had an apartment in Germany, and until this day, I see the boots of the Gestapo. When I have nightmares, I hear the sounds of those boots and I see them. They took away my father! And from before that, I remember the hush-hush conversations of the adults and the constant crying of my mother. My uncle came to warn my father that there were concentration camps and that we should all emigrate immediately. My father did not believe him and told him that he was a German patriot. He had fought in the First World War and gotten an Iron Cross for bravery. He was convinced that they would never harm him. How wrong he was. A few weeks later the Gestapo came to our house and took my father away. The only thing I remember was the shouting and those terrible black boots that made so much noise. Even today when I am anxious, I have these recurrent nightmares about that night.

Marjorie: You still have nightmares?

Renata: Yes, until this very day when I am anxious, at night or when I have a lot of problems, I will hear the sound of those boots and I will see them. My father was one of the lucky ones. He was detained at Buchenwald for about six weeks and released. One thing that I cannot forget is when my father returned from the concentration camp, my mother, my brother, and myself were supposed to pick him up at the railroad station. I will never forget that early foggy dawn. I did not recognize him when he finally appeared. All his beautiful curly hair was gone. He was completely bald, his hair all shaven off. I was in total shock and did not understand how lucky we were to have him back. He must have lost a tremendous amount of weight, so he came back as an old man, although he was gone only maybe two months, I don't know exactly. He left immediately for Czechoslovakia. His brother was already there and was trying to obtain visas for us to any country in the world that would accept us. As a young child, this was very traumatic to see my father come back this way. It was taboo in my house to talk about the concentration camp, about the time my father spent there. My father never talked about it. Never.

Marjorie: And your mother never talked about it either?

Renata: No. She did not talk about it. It was absolutely forbidden to discuss the topic at that time. We never spoke, and since both my parents died very young, we never really got to know about it.

Marjorie: And once you arrived in Chile, could you talk to your parents about that experience?

Renata: No. We did try, but they immediately changed the subject. They really did not want to discuss it. It was something that we learned never to ask them because it was an experience they did not want to talk about. So I remember coming to Chile and living in small boarding houses.

Marjorie: But first, you arrived in Valparaíso. Do you remember what you thought? You were just a little girl.

Renata: I was very young. Somehow, I knew nothing about Chile. I expected Indians with feathers to be living there. Indians with feathers! And then we immediately went to Santiago. Everything was so new, so different. I felt uprooted. I had no friends. It was very difficult.

Marjorie: Yes, people often arrived in these countries knowing nothing at all about them, the language, the customs. Immigrants were almost like sleepwalkers in these new cities.

Renata: We spoke no Spanish, not a word. My mother, my father, none of us knew any Spanish. We went to a pension, a boarding house. I remember that it had two beds which we moved close to each other and I had to sleep in the middle. It always opened and I fell through to the floor. They tried to put strings around the corners so I would not fall. It was very, very cold. It was wintertime. I got frostbite because it was so cold there. Also, we did not have much money.

Marjorie: Did you have a comfortable life in Germany?

Renata: Very comfortable. I came from a very comfortable, upper-middle-class family because my grandfather had the biggest umbrella factory in Germany. All the brothers were in the same business. I went to a Jewish school in Breslau, so I remember learning a little bit of Hebrew. I had learned to read in German and to write in Gothic script. My brother, Adolph, who is four years older than I, went to this Jewish school, too. Adolph was a very popular name in Germany at the time and had nothing to do with Adolph Hitler. Somehow I have always been ashamed of his name because I believe we all associate this name with Hitler. My brother's nickname is Ado and I only call him by that name. I remember trying to walk to school the day after the Kristallnacht and being told, "Go back quickly. No school."[1]

Marjorie: Can we talk a little about Kristallnacht? Please tell me how it affected you as a little girl.

Renata: I remember the day after Kristallnacht very clearly. It had happened on November 9th, 1938. The next morning, as usual, I walked to school by myself and I could not understand all the commotion on the streets. At the time you did not turn on the radio that early, I think, to listen to the news. At least, I don't remember doing that at all. When I got close to my school, I saw that the whole building was in flames. I was told, "Go back quickly. No school." Terrified, I ran back home as fast as I could. Then we learned that the school I went to was destroyed and there was no more school. That was the end of my education in Germany.

Marjorie: Yes, that night and all the broken crystal which signaled the advance of anti-Semitism. You said they destroyed your school? What happened to your routine, your life?

Renata: Yes, they destroyed the school and that was my end of going to school. It was burned down and we had no more schooling. I was seven and a half years old then. Since there was no school and I was terribly bored, I wanted to play in the garden of our apartment complex. It was a big back yard where I used to play with my friends. I wanted to use the swings and play with the other children when they got home from school. To my big surprise and dismay there was a big notice: "Juden und hunde verboten"—"Jews and dogs forbidden." We had to wait to get the visa, so I was eight when we finally left.

Marjorie: This reminds me of some places in Chile which, even in the 1950s, had similar signs, aimed at Jews and at Arabs.

Renata: It was the garden of our apartment building and I could not even go down and play there anymore.

Marjorie: So you lost your school and you lost your garden. Everything you loved was disappearing or becoming forbidden . . .

Renata: Yes, I lost my garden and my nanny, because Jews were not allowed to employ aryan workers in their service anymore. I remember this nanny that I adored and she adored me. She gave me the doll that I took with me. That doll, the doll I wanted so much to take with me. This is a traumatic experience, right here and now, going through these flashbacks. My brother was sent on a Kindertransport,[2] since he was four years older. He was sent to Belgium. He went alone. I cried so much because they were going to send me, but I refused to go, really refused, so I was not sent at the time.

Marjorie: And your brother also went to Chile and has remained there?

Renata: Yes, but my mother waited before sending for my brother. He was sent out of Germany on a Kindertransport, a children's train, maybe eight or ten months before Kristallnacht because already the atmosphere in Germany was very tense and difficult. It was supposed to be safer in Belgium. He went to the city of Antwerp, and then, when we all had to leave for Chile, my mother would not leave without him. My brother could not go through France. They would not give him a transit visa. He was considered, at that time (and this is a terrible thing to say of a ten-year-old boy) an enemy of the country. France would not give a ten-year-old Jewish boy a transit visa. Finally he was able to return to Germany, which was very dangerous at the time, in order to join us.

Marjorie: And he traveled back with your mother?

Renata: He traveled alone because he was alone in Belgium on that Kindertransport. He was sent to foster parents because they thought they would send the children out to save them, maybe. Since I was too young or too babyish, I cried so much and made such a fuss, they did not send me. So it was very, very hard for my brother to return. It was really . . . He could have died coming back.

Marjoric: You were waiting for him?

Renata: We were waiting for him with my mother because she would not leave for Chile without him. So when he came back, we left immediately. He had to come back to Germany and then we took the train to Italy.

Marjorie: And then Chile?

Renata: And from Genoa, Italy, we took the boat and went to Valparaíso and then immediately to Santiago.

Marjorie: And so now life in Chile is filled with these memories. Your brother also shares them since you often speak of him.

Renata: I still have those memories.

Marjorie: Of a world that is gone. Would you say that you were holding onto a vanished world?

Renata: Yes. A world that was gone. But I was too young to really grasp the meaning of it. Too young, and in a way, excited to start something new because living there was not so great at the end. It was actually terrifying. So, I was really eager to start a new life, to make new friends, to be able to play outdoors and be in a safe environment. Yes, to start anew. Of course, it was very difficult for my parents, who had lost everything. I mean, we brought our furniture; I remember a carpet. My father adored oriental carpets. He had a very big collection of oriental carpets, which I still have, as a matter of fact. I still have some of those in my house.

Marjorie: He brought them all the way from Germany to Chile?

Renata: Yes, and paintings too. We had paintings and carpets. I remember at the beginning my father selling every month one carpet and one painting in Chile so we could survive. So we could survive! It is very interesting how we made a living at the beginning, how my father made a living. Since there was no money, he had to start some sort of business. Someone told him about a business. They bought *un establo,* a stable, with another Jewish couple.

Marjorie: Really?

Renata: With nine cows. I even remember how many cows! Nine cows. There were two families living from what this stable produced—milk—and I remember helping my mother make cheese, cottage cheese, with the milk, and sell it right there. My father and mother had not even seen cows before that. They could not tell the front from the back end of a cow! Yet, there they were, making a living. They had a couple of people who took care of the cows and milked them. Eventually, they learned quite a bit about them. I used to help there, early in the morning, selling the milk at the pier. I remember the street. My father did this for the first two years. He sold out to his partner and then he got what they call a silent partner—a capitalist partner who put up the money—and again he started an umbrella factory. I was sent to school. I also was the one, I don't know why, who very often had do to the shopping. I was told in German what to buy. So there I went, on my bicycle in Santiago. We lived in the Barrio Alto and it was there and then that I learned Spanish.

Marjorie: You went shopping because you knew some Spanish?

Renata: No! I did not know any Spanish. So I would point and they would say what it was in Spanish. My mother had to work. I was eight years old, I had to try to help out with many things. So I would point and say, "potato," and they would say, "papa." Then I learned that this item was a "papa." Very quickly I started to learn Spanish, and I would then do all the shopping and bring it back on my bicycle, which I really enjoyed. Shopping did not bother me at all.

Marjorie: What was your neighborhood like then?

Renata: It was a good neighborhood. We started off by living in boarding houses, then my father rented that stable and a house in a nice part of town. We rented out rooms in that house. We rented three rooms to other émigrés and my mother provided them with breakfast and lunch. I had to help my mother clean the house and prepare the meals. That was another way of making money and we could stay in a decent place, a nice house with a garden. It had three bedrooms, a living room, and a dining room. My brother and I slept in the dining room. My parents slept in one of the bedrooms and we rented out the rest. I was sent to a neighborhood private English school, the Trewella Sisters. The teachers were not very understanding. On the very first day I went there, I was told to translate from English to Spanish and vice versa. Of course I didn't know either language and went home crying that I would never go to school again.

Marjorie: I know that school. It was a very prestigious school. That was a time when it was very difficult to be accepted at private schools in Chile.

Renata Brailovsky

Renata: You know the school? It was a little school with three, no two, sisters. It was a very interesting school. It had first through sixth grade.

Marjorie: How did you learn Spanish?

Renata: On the streets, in school. I didn't know any English, not much.

Marjorie: Did you have maids at home?

Renata: Yes. Later on we did, yes. We had some help and I learned some Spanish through her. I learned on the streets and in school. I remember coming home crying every day and saying "I don't want to go to school anymore! I do not know any English and I do not know any Spanish." I only knew German. The first thing I learned is, "May I go to the bathroom?" and then, "May I sharpen my pencil?" At least I could survive in school. And then, you know, children learn very fast, I think. I spent those first years there. I also remember having brought these German dresses, smocks, and no one wore things like that. It was completely not the style and as a young child I wanted to wear everything that everyone else was wearing. Then I made little holes in all of my dresses hoping my mother would buy me new ones. But there was no money to buy new ones! So, I remember having to wear the smocks that were patched up. I was not a very happy child at that time. I really was not.

Marjorie: And your parents, did they learn Spanish?

Renata: At home, we only spoke German. At that time, in Chile, you could not just go to a school and learn a language. So my parents decided that since they had to learn Spanish as they went on with their daily lives and business, they would never really learn proper Spanish. I, on the other hand, should learn proper German, which was the language they spoke fluently. As a matter of fact, my father also taught me about German literature. I read Goethe, Schiller, Heine.

Marjorie: How well do you feel you became integrated into Chilean society?

Renata: Our only friends were other German Jews.

Marjorie: So your whole world, would you say from age nine to fifteen . . .

Renata: Well, no. I made some friends in Chile, at school. It was hard because my Spanish was not so great. I had a German accent. It was not easy to make friends, so I spent a lot of time with the other German Jews. I went to an organization called Hashomer Hatzair where I formed my identity. I was nine when I joined them and this was my life.

Marjorie: So your world was that of a German Jewish refugee living an almost German Jewish life? This is very similar to the world my mother grew up in. She can even remember seeing you at Hashomer.

Renata: Yes, we led an absolutely German Jewish life in Chile. Our diet was German Jewish. We ate cold cuts for dinner, which is not a Chilean custom. Later on we incorporated some of the Chilean dishes.

Marjorie: How did you feel in that distant land?

Renata: How did I feel? It's hard to say. Different, alienated, a stranger. It seemed like I did not fit in, was not a part of Chilean society. I tried very hard to fit in.

Marjorie: What did you do?

Renata: I spoke Spanish correctly and fluently. I tried to say from the beginning that my favorite dish was *pastel de choclo*.[3] I tried that in my house. We tried to assimilate more, really, but my parents were . . . well, when I brought Chilean friends into the house . . .

Marjorie: Chilean Catholics?

Renata: Yes. It was difficult because my parents spoke a broken Spanish, grammatically incorrect. The food was not Chilean, not really Chilean. We adjusted and we assimilated. We had a Chilean cook and she would make some dishes when I invited friends to come over. It was difficult because they did not feel at home like they would feel with the Chilean customs.

Marjorie: How did they refer to you?

Renata: Just as "judía." The Sephardic Jews would call me a "yeque" [a Jew of German origin]. The Chilean Catholics called me "judía." I was not Chilean. I was "judía," not "alemana," because Germans were considered to be Catholic in Chile. I was considered "judía." So when I was growing up, I considered myself really "judía," always.

Marjorie: It reminds me that when I was growing up they always asked me,

"Are you Jewish or Chilean?" The answer was obvious, I was both, but that question never stopped bothering me. But let's talk about growing up as a Jewish girl in Chile.

Renata: First and foremost I was Jewish. All the time, growing up in Santiago. After 5 years of primary education, I transferred to a public school, Liceo number 1. Although by then I was completely fluent in Spanish I was always considered a foreigner. Some of the teachers were overtly anti-Semitic. I remember many instances of it. On the High Holy Days I did not attend school and I was told afterwards by some friends that our Spanish teacher had mentioned how wonderful it was to teach without the Jewish girls present. Well, we rebelled terribly against her. When she asked us to do things, none of the German Jewish kids would comply. Our French teacher . . . I will never forget that one, Madame Mirella, who taught us Racine. I was called upon. I loved French and was really good at it. One day when we studied "Esther" by Racine and I knew it really well, her comment was, "Jewish girls have a great facility for languages. So, although you gave an excellent presentation, I will not give you a seven, I will only give you a six." Seven is the equivalent of an A and six of a B. I remember. It still hurts up to this day. In all honesty we fought back and tried to annoy her as much as we possibly could. We would get together at recess, always at recess, because we could not participate very well with the other girls, and we would have our little clique—the German Jewish girls from different grades. And we would play our games and we would have a good time together. Another quite unpleasant incident was that we were forced to attend religion classes (Catholic, of course). We were supposed to make the sign of the cross, et cetera. My mother went to school and insisted that I should be excused (she could not write a letter because her Spanish was not good enough). I was made to wait outside in the courtyard, standing in the cold. I was not allowed to go to the library. I got a zero in religion, so when all our grades were added up to get our grade point average, mine was low. And all because I had not gone to the religion class. Most of the German Jewish girls stood up for their convictions.

Marjorie: That made you strong? Did it contribute to shaping who you are?

Renata: It certainly did make me strong. All of these obstacles have made me very strong and I am able to overcome all kinds of hardships. My Judaism was a very strong influence and we had many organizations in Santiago that we could belong to. If I had been asked in Chile whether I felt Chilean or Jewish, I would always have answered I am Jewish first and then Chilean. German Jews in Chile were a very united and cohesive community. The majority of our parents did not speak Spanish and spoke only German with their friends and with us.

When Hashomer Hatzair was begun, I immediately became a member of this organization.

Marjorie: Can you tell me a little more about Hashomer and how your experiences there affected you?

Renata: Hashomer was a very leftist Zionist organization. It had an enormous influence on my adult life. It was the center of my social life, and everything I did was affected by the ideals and methods of Hashomer. We met every Saturday afternoon and discussed Israel's war problems, anti-Semitism, et cetera. Each "kwutza," group, was made up of about ten people, divided up by age. We danced the horah and had a wonderful time like any other adolescents leading normal lives. On Sundays we would all get out our bicycles and go from one German Jewish house to another, collecting money in blue and white boxes for the KKL, the Keren Kajemet Leisrael. We all thought this a perfectly natural thing to be doing, and no one thought of it as giving up your weekend. We all participated. We would get up really early to get this done, and then we would get together to go hiking and go on picnics. I remember how much fun it was. No one had any money, and no one had any extra food at home during those early years there. We would sit in a circle and put all our sandwiches and fruit in the middle, and then we would all help ourselves from this common pile. We shared everything. We would sing songs in Hebrew, never in Spanish.

Marjorie: Tell me more about how you felt, being so active in Hashomer. How did this affect your relationships with other Chileans?

Renata: We felt really outside Chilean society. Our Jewish identity was very strong. In high school we were not accepted because we kept being foreigners even though as time went by we all spoke perfect Spanish. I was in high school during the war and found that the teachers, with very few exceptions, were deeply anti-Semitic. In general Chile was pro-German during the war.

I think that German Jews had a lot of difficulty in integrating themselves into Chilean society. It was not just a matter of language, but of our customs, our surnames. It seems to me that with a surname like Schnitzer one could never hope to fit in and be considered Chilean, but that one would always be labeled as Jewish. Jewish friends with surnames like Albala, Alvo, Pérez, González, et cetera, seemed to fare much better at integration. And in many of these cases, I didn't even realize until after I had graduated from high school that some of my companions were Jewish.

Marjorie: My mother often tells me about similar difficulties she had as the daughter of German Jews. It was really hard for her to feel part of Chilean groups, and not easy to make friends. My father, as a Russian Jew, had many problems when he was a medical student. Did your husband also feel discriminated against in medicine?

Renata: Yes, my husband, David, certainly felt discriminated against in medical school. Professors were always chosen by block votes. The Masonic block, the Catholic block, et cetera. At that time there were some specialties, like obstetrics and gynecology. No Jew could join in these specialties because they were dominated by non-Jewish Germans. That does not mean that we do not have good Chilean friends who over time learned to appreciate us for ourselves and not see us always in terms of our religion or our country of origin.

In Chile there was a lot of friction between the various different Jewish communities. The German, the Russian, the Sephardic, et cetera. For example, when I married David, our marriage was considered a mixed marriage, since he was a Russian Jew and I was a German Jew. We decided to make things easier for our daughters, and David founded the first multicultural congregation, where all the different communities were included. I taught Jewish religion classes at Santiago College, even though I didn't have much training for this, just the desire that all the Jewish girls at the school should have the same opportunities as the rest of the students, since there were Catholic and Protestant religion classes taught by priests and pastors. The priests and pastors contributed their time, but unfortunately rabbis wanted to be paid, so I ended up teaching the classes.

I found that Chile was less xenophobic and discriminatory after the sixties. My daughters were never aware of any anti-Semitism. I made my first seder at Santiago College. Both the students and the teachers received the presentation of the seder in the school auditorium with great interest, appreciation, and enthusiasm. It was the first time they had seen anything like this. The students and the teachers were completely ignorant about all Jewish observances. My daughters were the first to have their bat mitzvas in Chile. I was the one who introduced this ceremony of the bat mitzva in Chile.

Marjorie: All this that you're telling me is marvelous! What a wonderful story of your first seder. All these experiences must have made you who you are today.

Renata: I can be in any milieu, any atmosphere, and I think I am secure and that I can face anything and everything. Little things cannot bother me at all and I must admit that now, at this age, I am quite mature. I get so annoyed when women complain about a broken nail or a broken crystal, or soiled furniture. I have absolutely no patience. I cannot stand it! As a matter of fact, I cannot stand hearing all those petty things. People complaining about things like this. It made me so strong that I learned to really live every day. I am a very positive person because of it. The sun is out, I am happy. I will always be grateful for all the little things.

Marjorie: Like my mother. She says she is very grateful just to be alive and I have grown up with that belief. And now, Renata, can you tell me a little about Zapallar? You've mentioned that Chile in the sixties was a more open society, but what about Zapallar? It seems to me that this beautiful beach resort exemplified discrimination against Jews.

Renata: Yes, I do remember going on vacations, and once we went to Zapallar. Now in retrospect, I don't know why my parents chose that place. I thought it was the most anti-Semitic place ever. We went there . . . actually we only went there for a week. I remember it being one of the most horrendous weeks of my life. None of the youngsters would play with me. I think we were the only Jews there. Jews did not go there, but my parents wanted to go because . . . I don't know . . . because it had a beautiful beach. I can only think of that reason. What other reason could they have? And they went with friends. I was alone. I had no one to play with. I must have been thirteen at the time. They had these little dances always for the youngsters and of course no one would dance with me. Then, one young boy came up to me. I remember his name was Jesús María and he wanted to befriend me. Then all the other kids came up to him and said, "If you are going to dance with that Jewish girl then you cannot play or be with us anymore." Well, that was the end of that.

Marjorie: So it was the children also?

Renata: Yes, definitely. It was not just the adults. It was the children too. And from that moment on, I was alone.

Marjorie: What made you decide to leave Chile?

Renata: Being slightly paranoid, my husband and I decided to emigrate to the United States in 1970 rather than wait to see the outcome of Salvador Allende's regime. This time the adjustment was not so difficult. We were both fluent in English, and we both had professions and knew that we could succeed again. Again it was the Jewish community that received us with open arms, warmth, and love. We both became American citizens. If I were asked today what I am, I would answer that I am a citizen of the world. I am at home everywhere and nowhere. Home is where my children are. We lived in New Jersey for twenty years. Our three daughters went to school in Boston, met their husbands, and stayed in Boston. My husband and I moved to Boston when he retired, and this has been the easiest move of all. I still cannot get over the tolerance and respect that people have in the U.S. for the Jewish people. The way that plurality is stressed and taught in all the schools.

Immigration to the U.S. was much easier than our arrival in Chile. The Jewish community in New Jersey received us with open arms, as did our Italian neighbors. Since this is a country created by immigrants, there is no discrimination. Very few arrived in the Mayflower. There are so many Jews on the East Coast, and especially in Newton. Sometimes I think I am in Little Jerusalem. We feel very comfortable and happy in this country, where plurality is so accepted and respected. We feel that we are Jews first, and then Americans or citizens of the world.

SUSAN RUBIN SULEIMAN

July 18, 1939	Born in Budapest, Hungary
Summer 1944	Sent to live with farmers after Germany occupies Hungary
Fall 1944–Spring 1945	Lives with parents under false identity in Budapest, until liberation by the Russian army
August 1949	Leaves Hungary illegally with parents to escape the harsh Communist regime; settles in Vienna
May 1950	Leaves Vienna for Port-au-Prince, Haiti, via Munich, Paris, and Le Havre
December 1950	Birth of sister Judy in Port-au-Prince; family enters United States and lives in New York
Summer 1953	Family moves to Chicago; Susan enters high school
August 19, 1959	Father dies of a heart attack, age forty-nine; mother and sister move to New York, then to Miami Beach
1960	Bachelor's degree from Barnard College in New York. Spends post-graduation year in Paris studying at the Sorbonne; summer in Italy learning Italian
February 27, 1966	Marries Ezra N. Suleiman, an Iraqi Jew whose family fled Iraq in the 1950s
1966–1975	Instructor, then assistant professor, of French at Columbia University, New York, New York
1968	Fellowship year in Paris, with husband
1969	Doctorate in Romance languages and literatures at Harvard University, Cambridge, Massachusetts
April 9, 1970	Son Michael born in New York
1975–1979	Moves to Los Angeles with family; assistant professor of French at Occidental College
May 15, 1977	Son Daniel born in Los Angeles; mother remarries
1977	Sabbatical year in Paris, with family
1979	Moves to Princeton, New Jersey, with family
1980	Edits, with Inge Crosman, The Reader in the Text: Essays on Audience and Interpretation (Princeton University Press)
Fall 1981	Associate professor of Romance languages and literatures, Harvard; separates from husband and moves with children to Belmont, Massachusetts

1983	Publishes *Authoritarian Fictions: The Ideological Novel as a Literary Genre* (Columbia University Press)
1984	Fall semester in Paris with Rockefeller Humanities Fellowship.
	Named Professor of Romance and Comparative Literatures at Harvard; first trip back to Budapest (with Michael and Daniel)
1986	Edits *The Female Body in Western Culture: Contemporary Perspectives* (Harvard University Press)
April 18, 1988	Mother dies in Miami Beach
1989	Spring semester in Paris (with Daniel) with Guggenheim Fellowship
1990	Publishes *Subversive Intent: Gender, Politics, and the Avant-Garde* (Harvard University Press)
February–July 1993	Second trip to Budapest, as Fellow of Collegium Budapest Institute for Advanced Study
1994	Publishes *Risking Who One Is: Encounters with Contemporary Art and Literature* (Harvard University Press)
1996	Publishes *Budapest Diary: In Search of the Motherbook*, a memoir (University of Nebraska Press)
1997	Named C. Douglas Dillon Professor of the Civilization of France and Professor of Comparative Literature at Harvard
1998	Edits *Exile and Creativity: Signposts, Travelers, Outsiders, Backward Glances* (Duke University Press)

Like Susan Bendor, Susan Suleiman is a Hungarian Jew. She and her parents survived the war with false papers, in Budapest, her name having been changed to that of a Christian girl, Maria. When I first met Susan Suleiman a decade ago, I was struck by her restless, penetrating, generous gaze. A professor of French and comparative literature at Harvard University, and author of several scholarly books about modern literature, she is an extraordinarily successful professional and academic. Yet I suspected there was a mysterious side to Susan, a feeling reinforced when I read her essay, "My War in Four Episodes." This brief, intense memoir conveyed, poetically and profoundly, what war is like for a child. Her very powerful memoir, *Budapest Diary: In Search of the Motherbook*, inspired me to speak to her about the past.

On a January day in 1997, I returned to Susan Suleiman's house. I had visited her home eight years before, during the summer. Now the garden was covered by snow that had frozen and cracked, suggesting a pattern of little islands with silent spaces and crevasses between them. I longed to know more about the layers hidden beneath the surface of this cautious and vulnerable woman who had the courage to speak to me.

She invited me to come in and had prepared delicious coffee, which she served in demitasse cups in the best European style. She was wearing enormous slippers that caressed her feet. Susan greeted me, as always, affectionately and attentively. We sat down in the living room near some huge windows. Susan immediately opened the interview and moved willingly into the heart of her past.

Marjorie: Can you talk to me about the process of writing *Budapest Diary*? Did you feel you were preserving a memory of something gone forever?

Susan: Actually, I think it was more like creating the memory than preserving it. As I say in the book, I had shut out my childhood from my life in a very . . . I realized later just how prejudicial a way. That is, when I compared myself to other people, I realized that I very rarely talked to my children about my childhood, including some "really great adventures." You know, I could have made up great stories because I used to tell a lot of stories to my children, fairy tales I would make up, but I never made up a story or created a story about Mommy when she was a little girl and how she left Hungary. I had shut all that out of my mind. Then we went back to Hungary for the first time in 1984—I had decided to go back because my mother was sick and I realized she was fading. It was one of those weird moments when you suddenly have an idea in your head and you realize you have to act on it. Out of the blue, when I watched my mother, this thought popped into my head: we have to go back to Budapest. By "we" I did not mean my mother, because she was not going to come, but my children and me.

So we went back and spent two weeks in Hungary, and not all of it was nostalgia stuff. I was traveling with a fourteen-year-old and a seven-year-old, both of them boys, and they would not have let me wallow too much in memories. But there was enough there, and I think it was more the physical fact of being back in that place I had left thirty-five years earlier and that I could barely remember, except for a few things. I remembered very clearly the house where we had lived, not the outside, but the apartment, the inside of the building, the courtyard, the galleries above the courtyard, the staircase, the stairwell. I also remembered where my mother and I used to go hiking, just within the city limits, a lovely mountain where people still go today. Finding these actual, physical places was almost like a validation that these things still existed, these things were actually there. They have not disappeared. I think the way many immigrants experience their lives is that they leave things behind. And once they leave the thing behind, it somehow disappears.

It's almost like falling into a black hole. So to go back and to find that it was still there . . . for example, a book I remembered from my childhood, *The Boys of Paul Street*. I had often wondered whether it still existed. Well, of course it does. It's a classic. It's in every bookstore and on every kid's shelf. They read it in school. But I remembered it as something that meant a great deal to me and that had disappeared; maybe it never even existed. So, going back and finding the book, finding the house—the apartment—must have done something to me, because after the two-week vacation, when we got back to Paris, where I was doing research that summer, I found myself in a position of total constraint. I could not do otherwise: I had to sit down and write; it was an absolute necessity. I felt forced to sit and type about my . . . something, anything. I didn't know exactly what, but I knew I wanted to write about my experience during the last year of the war, when I was four or five years old.

Marjorie: Was this the first time in your adult life that you had a profound need to do this?

Susan: It was the first time in a long time that I had the feeling, "I have to write about this and it is not scholarly writing." In other words, "This is going to be a piece of literary writing, or this has to come out of me, whatever it is."

Marjorie: Would you say this felt more like creative writing? That maybe you felt like a writer and not a scholar?

Susan: In college I wrote a few things. I wrote some poetry and I have written poetry sporadically since then. You know, one or two poems, occasionally, but they are not particularly good.

Marjorie: But this was very powerful writing for you.

Susan: Yes, I keep thinking of a sentence that Georges Bataille wrote in the preface to one of his books,[1] where he says that no writing is worth anything except writing that was absolutely forced on you, writing that you were constrained to do. You had no choice but to do it. Books that almost . . .

Marjorie: Dictate themselves?

Susan: Well, it's not so much that. Dictated would imply a heavenly inspiration, or the muse of the poet. Instead, this is hard work. Almost like somebody locking you in a room and saying, "You will not get out of there until you have written this." There is a kind of violence implied; certainly in Bataille there is a violence that is almost like somebody hitting you on the head or whipping you and saying, "Do it!"

Marjorie: Were you frightened to feel that?

Susan Rubin Suleiman

Susan: We returned to Paris and the kids went off to see their father. I was alone, in August, in Paris.

Marjorie: Which was hot and crowded.

Susan: Hot and very crowded. I was in a borrowed apartment—actually a very nice apartment—and I would just sit there at the desk that I had set up as a sort of writing table and I was absolutely engrossed. The piece I wrote there was what eventually was published as "My War in Four Episodes." It was a short fragment. Well, not that short, maybe ten pages, about my experience of the war. And it had to be in fragments. I knew it would have to be, because I was so little then and remembering so little now, that I wanted simply to write down a few things that, for me, constituted the experience of that last year of the Holocaust, the war in Hungary. Which was an adventure; to me it was a big adventure.

Marjorie: That is what I find so intriguing; I find it revealing that your creative writing began with memories and the process of writing about the war in fragments, as if a fugitive memory came back to you when you began revisiting your past.

Susan: That, of course, is also part of a more general trend, I think, in academia today. Many of my friends, many of my contemporaries, most of them women, have this desire, what I call the desire to write as opposed to the desire to publish. Of course, when you write critical essays, you also want to publish, but publish in the academic sense, "publish or perish." This is different . . . the desire to write, to do what writing has always done, which is to communicate with readers who elect you as a voice or as a mirror. And at the same time, of course, to explore something that means a great deal to the writer herself.

I think there is a desire to communicate, which is different from writing a scholarly article. Of course, you want to communicate your research too, but on a different level. I think what you are hoping for is that readers will read you to look inward. I cannot speak for anyone else and I think all cases are different, but obviously age and circumstances play a role. When you are a mother with children you have to get off to school and do a million other things, and if you are a teacher and a scholar, there is very little time. In my case, when my children began to be somewhat older and they spent part of their time with their father, I had more free time. Or not even free time, but time to reflect on my life, which I think one doesn't always have.

When you are a woman, especially, there are so many demands on your time. If you have a full-time career and a family or children, there are all kinds of interruptions. I think maybe your case is different because you really think of yourself as, and are, a poet and a writer. Whereas my identity, certainly up to the time I went to Budapest, was that of an academic. Whatever free time I had, I would say, "I'm going to close the door and I will not deal with any of the demands. I will just write." It was always a scholarly thing. Now I may sit down and write my inner writing.

Some of the things I wrote in 1984 were included in the book and in that little fragment that was published separately. Some of it is exactly as I wrote it in 1984. But most of it, I would say, has been gone over and over and over, stylistically. By the time "My War in Four Episodes" was published, I had rewritten it about fifty times. Even though the main outline, the main idea, and the main structure were the same, it was the language that I kept having to redo. When I first sent it off to a few journals, I always got back a letter that said, "Well, this is good, but thank you, no." Then I began thinking that maybe it was not well written: maybe it's just not good. So I kept polishing it, especially a piece I had written about my father's death, which eventually found its way into the book. Nobody wanted that one, absolutely nobody, and I kept thinking, "This is very strange," I mean, when you are used to getting your things accepted by scholarly journals and then you send off something different and they are absolutely uninterested . . .

What really helped me or what determined, ultimately, the way this book turned out, for better or worse, was the second stay in Budapest in 1993. By the early 1990s, I had two things written and I had published this little piece about the war.

Marjorie: Had you written about your father?

Susan: Yes, but as I've told you, nobody wanted it. I finally put it in a drawer . . . I knew I could do something with it, but I had not found a way. Aside from that, I had fifty or sixty pages, which are now the first chapter called "A Brief Vacation," about the experience of going back to Budapest with my kids. And then, out of the blue, really out of the blue, I get this letter from Berlin which says, "We have started a new Institute for Advanced Study in Budapest. Would you like to go?"

Marjorie: So, out of the blue you began a new life?

Susan: Literally. It was in the mail. "Would you like to be one of the first Fellows?" I knew that they had no idea I was Hungarian. It was just one of those invitations you get as a scholar, to go to this place or that place. The minute I got the letter, I said, "This is it. I have to go. Of course I have to go. This will allow me to finally write more." So I immediately accepted. I spent six months in Budapest, from February to July 1993. When I went I already knew that I wanted to write something.

I was finishing *Risking Who One Is*, which was a scholarly book, a critical scholarly book, but I also knew that I had to do this other project, whatever it was. And I must say, it was like a dream. The Collegium Budapest is in a beautiful building, with computers, fax machines, a library. The Fellows all had their own offices and comfortable apartments in the city, a very privileged life, certainly compared to the normal Hungarian's. And I was not teaching, so I could spend my time exploring Budapest, getting to know people, and writing. It was ideal!

Marjorie: So, in a way, it was an incredible gift that brought you back home. Was it really home?

Susan: It was a gift and maybe that is why a few readers who have read the book have said to me, "But you have idealized Budapest in a way I don't agree with. You met the most wonderful people, but actually I think many Hungarians are racists, nationalists, narrow-minded," or, "What a pity that you didn't meet more ordinary people!" It's true that I idealized Budapest somewhat. I was so lucky. I met absolutely marvelous people. Not that I wasn't aware, of course, in 1993, during the post-Communist period, that there were many problems—with the economy in particular, as in the rest of Eastern Europe. And also, there was a rather ugly anti-Semitic discourse forming in Budapest, and all over Europe . . . Eastern Europe. I was very much aware of that and I wrote about it. I was also very much aware of the destruction of the Hungarian Jews during the war. You need only go to any city outside of Budapest to see how much was destroyed—so many synagogues, once beautiful, now empty or in ruins.

Marjorie: I have also seen that there are very few synagogues left in the city. What was Jewish life like in Hungary during your visit in 1993?

Susan: Well, the synagogues are there. In the provincial cities, the buildings are there, but some of them are crumbling. Others have been restored, but put to some other use; or else there is a synagogue, but you have fifty people attending, whereas it used to be a vibrant community. It's a very sad thing. In Budapest, though, there is quite a thriving Jewish life: schools, synagogues, magazines of Jewish culture. The Jewish population in Budapest is the largest in Eastern Europe, approximately seventy thousand. On the whole, I have to say that for me the experience of being there was euphoric. It was euphoric in great part because of the writing. That is, the euphoria was produced not only by the city and meeting people, but by the almost simultaneous turning of that experience into words.

It became the diary, and that's what you were referring to earlier about the documentation: I wrote all of that 1993 experience in the form of an actual diary. When I came back from that trip I had five hundred pages which I had not even printed out yet. And when I printed it out, I said, "Oh, this is impossible. Even I am bored to death!" There was too much, too much detail, too many names. So then, I spent two years editing the diary down so that it would have a coherence and a shape, and only the relevant material would be there, not every single thing.

Marjorie: When you started the diary, did you know that you were writing a book?

Susan: I was hoping it would eventually become a book, but I didn't know exactly how to go on from there. What I was trying to do from the beginning was to find a form for the book that would correspond to the kind of experience I was trying to get at, which was one of fragmentation and nonintegration, or at least a certain dispersal of the personality. It's what I talked about before, leaving each place behind and then having it fall into a black hole. That suggests a life which moves, but at the same time the pieces don't all fit because each one was left behind.

Marjorie: In the process, did you have this very conscious idea, not only when you were writing, but when you were living there, that this is where your mother and father lived and met? The pages where you talk about finding their marriage certificate and then your mother's birth certificate, it's as though you knew they were real, but you somehow needed the physical evidence. And as you said, maybe these pieces of paper will not matter to other people, but they matter to you because it is your story. Did you, in a way, try to understand your parents' life so that you could understand your own?

Susan: I think it's hard to put a single reason to it. I don't feel that I have really understood their life. Yet this desire to track down might explain why I find the "motherbook" such a wonderful coincidence. The Hungarian language has an expression, a very ordinary phrase, "motherbook," which refers to the registry where records are kept. The registry is the "motherbook office," and official documents are "excerpts from the motherbook." For Hungarians, the word has no poetic significance whatsoever. But obviously, for an English speaker, if you translate it literally, "motherbook" is full of suggestive imagery and resonance, especially if you are looking for your family background! My search for these "excerpts from the motherbook," my parents' marriage certificate, my mother's birth certificate, my *own* birth certificate, took a while. Then my father's, which I never did find because he was born in Poland and the records were completely destroyed . . . It's very hard . . . how shall I put it? There was a real need to do this . . . To get my mother's birth certificate, I had to travel to northeastern Hungary, near Ukraine, where she was born.

Susan Rubin Suleiman

Marjorie: But that was very important to you, the actual encounter with a physical space?

Susan: Yes, it was very, very important. It's what I said earlier about materiality, of actually walking along the streets or seeing the building, being in the city where my mother was born. She was born there because her family went there from Budapest every summer (she had several uncles living there) and she was born in the summer. Going there wasn't like trying to recreate her whole life, but it was a connection that could only be fully established by the experience of looking. It's not so much what you find, because usually you don't find much. It's the experience of walking and trying to find something; taking the train and getting off the train and finding the city hall and trying to see whether you could even find the house where she was born. Does it still exist? The experience of the search was what was interesting or compelling or irresistible or necessary, rather than what you actually found when you got there.

Marjorie: Susan, tell me about your childhood. When were you sent away and reunited with your parents? How has this had an impact on you?

Susan: My parents sent me away in 1944, after the Germans occupied Hungary (in March), to live with farmers. And then they came and took me with them— they had decided we would try to live this out together. We had false papers, and my parents found a job as caretakers on an estate in the Buda hills. It was almost like a big play-acting adventure for me, pretending to be someone else. That and what I wrote in the last chapter of *Budapest Diary* about my father's death, are the two things I remember most vividly. My father died much later, when I was in my last year of college. I was still mourning when I graduated. But the two events—the war, and his death—were linked, because for a long time I had to put them both out of my mind. I had the feeling, as I say in the book, that I would have to forget about him so that I could go on with my life. His death closed a chapter. It was the beginning of my adult life, the life I would live on my own.

Marjorie: Do you feel, because of your past and your history, that you are a displaced person? Have you always felt as a child, and later coming here, that you were an immigrant, a Jewish immigrant?

Susan: No, no. Maybe it's because I came here when I was still young enough. I was ten when I left Hungary and I was eleven and a half when I arrived in New York (we lived in New York for the first three years and then moved to Chicago). A strange thing happened then: I became an American, or at least that's what I thought at the time. It's true that I have a facility for learning languages, the way many Hungarians do, and I immediately started devouring books in English. By then I also knew French quite well.

Marjorie: Because of Haiti and Vienna? You were very well trained in languages and cultures.

Susan: Yes, even in Vienna I went to a French school. And I continued to speak Hungarian with my parents. Later, whenever my children heard me on the phone speaking this weird language, they knew I was talking to my mother or my aunt. So I knew Hungarian, I knew French, and I knew some German. I learned English very largely through friends—I made friends in school, I was in the sixth grade—and through the public library. I became deeply enamored with English.

Marjorie: In my own exile, I became deeply enamored with Spanish. For me, learning English was not so important because I was always concerned with keeping and preserving the essence of Spanish. I understand that you write in English.

Susan: Yes. That's an interesting point, that I did not feel like a foreigner after a while. Maybe because New York is such a melting pot. New York is a town where everybody is from somewhere else. That contributed, I think, to my sense of assimilation, to the point where I was able to forget all those earlier years.

Marjorie: Did you forget Hungary when you were in New York City?

Susan: Well, not "forget," because my mother, and my father too, had a very thick Hungarian accent. So it's not as if it were possible or that I wanted to completely obliterate my past, but somehow . . . Did you mean, do I feel totally at home?

Marjorie: That was my next question.

Susan: No, obviously! But then I think that not feeling totally at home may also be part of the American experience. It's true that many people in the United States are born, live, work, and die in the same place. Or at least some, certainly. I now live in a small town, a small suburb of Boston. There are people in Belmont who went to elementary school and high school here, live here, have children here, and will probably die here. But I think that the American experience in general has been one of moving from place to place. It took me a while to disentangle my own past from that more general American experience.

Marjorie: You grew up speaking Hungarian and French. Yet you seem to be at ease with English.

Susan: Well, English became my—as I say in the book somewhere—stepmother tongue. It's not my mother tongue, but it's my stepmother tongue, a kindly stepmother. And she has a twin sister, French, because I speak French almost as well as I speak English.

Marjorie: And what is the place of the Hungarian language in your life? Is it the language of memory, of affection? Where does it fit in?

Susan: That was part of the euphoria I felt in Budapest in 1993, when I learned to feel comfortable in Hungarian. Until then, it was a language I spoke only at home, and even that no longer because my mother was dead by then and my father had died years before. I have a few aunts in Toronto, my father's sisters, and I usually spoke it with them. But not very well—my syntax was OK, but I had no vocabulary, really. I had very few words that could express any kind of complex thought in Hungarian. In 1993, over the course of my six months in Budapest, I found myself able to converse in Hungarian with scholars, writers, and intellectuals—people I felt some kinship to. That gave me a huge feeling of pleasure, because during those months, I discovered Hungary as a place where there were people like what I am now, as opposed to people who only hearken back to my childhood or past.

Marjorie: Your story differs from that of many other immigrants because you were happy to return to Hungary. I found that very interesting: even though there was the Holocaust and Communism and your narrow escape, you feel no resentment. Do you know what I mean?

Susan: Yes, I know. And it's funny because there's a Hungarian . . . a very well-known Hungarian intellectual whom I mention in my book. He was minister of communications at one point. He is now in California on a fellowship for a year. A friend of mine gave him the book and he E-mailed me. He said, "This is quite extraordinary, that you can be so gentle." He used the word "gentle." He said, "If my family had gone through what yours did, I would be less forgiving. I would be more angry."

Marjorie: What made you more forgiving?

Susan: When I went in 1993, I was not "going back" or living there as a returnee. I was invited by people who did not know that I was Hungarian, that I had been born in Budapest. I was invited as an American scholar, a literary scholar from Harvard. So, my way of being there was not only as a person look-ing for her past. It was also as an American scholar spending six months in this marvelous research institute, where they let you do whatever you wanted and you could have a perfectly fine atmosphere for doing your work and also meet other scholars. The people I met in Budapest have to do with my life now, and that was the exciting part for me. That is why I decided to keep the central sec-tion of the book, the 1993 section, in the form of a diary, even though some people advised me against it: "Who wants to read a diary?"

Marjorie: But the diary helped you trace . . . the present. The diary was also a bridge to the past and your connection to the future.

Susan: Exactly. The diary was a simultaneous account, and I purposefully kept that characteristic of the diary, which is that it is heterogeneous. In a single day, on a single day, you can relive a memory about your father and you can also go to the movies and have dinner with a friend. That's the whole point of a diary. If you do it right—that is why it took me two years to edit it—if you manage to pull it off, then the reader will not lose you. The reader will follow you through those days when you have lunch and discuss politics with this one, then go on a pilgrimage to your former apartment, and then, in the evening, go to the mo-vies. Somehow it works, if it is properly done.

Marjorie: It also made it very real for the readers because they knew they were reading a true account, a real life.

Susan: You said you liked the fact that I don't say everything. That so much is only hinted at, or evoked briefly.

Marjorie: The part that moved me the most as a reader was your willingness to leave me room to invent. It's a book that documents, but on the other hand it also meditates. I like that. Has your identity been somehow connected with dis-placement?

Susan: As I said, for many years I thought of my own sense of estrangement as part of the American experience, and I think it does take a while or a kind of shock to realize that it was more than that. Let's take a very clear example: I have never thought of myself as a Holocaust survivor. I would always say to myself, "No, that's not me. I was not in a camp. My parents and I, and even my grand-mother, came through the war. It was an adventure. I am not a Holocaust survi-vor." And this is true, I am not the typical Holocaust survivor. But technically I am a Holocaust survivor, right? I mean, I was alive in 1939. I was still alive in 1944.

Susan Rubin Suleiman

Marjorie: You were born at the very beginning of the war.

Susan: I was born six weeks before the war broke out, in July 1939. And I was in Hungary in March 1944, when the Nazis marched in and rounded up all the Jews. I remember events from the last year of the war, 1944–45. So to say that I am not a Holocaust survivor is, in a way, an incredible kind of denial. But I understand it too, because I don't like the idea of being a professional Holocaust survivor. My attitude has been that I am not a Holocaust survivor because I was not traumatized in a major way. I don't have nightmares. I don't wake up screaming about flashbacks and things of that sort. But does that mean I wasn't affected? Does it mean I have the same kind of relation to people that I would have had if I hadn't gone through that original trauma?

Marjorie: You mentioned you always fear that people will not come or show up, that you are going to be left alone. Maybe you were affected and now you realize it?

Susan: I am always ready to believe that if somebody is five minutes late . . .

Marjorie: They will not come? They will forget you and leave you forever?

Susan: They will not come, either because they forgot or because, in fact, they are letting me go. I think one of the things this book has helped me to understand is that I cannot think of the past like everybody else. But, you see, the problem is that I am opposed to affixing an identity to myself and saying, " I am the way I am because I am a displaced person" or "I am a survivor" or "I am this or that." I say that at the very end of the book. once you remember, you have to move on.

In other words, it's a very complicated movement. There is the drive on the part of the immigrant, or on my part, let's say, to move on constantly and never look back. You know: adapt, survive, and never look back. That's why everything falls into a black hole, because you are never looking behind. Once you leave a thing behind, it disappears. It sinks into nonexistence.

I think you have to be able to return and discover that those things don't disappear. People don't die just because you leave them and people don't disappear. It's a good idea to keep sending them little postcards from time to time. So the first step is to recover, in some partial way, what you have left behind. Partial, I say, because you can never fully recover anything. We have to recover connections—not the past, but a connection to the past. The next step has to be that you can't linger and stay in that mode, because you really do have to move on in your life to new experiences. Not toward new forgetfulness, but new experience. We move on and yet maintain the connection to the past that we have now reestablished, or are trying to reestablish.

Marjorie: I would like to make another point about identity. I know exactly what you mean because I don't want to be known only as a poet who writes about human rights. I want to write about love, I want to write stories. I do not want to be fixed in one category. I also think this society likes categories too much. I know what you are saying when you don't want to be labeled a Holocaust survivor. And yet, we cannot escape the labels and our identity is mingled with these labels. Maybe memory and its arduous paths of retrieval are ways to invent ourselves.

Susan: That's right. The successful model for the surviving immigrant or emigrant is displacement-replacement. You leave a place behind, and you replace it with another place. But that's part of the black hole phenomenon because you have left it behind in order to replace it; it's substitution. In other words, you have to get rid of that one and replace it with another one. Now, the other possibility is not replacement but addition. Then the metaphor becomes not the zero sum game where every x has to be arrived at by the elimination of a y, but a series of additions, x's along a thread. For me, Budapest had fallen into the black hole—I had almost no memory of it—but now it has become a city that lives and, in fact, changes and evolves and is familiar. It is *a* home, not *the* home. I make that very clear. I could never go back there as *the* home. But it is one of the places where I now feel at home—or at least, pretty much at home.

Marjorie: Where is home for you?

Susan: I don't want to say it's the house or it's Belmont, Massachusetts, because if I move tomorrow I am not going to feel homeless. And I very well may move, although I have lived here for more than fifteen years. [Long pause.] I think probably it's true that the most constant home is my study, which is not necessarily the same everywhere. It doesn't have to be *that* particular study. It can be a different study in a different place. The setup, which is that of sitting in front of a desk, in front of a computer, with books all around and papers spread out, that is one of the places where I feel I can always go to and feel like me.

Marjorie: And that you belong.

Susan: I think home is where you can feel like yourself. Home is a place where you don't have to . . . where you don't feel alienated from yourself, where you can have the sense that there is a rightness about being there. You don't have to look for yourself there because you are there already. You are there.

Marjorie: All the women I have chosen to interview are Jewish because the Jewish people and their identity are a part of a universal diaspora, a movement of people, of emigrants and immigrants. Your writing ... I am trying to understand what the connections are. How does Judaism take its particular place in your life as a writer or in your search or in assembling your past?

Susan: When Joyce wanted to write the modern *Odyssey*, why did he choose Leopold Bloom as his protagonist? In some way you could say "we are all German Jews," as the slogan said in May 1968 in Paris.[2] The Jew is, for some people, the very emblem of the "rootless cosmopolitan." But the other way of putting it is the very emblem of the one who is able to carry his home around with him, that is, his books, but who is not fully anchored in any one place, or is always there as a visitor, or is always having to pick up and move on to some other place where there will be fewer pogroms. It's interesting that you should ask this because I actually have edited a rather lengthy volume of essays called *Exile and Creativity*. This was done over a number of years and I didn't ask only Jewish people to contribute. In fact, it's not even about Jews, but it was astonishing how you ask a whole bunch of different people to write about creativity and exile and three-quarters of them write about Jews.

Marjorie: Even the non-Jews?

Susan: Yes, even the non-Jews. The volume is very much in a Western European perspective. What this leaves out, I realized, are those other parts of the world where the metaphor or emblem of displacement, and all of the things we've been talking about, homelessness, alienation, however you want to formulate it, doesn't take the form of a Jew. Look at Rwanda or India. A writer like Rushdie is profoundly aware of what it means for Indians to be living in Britain or far-flung places. Not to mention, of course, the concept of the African diaspora, which allows African-Americans to feel that they are diasporic, even though they've been in the United States for hundreds of years. So, I do think we need to put things into perspective and not say that Jews are the universal emblem of displacement. Universal within the West, within Europe and the West, and maybe Latin America.

Marjorie: It's also Latin America. I think that in the popular culture of Latin America, the Jew is this wandering being. "The wandering Jew." It's part of the language.

Susan: Right. That's because Latin America in that regard is turned toward Europe. What about the Mexican population, the Mayas?

Marjorie: That would not enter their view of the world.

Susan: That's right, but they have their own image of destruction, cultural destruction and displacement. Another example would be the Vietnamese boat people. That was their specificity and it had nothing to do with being Jewish—it had to do with history, with the very precise events that forced many Vietnamese to leave Vietnam, or Cambodians to leave Cambodia. I think that one of the things multiculturalism and cultural studies have taught us is never to think that just because it seems universal to you it's really universal, totally universal. You always have to qualify. Yes, it's universal for the Western canon, or in the Western tradition.

Marjorie: Do you consider yourself a Jewish writer?

Susan: It so happens that in the twentieth century, Jewishness is not just a metaphor for displacement, but from the 1920s on—or certainly from the 1930s on—Jewishness was also the specific historical condition that forced certain people into mass migrations, huge displacements which were experienced as deeply personal and individual, but also as collective. That's one of the things I was very aware of when I was writing my Budapest book: every life story is part of a larger history. I think that being Jewish in the second half of the twentieth century, you cannot help but feel connected to that collective experience. Even the most placid American Jews at some point have to ask themselves, "What is my relationship to all this?" And it's interesting how the Holocaust Museum in Washington elicits that. I have heard people in the bookstore saying things like, "Gosh, if my grandfather had not migrated to New York . . ."

Marjorie: That's right. I visited the museum with some friends and they said, "Look, you could have been born in New York City if your parents or their friends had come here." So, I realize that they see themselves as a part of it.

Susan: Sometimes what they say is the opposite: "We could have been in Warsaw if . . ." or "We might have perished in Auschwitz if . . ." In other words, they realize that even though they are here, and maybe their families have been here for generations, there is a historical connection to European Jewry, and their own lives are part of that connection, even if at other times they may think, "My life as an American Jew has nothing to do with those major world historical events." So they suddenly feel the connection. I think that if you are a Jew born in Europe between 1930 and 1940, or even 1930 and 1945, you don't have to go to the Holocaust Museum to realize that your personal life is part of a much larger collective history.

Marjorie: So you feel that there is a strong connection now more than ever, after you wrote the book? Or have you always felt this?

Susan: I didn't always feel it, but I certainly feel it now very much. You asked earlier whether it was because I had reached a certain age. I think it is an awareness that comes as the century moves on to its end. And, of course, as we ourselves move on toward late middle age, or even old age.

Marjorie: Adulthood.

Susan: You know, you suddenly realize the presence of the big "H"—history—and its weight on individual lives.

KATHERINE SCHERZER WENGER

April 12, 1950	Born in Satu Mare, Romania
June 1962	Receives visa for Israel
January 1963	Leaves Romania with family for Vienna
June 26, 1963	Mother dies in Vienna
October 1963	Leaves Vienna for the United States, arrives five days later in New York City; stays at the Broadway Central Hotel for two weeks, then moves to Brooklyn
1968	Attends State University of New York at Buffalo; grandmother moves out on her own, brother marries; father moves out on his own
1972	Bachelor's degree in psychology and languages; spends summer traveling in Europe
1974	Master's degree in counseling education; returns to New York City; lives with father and then moves in with a friend
1975	Begins work in geriatric field
June 25, 1979	Marries Harold, honeymoons in Romania, but doesn't visit home town
September 1979	Moves to Chicago, Illinois, for husband's surgical internship
June 1980	Master's degree in social work from University of Illinois
September 1980	Moves to Boston, Massachusets, for husband's second year of internship
January 27, 1981	Daughter, Julia, born
July 14, 1984	Son, Alexander, born
May 8, 1987	Grandmother dies at the age of one hundred in a nursing home
December 3, 1993	Father dies
January 8, 1994	Julia's bat mitzvah
1995	Visits home town in Romania with brother
1996	Completes psychotherapy training program at the Boston Institute for Psychotherapy

Like other less powerful nations in Eastern Europe in the 1930s, Romania recognized the need to align itself with other Balkan states in order to buffer the aggressiveness of Nazi Germany and the Soviet Union. The Little Entente (Czechoslovakia, Romania, Yugoslavia) formed in Geneva on February 16, 1933, to solidify an economic front in the face of Germany's mounting prominence in Central European politics. Austria, Italy, and Hungary signed the Rome Protocols as a retaliatory gesture the following year.

During the latter half of the 1930s, Romania's King Carol II witnessed a complete shift in his government from left to right. The right wing was strengthened by the formation of the Christian League, which collaborated with the fascist party of Romania (the Iron Guard) to defeat the National Liberal government in the December 1937 elections.

Romania entered a ten-year economic contract with Germany in March 1939, ties that were strengthened the following year. In June 1940 the Soviet Union issued a twenty-four-hour ultimatum to Romania to hand over the regions of Bessarabia and Bukovina. Britain and France, despite earlier promises to help Romania maintain its territorial integrity and political independence, did not intervene in the conflict. In hopes of protecting itself from Soviet invasion, Romania joined the Axis nations in the first week of July. Politically allied to Germany, the Romanian government began instituting anti-Semitic legislation later that summer.

The new Axis alignment did not prevent Hitler from parceling out Transylvania and other Romanian lands to Hungary at the end of August. King Carol II fled and a puppet government was established with General Ion Antonescu as prime minister and Horia Sima, the Iron Guard leader, as deputy prime minister. On September 14, the Iron Guard became the only legal political party in Romania. In October, German troops occupied the country; the following month, the Iron Guard began to massacre its political enemies, including Jews.

Although the Antonescu government curbed the wide-scale violence of the Iron Guard (which was disrupting its capacity to rule), it still cooperated with the Nazis in establishing Jewish ghettos in cities and towns across Romania. During the war, Katherine Wenger's family lived in the Chernowitz ghetto, where her brother was born in 1942. She was born in 1950 in Satu Mare, Romania. Although her family survived the war, two-thirds of the Jews of Chernowitz were murdered by the Nazis.

My first encounter with Katherine was in February 1997, when she described her Romanian childhood to an assembly gathered at my children's Sunday school. She disclosed that her mother had died of breast cancer in a Viennese hospital shortly before the remaining family members emigrated to the United States. At the vulnerable age of thirteen, Katherine lost both her mother and her homeland. The audience, a very polite group of North American Jewish women, asked questions that avoided touching this obviously painful transition. I wondered whether they really understood what it meant to come to a foreign land without a usable language and without a mother.

Katherine and I decided to see each other again, to get to know each other better. She is a very private woman, often withdrawn and silent, but I hoped to draw her out. I knew that her family members were among the few Romanian Jews to survive the war, and that although she was born in 1950, those terrifying years play a role in her life. I asked her if she felt like a daughter of the Holocaust. She paused, taking her time to digest my question, and finally replied that the need for survival has dominated her whole life. Katherine ran a hand over her beautiful ash-colored hair, and told me that her whole life has been turbulent and oriented toward the future.

Although private and self-protective by nature, she was eager to tell her story. She spoke with thoughtful candor about her world at thirteen, evocatively recalling both the pleasures and pains.

Marjorie: What do you know about your own family's history?

Katherine: Both my mother and father lived and met in Chernowitz. My paternal grandmother was born in Berlin into a middle-class, educated family. My paternal grandfather came from an Orthodox family close to Chernowitz. On my mother's side, my grandmother who lived with us all my life came from a large, religious, very poor family in Poland. She was one of eleven children. At the age of thirteen she had to leave home to live with an aunt due to food shortage. There she started working and became apprenticed to a seamstress. Life was grueling and grandmother continued a life of deprivation. She married a horse trader at an early age and had two daughters, my mother and a younger daughter. This daughter died of tuberculosis at the age of twenty-eight. Shortly before that, grandmother lost her husband and became a widow in her forties. During the German occupation, Jews were herded into one part of the town, which became the Jewish ghetto. My paternal grandmother lived there already, so they were somewhat better off than the others. Three adults shared one room, several families to one apartment. It was not uncommon for extended families to live in two rooms all sharing a common bath and kitchen. My brother was born in the ghetto in 1942. The story goes that he was born prematurely and the doctors told my maternal grandmother to give up on him. She stubbornly kept him alive by forming a cocoon around him made up of warm water bottles and cotton. She did the same for me eight years later. After the war, in 1945, my two grandmothers, my father, mother, and brother left Chernowitz in search of safety. Family story has it that my mother would get off at every train stop and inquire whether the town had a Jewish community and food.

Marjorie: Where did your family finally decide to settle?

Katherine: The town of Satu Mare, because it fulfilled her two requirements. It had a population of sixty thousand, two thousand of them Jews, most Holocaust survivors. Many of them became nonobservant as a result of their horrifying experience. This became home. Twelve Stefan cel Mare, my address in Satu Mare, Romania, cobblestone street, where I lived till the age of twelve. It was twenty square miles. Much of this was farming land, rich in corn and wheat. The town also had a locomotive factory and four high schools, sex segregated, half of them Romanian and the other Hungarian, just like the population of this town. There was one cinema, indoors in the winter and outdoors in the summer due to lack of any ventilation. The shows changed infrequently, but being the only show in town people eagerly attended whatever movie was passed down from the larger cities. When they moved there, transportation consisted of horses and carriages, later on buses enhanced travel but took away some of the quiet and slow pace of life. The river Somes ran through Satu Mare and divided the town in half. In the summer the beach provided us with fun and relief from the heat. Indoor plumbing was for very few people, most used outhouses, some more privileged had their own private outhouse. All homes were equipped with wood-burning stoves. These were used for cooking, heating the house, and the water used for bathing and laundry.

Marjorie: What was postwar life like for your family?

Katherine: My world included our three rooms, that my mother, father, brother, and maternal grandmother shared. These were in a courtyard with six other neighbors. We lived closely packed together, yet, as I only came to know much later, very far apart. There was only one other Jewish family in this courtyard. The other families were also poorer, with smaller dwelling places. These differences kept the adults at an uneasy distance, filled with envy and jealousy about imagined luxuries the Jews enjoyed. As a child these differences were nonexistent for me. My courtyard was my world. We spent hours together playing in the mud, exploring forbidden places under porches, basements, and our bodies. We knew no divisions or differences. In the bitter winters of Eastern Europe, the snow and ice provided us with endless hours of pleasure. My brother would sometimes make me feel privileged by taking me sledding with his older friends. We rode the steep hills just outside the town that appeared like mountains to me. The speed was exhilarating and I could hardly wait to go back up to the top and start again.

Marjorie: Which of the three was your favorite room?

Katherine: My favorite room was the kitchen. It was the warmest of the three rooms, the one which remains most connected with pleasure. The fragrances of my grandmother's cooking remain vivid for me. At times my mother would join in and create magic with her baking skills. Culinary wonders were created there by my mother and grandmother. So much time was spent in the procuring and preparing of food that it seemed always present. I was sent daily to get the black dense Romanian bread, often still warm from the oven. This bread was rationed, so I was made aware from a very early age of the value of food.

My family had also in the not too distant past lived with the daily reality of food shortages. Taking food for granted was not an option in our home. To do so was sacrilegious.

Marjorie: Your memories are so specific. Did you remember having a favorite day of the week?

Katherine: Friday morning was by far my most favorite day. My grandmother would always be the first up in the morning. She started the fire in the stove while the other rooms remained shrouded in cold. I took a deep breath and with determination grabbed my freezing clothes, racing for the kitchen and the stove. The bread would already be kneaded, almost ready to go into the oven, and the room was fragrant with the smell of baking bread. My grandmother handed me the roll (*flam pletzel*), hot out of the oven, and cutting into it, I watched the fragrant steam rising, filling all my senses. To this day warm bread remains for me the one food I cannot do without. The challah was on its way and the serious cooking for Shabbat [the sabbath] had begun. This was a race for time, to clean, to prepare everything for the evening meal and the following day. Shabbat was the one day in the week that my grandmother and mother rested. I think this day was created for them.

Marjorie: Things that awaken our five physical senses very often leave the most lasting memories. What role has the smell and taste of food played in your memories—your ability to remember?

Katherine: My happiest memories are food-related, menus for events, intertwining taste and color. Food is such an elemental part of us. It was for me a source of nurturing, where affection and warmth were more scarce. Food—unlike people—never disappointed or hurt me. It was also given to me by the two women with whom I could not have a close relationship, my mother and grandmother. Dinner eaten together reminds me of at times being able to sit in my father's lap and share his food. This of course was frowned upon by mother and grandmother, their perception being that I was spoiled.

Marjorie: What kinds of food did you eat?

Katherine: Friday night was chopped liver surrounded by tomatoes. This was followed by chicken soup with noodles made by my grandmother. There was always challah slowly cooking in the stove for Shabbat, the stove stocked by a Gentile neighbor. Goose liver paté created by my grandmother's steady force-feeding of geese. The farmers' market provided us with fresh vegetables, fruits, and poultry. We ate what the farmers grew. Once in a while some exotic food would be shipped to our town. One time there was such a shipment and my mother sent me on this particular expedition. As for many of the staples we used, there was a large line. After waiting for at least an hour, my turn came. I had no idea what the strange fruit before me was, but I couldn't very well leave after having waited this long. I bought a bunch of something I had no name for, and proudly went home with it. They were slightly green but we had to try them right away. With great anticipation I took one, peeled it, and bit into it. It was tasteless and somewhat slimy. My mother was furious with me for having spent money on something so awful. It was much later, in this country, that I understood that what I bought that day was bananas and all they needed was time to ripen. Oranges were rare treats, that I received once in a while as a gift. Sometimes on a Sunday we would go to our local café, and I would be treated to ice cream or some store-made pastry. My dress would be freshly starched and ironed, lace knee highs, hair combed and pulled back with a ribbon. Politely I would point out the pastry I wanted and sitting at a small wrought-iron table, would try to savor every bite while paying close attention not to get anything on my pretty dress. A tortured pleasure.

Marjorie: What was your relationship with your grandmother like during this time?

Katherine: In the fall my grandmother would let me help her can fruits and vegetables for the long winter months ahead. This would offer both of us brief reprieve from the daily battles that she and I would get into. My brother and I were the second set of children that she was raising. She was older, over-worked, and bitter from the many losses she had endured. I was feisty and challenging like children tend to be. Grandmother had no patience or time. Much of my anger at my mother and father were often vented at her. I was told that at least on one occasion that I bit Grandmother's hand and on many occasions I was known as a *wilde chaye*—translation: a wild animal. She in turn vented her anger at her situation and circumstances on me. My brother was both my mother's and grandmother's favorite, he could do no wrong. And so we came together for brief periods making food together. Jars would be boiled, fruits pitted by the gallon it seemed. My whole body would be sticky from pitting and slicing.

Marjorie: It sounds like these are pleasant memories for you, in spite of the food rations and cramped living space. Was it like that for your friends and neighbors?

Katherine: The other children and I ran around barefoot with only panties on, through the hot summer months. I loved eating the simple fare of one of our neighbors, potatoes with paprika. This was a very poor family, some seven people to one room. That included an adolescent daughter with a set of twins. The dirt and chaos in that house was a welcome relief from the regimented life in my home. There was very little to eat but it was shared and the food there tasted better than anywhere. That I didn't have to sit down at a certain time and eat whatever was placed before me with many admonitions was a relief. The food that my grandmother would cook for dinner or some future time would be stored in the pantry or in our basement. All the canning was here as well. Father would buy large fresh apples when in season and wrap each one with care in newspaper and box them. They too would be placed in storage, to be parceled out later when the cold came. The basement was sacred. It was a refrigerator, the cold cement keeping things cool in the hot summer months, and fresh in the winter months. It was also a storage bin for the tons of wood shavings, wood, and coal that were delivered regularly to heat the house. Nothing could be touched in this shrine, or punishment would be meted out by Grandmother.

Marjorie: Tell me about a childhood experience that may have helped shape your view of life and death. Was death something that was real to you, even as a child?

Katherine: Harry, my brother, was squeamish about blood and so I was entrusted with the responsibility of taking chickens, every week, to the Shochet. This was one of the slaughterhouses in our town. A shochet was trained in the ritual of kosher slaughter. Upon entering this hall, one was greeted with the flapping and shrieking of the chickens waiting or being taken in hand by the shochet. With one hand he would pin their wings, pull their heads back, pluck a few feathers from the throat, and with a single clean gesture slice their throats open. The chicken would struggle to no avail, till at last its life blood was given up. The chicken would then be inspected and declared either kosher or tref, spoiled. This would only be the beginning of the process of making this a kosher chicken, fit to be eaten. Grandmother would pluck the feathers, clean the inside, discarding all but the liver, neck, stomach, and feet. For the next two hours the chicken was salted and then soaked in water. We lived close to life, death, and all that lies in between. As children we saw too much and were too young to understand and make sense of much of it. The opportunity for privacy was nearly nonexistent.

Marjorie: How did your family deal with such a small living space?

Katherine: My brother, grandmother, and I shared one room and my father and mother had the last room, which also doubled as my mother's workshop.

Here from early in the morning into the night, with almost no rest, she would make shirts, pajamas, and bed linens. My grandmother would help to hand embroider the monograms. Some of the work would also be sent out. She had learned her craft as a young girl and she was very good at it. Her reputation had spread far and wide and she would be inundated by work. Her work was our major source of income but it also insured that Mother would have no time for me. We had money that could not be spent, saved for a future life that awaited us once we left.

Marjorie: Was family life all work, or did you also play?

Katherine: When my mother sewed there were several benefits for me. I would be allowed to keep some colorful scraps of fabric out of which I made my numerous rag dolls. Of course they had to have accessories and a home to live in. The home was a cardboard box, with windows and doors cut out accordingly. Hours were spent playing with these dolls with friends and by myself. The leftover fabric was also woven into rag rugs. Nothing was discarded. The one luxury item that we had was a grand piano. There was much excitement initially, till it became clear to me that I was expected to practice daily, alone. I would sit, for hours, hating every minute of practice. Alone, I would sit and move the clock ahead, so the hour would end faster. I can imagine my mother and father feeling frustrated and angry at my lack of appreciation, and for me this was one other place to feel alone. They finally gave up and the piano was sold. Somehow I felt betrayed, even though I had no interest in the instrument. What I wanted was to be heard, to be paid attention to. It took me years, when older, not to fall asleep when listening to piano music.

Marjorie: What role did holidays and religious observances have in your daily life?

Katherine: Holidays and special occasions took on important meaning, given the life of toil each day held. It was a celebration for the passing seasons, giving thanks and praying to get visas to emigrate to Israel. Paradoxically all this entailed a great deal of work for the women. My brother's bar mitzvah was celebrated at home. The table was laden with food and the photograph of my aunt, my father's older sister, living in America, strategically placed in the center of the table. She held much hope for us and was instrumental in our eventually being able to resettle, not in Israel but America.

Marjorie: Did your family go to the synagogue?

Katherine: There were seven active synagogues in our town. Like most Jews in Europe at that time, we practiced Orthodox Judaism. I thought that the synagogue we belonged to was the most beautiful one. These synagogues were always open, used daily for prayer. On the High Holy Days the adults would dress in their best and spend the entire time in prayer. On the eve of Rosh Hashanah the synagogue was brilliant, illuminated and made fragrant by rows and rows of yahrzeit candles. Men and women were separated, the men downstairs and the women upstairs. Children ran in and out, mostly playing out on the street.

Marjorie: What hopes and dreams did you have as a child?

Katherine: Two prayers pervaded my childhood, the first was that I was the daughter of royalty, and had been temporarily placed with these people, waiting to be reclaimed by my good parents. The other was more of a family prayer, it being that we would finally receive our visa and leave for the land of Israel, the home of all Jews. We were torn by the glamor that America held for us. We had world books and I would gaze with awe at the tall buildings in New York. Even in Romania it was considered the land of opportunity, while Israel was the land of our people. The split was always there, which master to serve. The pull of New York was also my aunt, my father's older sister, an accomplished poet who had lived there for some twenty years.

Marjorie: How did these illusions of America fit in with your life in Romania?

Katherine: Our discussions of these hopes were always in tandem with the daily realities of our existence. Everything we did in our daily life was translated in the context of emigrating, someday. It was the backdrop for everything my parents did. Although there were almost no discussions about plans or expectations to leave, money was saved for this purpose, my mother worked harder, some clothes they bought were stored. There was no way to know how long this process would take.

Marjorie: Under what circumstance did your family finally receive a visa and decide to leave? What were your feelings during the time of preparation?

Katherine: Mother's cancer and our visa came at about the same time in 1961. Days that Mother spent sewing were now filled with doctor's visits, injections, travel to Cluj where better medical care was available. Our daily rhythm was shattered by these two events, the prayer for our visa mixed with the pain of her illness. Mother's mastectomy and the preparations for our departure went on at the same time. Neither were discussed nor grieved. My memories of that time are often chaotic and confused, walking alone, sad, scared, selling furniture to neighbors, acquiring new garments for our travel, Mother's absences, adults' complete preoccupation and unavailability.

Marjorie: What do you remember about the actual day you left Romania?

Katherine: The things that we could keep and take with us: bed linens, clothes, kitchen items, photographs. What we could not bring along was the money that my parents, especially my mother, had toiled so hard for, and jewelry outside of wedding bands. The train would bring us to our first destination in Vienna. At the Romanian border we were thoroughly searched and much was taken away. I was angry with Mother for allowing the guard to take away a ring that I loved.

Marjorie: What was happening to your mother during this time? How did you feel about her illness?

Katherine: In January of 1963 we were given shelter in a hotel in a seedier part of Vienna. Mother went to the hospital almost as soon as we arrived. The cancer continued to spread. I only knew that Mother needed to be in the hospital, any discussion of this was avoided and discouraged. After her second mastectomy she became increasingly worse. My visits to her were infrequent, memories of her pain, baldness bring waves of sadness for me still. My helplessness was overwhelming. Every day was filled with magical rituals of trying to beat the light crossing the street, not stepping on cracks, making bargains with God. My thirteenth birthday came and went. We were living in our own apartment at that time, a five-floor walkup. My mother happened to be home for a brief visit. Father didn't want to buy anything in celebration of my birthday. What I had asked for was a bra and pantyhose. Mother intervened on my behalf and I was grudgingly given a birthday gift. Later I felt selfish about this request.

Marjorie: Thirteen is a difficult age for most girls, and yet you were also losing your home and possibly your mother at the same time. How did you respond to these changes?

Katherine: We were in limbo, Mother was suffering in the hospital, in pain most of the time. We lived for a brief period of time in the seedy hotel, getting our meals from kosher soup kitchens. Mother was dying and *West Side Story* was playing in the Viennese cinemas. My adolescence and sexual awakening crashed head on with the loss of all stability. Becoming acclimated to Vienna was made easier by my having spoken Yiddish and German at home. What I remember most vividly is the aloofness, feeling outside of and different from the other children. Not even my body provided me with any constancy as I entered adolescence. We were coming undone, Mother's death unraveling the fabric of our family.

Marjorie: How did other family members respond to your mother's cancer?

Katherine: Grandmother's reaction to mother's illness was anger. She blamed Father for having allowed Mother to work too hard, she blamed me for the aggravation that I caused our mother. Father seemed lost and helpless without our mother, preoccupied and unavailable. My brother worked throughout this period driving cabs in order to supplement our very meager funds. However, this took away from him his young adulthood. He would often say that the long hours he worked prevented him from visiting Mother in the hospital. He tried to spend time with me when he could, to relieve our dreary and lonely life.

Marjorie: What you can remember about the day you found out your mother had died?

Katherine: One day in July, my brother came home carrying a bundle of clothes. I was in the other room. The scenario is ingrained in my mind, like a recurring bad dream. I heard him speak to Grandmother. Nothing, that I can remember, was said to me. I felt as if the room I was sitting in was in the dark and my brother and grandmother were in the other, lit room. I knew Mother had died, those were her clothes. There was this nothingness, numbness. I didn't count, I was not important. I was too young to be of any help and too old to be a child.

Marjorie: What was your relationship like with your father after your mother was gone?

Katherine: Father was heartbroken after Mother's death. She had been a replacement for his beloved mother. He had lost his father when he was thirteen, and he was rapidly thrust into the role of caretaker at a very young age. He felt both responsible and deprived. Having to take care of another thirteen-year-old was overwhelming for him.

Marjorie: How did that make you feel?

Katherine: I felt endangered. I have a memory that is completely unclear. My father and I are riding a bus and I beg him not to send me away. I feel frightened that I will be abandoned by him. Is he trying to rid himself of me? For a very long time after my mother's death I had a sense that she just went away and that I would find her somewhere, sometime. How could she be gone forever?

Marjorie: What circumstances finally determined that you would go to America?

Katherine: Aunt Osia encouraged father that changing our destination to America would provide us, the children, with a better future. Being an American citizen, she was able to bring the change about. In October of 1963 we set sail on the *Queen Mary*, emigrant class. The bunks were on the very bottom of this opulent floating city. For me it was all wondrous.

Marjorie: How did your actual arrival in the U.S. compare with the images you had of it as a child?

Katherine: After five days of a fairly rough ride, we approached our destination, New York City. There is a photograph of myself, in an old coat, with a scarf covering my pigtails, ahead of me the Statue of Liberty. Nothing prepared us for the hardships and confusion that lay ahead. We were placed temporarily in the Broadway Central Hotel, a holding pen for new immigrants. It was in the lower part of Manhattan, an old rundown relic.

Marjorie: Tell me more about your aunt. Did she become a mother figure for you?

Katherine: My aunt was an elusive and inconstant presence in our lives. She left Chernowitz at nineteen, shortly after her father died. According to her this was something that her mother wanted her to do, no longer being able to afford the college education that she had begun in philosophy. She was intelligent, outspoken, and headstrong, but she couldn't overcome losing both her mother and father at such a young age. In a way she felt driven away from home. She wrote poetry in German, poetry filled with pathos and yearning. I felt no connection to her. I remember her as a cold, moody, and critical presence. She had no sense of the terrible loss that we had all suffered.

Marjorie: What happened to your brother?

Katherine: He was twenty-one at the time, a young man, expected to continue working and supporting all of us, as he had in Vienna. There was no thought of his needs for friendships or pleasure, or the pain that he was feeling about the loss of his mother. His kindness had sustained me during very those difficult times in Vienna, when he would take me for a ride in the taxi he drove, or take me to play Ping-Pong with him.

Marjorie: It sounds as if you were still very isolated and lonely. Did you make any friends?

Katherine: Vera Hacken, a friend and admirer of my aunt, became an important person in my life. She was five foot three, round, and seemed comfortable and happy with herself. She was bubbly and enthusiastic about everything. She would rescue us at times from the squalor of our circumstances to her home in upstate New York, where her husband was head of the psychiatric hospital. From her I felt the first possibility of hope beyond our present situation. I dreamed of becoming like her, having regular poetry readings in my home, living in the country, surrounded by trees, flowers, and beauty. She offered me kindness, friendship, and a brief respite from motherlessness. On some weekends, Vera would bring me to her home. She lived in what seemed to me a mansion. Indoor plumbing, bathrooms, separate bedrooms covered in beautiful linens. Life was peaceful and predictable. I was keenly aware and observant of everything around me, trying to ingrain in my mind what I hoped for someday. At that time it felt unattainable. We would take short walks together and although I don't remember the content of our conversations, I remember her pleasant, engaging manner.

Marjorie: Were you aware of your Jewishness, of being "different"?

Katherine: We found ourselves in somewhat similar circumstances as my parents did when they first left Chernowitz. Where to find safety and a Jewish community. Borough Park became our new home.[1] There was a community of emigrants from Romania. My first group of friends came from these families. This group of adolescents provided me with the safety of making the transformation from the poor emigrant to the acclimated American. Television became my most important source of learning. Not only did I learn the language, I also learned about the American way of life. School was both a refuge and torture. I did not fit in. My clothes were different from those of the other children, and I spoke with an accent. My one dream was to look and sound like the others as quickly as possible. On the other hand, I quickly mastered the language and became an excellent student. This was a great source of self-esteem for me and made my father very proud.

Marjorie: What languages did you speak?

Katherine: From the very beginning of my life I had been thrust into a multi-linguistic world. At home we spoke German and Yiddish, with the children in our courtyard Hungarian, and at school Romanian. Shifting back and forth in these languages was a perfectly natural matter. By the age of ten I had finished reading most of the children's books and taught myself to read Hungarian. I loved books and they provided me with hours of comfort and pleasure. The love of books continued to serve me well in the middle school and later in high school. I don't quite remember the process but it almost seemed one of osmosis, absorption by immersion. There was no escape from the need to interact in this new language. Initially the process was one of simultaneous translation. I would hear the English word, translate it for myself into German, and respond to the message. Speaking, I would think in German and then translate, as best I could, into English. Over time this process became increasingly frustrating and time consuming, therefore the impetus to learn to think in my new language.

Marjorie: How did you respond to having new friends? What did you do to try to fit in?

Katherine: The driving force at this time was for me to shed, as quickly as possible, all that could identify me as an immigrant. I wore miniskirts, fishnet stockings, and straightened my curly hair. I smoked cigarettes, loved Elvis Presley, and shaved my legs. My only friends were other immigrants. In the safety of this group I practiced being an American teenager and seemed to succeed in hiding behind this new persona. I didn't think of it as hiding at the time, rather feeling drawn to what other teenagers did. Our small group of friends had parties, went into the city together, to Coney Island beach in the heat of the summer. We spoke English, as if we had always belonged to this country.

Marjorie: What was your family life during this time?

Katherine: At home, our family continued to fall apart. My grandmother's animosity towards my father grew and old recriminations surfaced daily. I remained a staunch supporter of my father, putting me at odds with Grandmother, while my brother who had few feelings for Father, remained on Grandmother's side. My brother and I, however, remained close. Within this tense home situation, school and friends became a lifesaving refuge.

Marjorie: So school and friends had become an escape for you from your family and the pain of past memories. Were you successful in academics?

Katherine: In high school, my interest in language and communication fueled my wish to become a foreign diplomat. I had my sights set on George-town University. Although I had excellent grades, I tested poorly. I eventually realized that Georgetown University was out of my financial and scholastic league and that I had to settle for another school. I was very disappointed and once again alerted to the reality that wishing for something has nothing to do with getting it. SUNY at Buffalo was able to offer me a scholarship and work study. I wanted to leave home and go away to college, something that none of my other friends aspired to. The hope was to distance myself from my family's pain.

Marjorie: Were you able to escape your past in this way?

Katherine: In 1968, at the age of eighteen, I left for SUNY at Buffalo, my brother married shortly thereafter, my father and grandmother each moved, and I lost my home once again. This was also the beginning of my depression that would last for twenty-three years. As soon as I left for Buffalo, I was thrust into American culture, something that I had managed to keep at a safe distance as long as I had my Romanian friends. I found myself once again on the shaky terrain of feeling the outsider as I did at thirteen, but this time without any safe haven. I had managed to avoid dealing with the loss of my mother during those first five years as well as with the impact of our move and the painful beginning of my life in this country. The refuge and self-esteem that I had derived from having been a good student became lost to me as well, when I could only do C work in some beginning courses. In my attempts to shed my immigrant identity, my shame about my helplessness, I now found myself with no resources to fall back on. I felt different from the other girls, inferior to their smooth navigation of the social scene. I experienced my difference as that of an immigrant, that is not belonging to this place, but not necessarily belonging elsewhere either. Rather it was being a motherless person without a home. I believe this was a large part of the shame and isolation that I felt at that time. Religious differences seemed less relevant.

Marjorie: So you do not think being Jewish contributed to your isolation, but neither did it help give you a sense of identity or place of belonging. Who or what did you turn to next for refuge?

Katherine: The road to healing was long and arduous. It took many unexpected twists and turns, some chosen by me and some simply by the serendipitous nature of life. I needed help and found the counseling center at my university. A new world of the unconscious opened for me and I became a psychology major instead. I also rediscovered my love of languages, taking Spanish and German literature courses. This became my second major. I did well in these courses, finding emotional and intellectual nourishment in my studies. I continued with graduate work in Buffalo and earned a master's degree in education in 1974. I returned to New York City at that time but couldn't find any work in my field. My interest specifically was to work on a college campus in the counseling center, to do the work I had come to love. The only work that I managed to find was in geriatrics. In time this led me to pursue graduate studies in social work. I became a clinical social worker and, in the course of working with others in pain, I could also address my own.

Marjorie: Perhaps the immigration was hardest on your grandmother, since she had lost the most by leaving her home country. What happened to her after she moved away from your family?

Katherine: My grandmother at the age of eighty had moved in with another elderly woman. She was illiterate, having learned how to sign her name in Vienna. Perhaps it was the living apart from one another or perhaps age and quiet mellowed her, allowing both of us to have a chance to grow to love one another. Living in Buffalo left all the caretaking to my brother, but on rare occasions when I did come back to visit, I would become involved in small, intimate aspects of her life, cutting her nails, her hair or threading a needle for her. I witnessed her growing old and frail and had opportunities to hug and comfort her. In this important experience I felt some healing, in small measure being able to have with my grandmother, my mother's mother, something that I did not have with my own mother when she was ill and dying.

Marjorie: What lessons have you learned now from having your own family, being the mother you lost at such a young age?

Katherine: I married at twenty-nine a young man whom I met shortly after having returned to New York City from Buffalo. His parents had also come from Eastern Europe, arriving in 1951 when he was three weeks old. Our daughter was born in 1981 and our son in 1984. They were my most important teachers. I learned about love, needs, and attachments. I remained, however, split from the strength of my immigrant roots for some twenty years, and deeply ambivalent about my Judaism.

Marjorie: Yes, you don't talk much about your Jewishness. What does it mean to you?

Katherine: My family of origin as well as that of my husband provided us with temporary connections to our religion. I had lost faith in God after my mother died, when my fervent bargains were not accepted. For many years I carried deep anger and resentment towards God and to this day I have an uneasy connection with my religion. As our children grew older I felt pressed to pass on to them a sense of Judaism. I felt comfortable being a Jew, but not a very religious one. My brother had continued with our conservative family traditions. I was uncertain how or what to pass on to my children. What remained deeply meaningful were the holidays, the rituals, and the food. I found observance to be much more connected with the prayers and the belief in God, something that I was having great difficulty reconciling. In my family I didn't see joy and pleasure connected with observance but rather mostly obligation. We joined a reformed temple, where I found less rigid religious boundaries and a great commitment to community service. It also provided a nursery school for our children within a Jewish community. The songs and the Hebrew chanting within the context of other Jews provided some sense of comfort and belonging. Once our children joined the public school system, an important religious link was lost for me. My husband's lack of interest in any aspect of religion left me alone in the task of defining this for myself and our children.

Marjorie: Did it ever seem an important part of your own healing to go back to Romania? What kept you from going and what circumstances finally led up to it?

Katherine: Over the years I had often thought of returning and revisiting my beginnings. Ambivalence about returning to a past that held grief and loss did not make this journey a reality for thirty-three years. My brother was the only remaining link to my family of origin. My grandmother had died at the age of one hundred in 1987. Father died only a year and a half earlier, three weeks before my daughter's bat mitzvah. At this particular point in my life I was in the middle of a clinical training program. This was an intense experience. We were provided with opportunities to confront and to become intimately reacquainted with ourselves. In this work, I had often journeyed back and forth over time, tracing and retracing my past and present, to make meaning of it. I saw this trip with my brother as another way of regathering parts of myself, this time as a forty-six-year-old woman, not the vulnerable child I had been.

Marjorie: What did it mean for you to actually be back in Romania and Vienna? How did the trip compare with the expectations you had been building for over thirty years?

Katherine: In retrospect, I realize that the time we allotted to this was too brief, ten days, four countries. It was just enough time to see, but not quite long enough to reflect. I was particularly anxious to go back to Vienna and my home town in Romania. My brother tried to arrange for our arrival in Vienna to be at the same train station as our initial one in 1963. This did not turn out to be possible. Nor was it possible for me to reexperience those initial feelings that I had often recaptured in dreams and therapy. Time and reflection had worked and molded those early feelings into more palpable material. I recognized neither the street nor the apartment building we had stayed in while in Vienna. I felt deeply disappointed. My mother's grave was the one existing reality that tied me to this city and to the past. On a sunny, warm Friday morning, we took the tram out to the Jewish cemetery. The day was very much like the one thirty-three years ago, when I walked these paths as a thirteen-year-old. The first thing that I noticed was the strong fragrance of the linden trees. I remembered that sweet, soothing fragrance from long ago. Now, standing by my mother's grave, I spoke to her in Yiddish, our language. It was perhaps the first time that I was able to say goodbye to her, and let go of many years of sorrow.

Marjorie: What other significant experiences took place during that trip?

Katherine: From Vienna we traveled to Budapest and then took the train to Romania. As it turned out, I inadvertently recaptured the experience of leaving my home thirty-three years earlier. At the border, between Hungary and Romania, our passports were taken by the Hungarian border police, without explanation. My fantasies immediately went to our being taken off the train, being separated from my brother, and ending up in jail, once again stripped of everything. The helplessness of that time infuriated me now. This time I got off the train and asked what was going on. They returned the passports and waved me back on the train. In some small measure I regained some of what I had lost then.

Marjorie: What happened when you reached Satu Mare?

Katherine: Entering my hometown, I again experienced this lack of recognition. Despite my earlier resolve to let go of expectations, it was harder not to feel anxious. I feared that things might have changed so much that I would not recognize my one-time hometown. As we approached the center of the town, there was this unfolding of the place as it was then and with that, a sense of joy at having remembered accurately: a sense of truth. The broad Corso remained, the beautiful hotel with its bright blue ceramic inlay and roof. Across from it the park seemed even larger with its numerous trees and large water fountain. My grandmother had sat here on one of these benches, on those rare moments when she allowed herself some rest, while I ran, played, and returned to her to eat the cucumber sandwiches she had brought along for me. Around the corner from the park, halfway down the cobblestone street, stood the old building I called home, changed by time and circumstances. Neglect and poverty were evident everywhere. How much of this had always been like this? Not having known anything else I couldn't have looked at it from any other perspective. The massive wooden gate to the courtyard looked neglected and dented. I had stood at this gate before we left, selling some last remaining items we could not bring along. Inside the gate, the large cobblestones had been removed and covered over with cement. Dogs were barking furiously from somewhere above us. I felt intimidated, a stranger in what was my home.

Marjorie: Were there any people around, some of your old neighbors even?

Katherine: A young gypsy man stared at us curiously and followed along. He lived in the back part of the courtyard in a single room with his wife, a dirty lace curtain doubling for a door. An older woman appeared from the upstairs apartment. It turned out to be Dora. Her sister and I were friends. Although she is my brother's age she looks old beyond her years. Excited and overwhelmed by our unexpected appearance, she tells us that her sister had emigrated to Israel some years ago but she decided to stay. The dogs are hers, to keep intruders away. She doesn't feel safe but is used to this lifestyle. She tells us that there are only a handful of Jews left and the temples are now silent.

Marjorie: In what ways was the trip disappointing or different from what you expected?

Katherine: Before we started our journey, my brother and I spoke about wanting to see the Jewish quarters in the cities we were to visit. With little contrast, the synagogues we saw, once vibrant, were now emptied of the life they once held. Many synagogues had been destroyed and ransacked throughout the Holocaust years. Some had become museums, relics of a past, their meaning extinguished. It was paradoxical that both the evil as well as the life of that period were destroyed. This was most evident in Prague. On a small side street, tucked away from the center of the city, the synagogue, cemetery, and houses huddled closely together. Even the cemetery is twelve deep; space having run out, the dead were buried in layers. Vendors lined the narrow street, selling Jewish artifacts. The synagogues were now museums, with hourly tours. It was painful to see such emptiness in what had once been so filled with life. The next generation would not even be able to feel this pain, not ever having been part of this. In my hometown the two temples stood behind locked fences, still beautiful and imposing, but now silent.

Marjorie: Yes, physical places have both the ability to validate and to deny our past experiences. What did the trip teach you about the past?

Katherine: I realized that I wanted to find what I had left and have it magically restored. I wanted to find my parents and my home as it had been, touch all that I had to leave behind without a proper farewell. It's painful to realize that cannot be. The physical world, although somewhat changed, remained—the street, the buildings, the city. What it lacked was my life then. It was devoid of people with whom I could reconnect and retell the story. It deepened my memories but I didn't rediscover anything new.

Marjorie: What are some lessons you have learned from your travels?

Katherine: What I have come to value is that the journey goes on every day. It does not require traveling distances. Learning and seeing is available every day. To keep my eyes open even when the sights are not the most pleasant, because the opportunity for learning is always there. Throughout my life what was most difficult was to live behind a wall of depression through which so much of what I lived was filtered. My world was shrouded by much grayness with only occasional colors. The pleasures in my days are actually small ones. In reviewing each day I want to be able to know that I had been of some help, have treated my family with love and respect, and have not compromised my feelings in order to appease others.

Marjorie: In which country do you feel most at home?

Katherine: I feel connected to this or any other place by the friendships that I have, and the freedom with which I can live my life. With only occasional lapses I feel terribly grateful to live in this country. My personal rights have never been curtailed and many opportunities have been made available for me.

Marjorie: Is there any good in your life that you think resulted from your past struggles?

Katherine: I'm certain that my early beginnings and the paths I traveled as a result have opened my heart to the misery and pain of others. I value the different strengths that I have inherited from the three women that I was connected with in my family—my mother, grandmother, and aunt. Although I don't live a religious life I feel that I live a righteous one, feeling very connected to my roots and my people. Without living in Israel I consider it another home. Though not having directly gone through the Holocaust, I believe that the reverberations of that event resonate in our soul if not in our conscious mind. There is still a longing in me to find a meaningful way of living a Jewish life. Although I feel I once again own my multicultural and multilinguistic heritage, I continue to struggle with my religious identity. I have some worry that the Yiddish language and the vibrancy of the prewar Jewish life will become only a memory rather than an act of remembrance for the generations to come.

SILVIA ZELDIS TESTA

1915	Maternal grandmother flees the pogroms in Poland and arrives with her parents and brother in Tucumán, Argentina; moved to Oruro, Bolivia; eventually settles in Valparaíso, Chile
1922	Paternal grandparents flee Russia; Silvia's father born in Romania, en route to Amsterdam to take the boat to America
1923–1948	Paternal grandparents arrive in Buenos Aires, Argentina, and stay for seven to eight years. Eventually they move to a small town in Chile, on the outskirts of Viña del Mar; then they move to the closest big city, the port of Valparaíso, where grandmother and uncle run a jewelry store. Grandfather dies there. Only two of the five brothers can pursue higher education: Silvia's father becomes a doctor
1927	Maternal grandparents marry in Valparaíso and return to Tucumán two years later, where Sylvia's mother is born
1949	Parents marry in Valparaíso
April 1950	Silvia born in Valparaíso; when she is two, her family moves to Viña del Mar, also known as the "Garden City"
1955	Attends the elementary school in Valparaíso
1956	With two siblings, moves to grandparents' apartment in Buenos Aires and attends school while mother and father are in England for his medical fellowship
1957	In the third grade, switches, along with her sister, to St. Margaret's School for Girls, an English immersion private school
1964	Attends Liceo de Niñas de Viña del Mar, the public high school
1967	Begins medical school in Valparaíso
1970	Moves to Santiago to seek better professional opportunites. Enters the University of Chile Eastern Campus
January 22, 1972	Marries
February 1974	Graduates from medical school. Enters the field of pediatrics
July 1974	Daughter, Andrea Patricia, born
1976	Starts working in neonatology
1977	Moves to Boston, Massachusetts; husband begins internship and residency required for all foreign medical graduates
1980	Son David Enrique born
1983	Begins medical training

1986	First visit back to Chile, with children; begins traveling more often so that children become close to their grandparents, aunts, uncles, and cousins, and remain bilingual; moves to Newton, Massachusetts
1987–present	Begins work as neonatologist, first as director of a level two nursery (intermediate care) for eight years, and then as a staff member in a level three (intensive care) nursery and other level two nurseries in the Boston area
1989	Son Daniel Alexander born

Before the twentieth century, few Jews emigrated to Chile. Those who did came from Eastern Europe in the 1870s and 1880s and immersed themselves in Chile's economy as peddlers, traders, and merchants. Anti-Semitic sentiment in this period, linked to concerns that the Jewish immigrants threatened Chilean Catholicism, sharply increased with the 1904 publication *Raza chilena* (The Chilean race), by Dr. Nicolás Palacios. This book, a founding work of Chilean nationalism, praised the nation's native Araucanians and Spaniards while lamenting Chile's economic dependence on Europe. Jewish immigrants to Chile and their children came under suspicion as nonnative, non-Hispanic, non-Catholic aliens with strong cultural ties to Europe.

The worldwide economic depression of the 1920s and 1930s exacerbated anti-Semitic feelings just as additional Jewish refugees began arriving from Central and Eastern Europe. In 1933 the Movimiento Nacional Socialista (MNS) was formed. The Nacistas, lauding Nazi persecution of the Jews, sought to establish a hierarchical order in Chilean society that would promote national interests. Unable to overcome the Chilean Catholic Church's antipathy to racial genocide, the Nacistas instead accepted Jewish immigration on the condition that Jews work hard for the advancement of the Chilean nation.

Anti-Semitism, embedded in Chile's political framework, remained a volatile issue in the years to come. The late 1930s were marked by political disagreement over the Jewish immigration issue. Left-wing Carlos Vicuña Fuentes wanted to allow more Jews access to Chile, while Foreign Relations Minister Miguel Cruchaga adamantly opposed such a policy. He, along with many other nationalists, feared that Jews would take over local merchant jobs instead of working in agriculture and mining, the two areas considered necessary to Chilean modernization and development.

By the early 1940s only twenty thousand Jews were living in Chile, the majority of them in the nation's capital of Santiago. Only fifty Jewish families were permitted to enter the country each year, although others entered illegally. Even so, Jews accounted for under 3 percent of the population of Santiago by the end of the war. Despite this small figure, Jewish immigrants aroused fear and suspicion and were criticized for failing to assimilate swiftly.

Postwar Chilean politics were based upon a multi-party electoral system. In the aftermath of the 1959 Cuban Revolution, the rightist Liberal and Conservative parties joined forces with the Christian Democrat party to block the 1964 Socialist presidential candidate, Salvador Allende Gossens. Allende successfully ran again for the presidency in 1970, under the aegis of the Popular Unity (UP) coalition of the Socialist, Communist, and Radical parties. Allende's presidency and Chile's "socialist experiment" captured the world stage. Allende moved to reform Chilean agriculture and to nationalize its copper mines.

The pace of Allende's reforms, well received in his first year, continued to escalate. Workers took control of factories and *hacienda* plantations. Chilean socialism aroused hostility from the Nixon administration, which exacerbated woes caused by disinvestment in private industry. Economic disaster loomed on the horizon for Chile. The "March of the Empty Pots" of December 1972, staged by upper- and middle-class women in Santiago to protest food shortages, proved a major embarassment to Allende during Cuban dictator Fidel Castro's state visit. Strikes paralyzed the government in July and August 1973, and Allende committed suicide during the military coup of September 11.

The leader of the junta, General Augusto Pinochet Ugarte, became Chile's next president in June 1974. Under Pinochet's sixteen-year regime, the congress was dissolved and political parties were outlawed. The agrarian reforms of Allende were reversed as the *hacienda* estates were returned to former owners and farm workers' wages were cut. Terror tactics spread to keep the populace in line. As in Argentina, any opposition to the government was severely punished, and thousands of Chilean citizens disappeared.

With the subsequent Christian Democrat governments of Patricio Aylwin Azócar and Eduardo Frei Ruiz-Tagle in the 1990s, Chile began to adjust to the political and economic instability of the previous decades. It continues today to move closer to a full democracy.

During the beginning of the twentieth century, many families fled pogroms and conscription in the army of Czar Nicholas II. Some went to Argentina, to the port of Buenos Aires (the entry port to South America), and some went to Uruguay. Only a few went to Chile because of the difficulty of crossing the Andes. From 1915 to 1922, Silvia Testa's grandparents fled to South America from Poland and Russia. Her mother's family eventually settled in Valparaíso, Chile, while her father's family settled nearby in the beautiful city of Viña del Mar.

Silvia and I had not seen each other for almost twenty years when we were reunited in Boston. Our families had been friends for three generations, had gathered for Passover and attended each other's weddings. We share a Chilean past, although she was educated at an English school, St. Margaret's, while I studied at the Hebrew school in Santiago. Our language is Spanish and Chile has shaped our identity. Yet being Jewish and European also matters. At a family gathering in Boston, Silvia's father told his granddaughter Andrea that she was not Hispanic, but rather a European Jew. I can understand his reaction; in Chile we were always viewed as Jews, not Chileans.

Silvia spoke to me at my home in Wellesley, Massachusetts. A modest and reserved person by nature, she was nervous about this interview. On several occasions she asked me, "But do you think that this could interest anyone?" She had read *A Cross and a Star*, my biography of my mother, which was the catalyst for her to recall her own past. We had a leisurely conversation on a glorious autumn day and, while our children were in school, we remembered our childhoods.

Marjorie: You said earlier that you identified with my mother in my book *A Cross and a Star*. In other words, you thought that something in her story might be part of your own history. Did you see yourself there?

Silvia: Many of the experiences described are the same as mine. Some are related to anti-Semitism, or to the fact of feeling myself to be a minority, of having to explain things that for me were part of ordinary life but which were unfamiliar to other people—the religious part, the Jewish part. Besides, I could recognize real people and their lives as Jews, as a people who both were and were not integrated into Chilean society.

Marjorie: My sense of what it was like to be a Jew in Chile is very clear and I can recall my first awareness that I was Jewish. At recess time there was a song about who robbed the bread out of the ovens, with a cheerful chorus where everyone sang, "the Jewish dogs." I was six years old, in first grade. My parents reacted by immediately removing me from English school and sending me to Hebrew school. That song is still sung in Chilean schools. Friends of my mother tell me that on Jewish holidays teachers talk about how they are going to have a wonderful class because there are no Jews present. This was happening in 1939 and still in the 1960s when you and I went to school. Yet your experience was very different from mine.

Silvia: I will tell you how it was that I found out that I was Jewish. For first and second grade, I went to a Jewish school, a Hebrew school in Valparaíso. Later, my sister and I went to an English school. Mainly because my parents thought that it would be a good idea to learn English as preparation for the future. Besides, the school was considered to be a good school, better academically than the Hebrew school. So I switched over to the English school for third grade. Of course I had no idea, and the second day of classes, there was a religion class. The inspector came by to tell the Protestant girls to line up to leave class because this class was for the Catholic girls. She instructed: "Protestant girls, here in a line." I did not understand what she said. The girl who was sitting beside me asked if I was Protestant. I said no, and so I stayed on in the class.

I stayed in the Catholic religion class. When they began to pray the Our

Father and the Hail Mary, which of course I had never learned, the girl beside me elbowed me and said, "Next time you had better go with the Protestant girls." So the next time I went out with the Protestant girls. The Protestant pastor gave me a notebook to make me feel more comfortable, and he gave me some religious stickers to put into the notebook. I had never seen such things before in my life. I got home, I was seven years old, I told what had happened to me in the first class, which was not where I belonged, and I told about what happened in the second class, where I did not belong either, and I found out that I was Jewish. I had lived my whole life with Jewish people all around me: that was my world.

Marjorie: How did that make you feel?

Silvia: It was then that my parents realized that there was something missing, and they explained to me that I was Jewish and I asked what I was supposed to do during the religion classes. There were two or three of these classes per week, and so they let me choose. In general what happened was that I had the hour free. I went to the office and read.

Marjorie: This experience of yours is very similar to that of other Jewish girls in Chile, where the population is 97 percent Catholic and 1 percent Jewish. My mother told me the same sort of story, but she says she enjoyed it because she got to play. It is curious that in Chile there is still no separation between education and required religion classes.

Silvia: The rest of the class envied me. Years later I stayed on in religion class. What I learned about the Catholic religion I found out in school, because I found that for me it was necessary to know about the world in which I was living, to learn about those who were all around me. Then for several years I used that free hour to paint or read. Sometimes there was another Jewish girl whose parents were stationed in Chile for one or two years, or something like that. I no longer even remember the names of these girls. The father of one of them was a representative of the Encyclopaedia Britanica. The family spent two years in Chile and this girl went to school with me during those two years. Then there was a Hungarian family, and for another two years I had a companion. But in general, the rest of the time, I was the only one.

Marjorie: What was it like to be a Jewish girl in a Catholic school?

Silvia: The school itself was Protestant, Anglican. The teachers were English women, most of them brought directly from England. Most of them were Anglicans, but the friends of mine who attended the school were predominantly

Catholic because they came from the community, that is from Viña del Mar, and they weren't necessarily English. It was in grade school that I began to hear insults related to being Jewish. The first few times I didn't understand what they were saying. At home we did not use swear words, so I had no idea what those meant either. I was very innocent. The instructions I remember getting from my parents were to pay no attention to them, and not to answer back. So people would yell at me and say things to me, but I pretended not to notice. For the lower class, the problem was seen from an economic point of view. The Jew was the one who was rich, who had money, who oppressed the poor. That was the idea lower-class people had of the Jew. I still don't know exactly what upper-class people were referring to when they insulted Jews, but it had a lot to do with how the Catholic religion was being taught. Another experience I had in the street where we lived: there were two girls, neighbors of ours, who were studying at a nuns' school and we always played together. One day we were playing school, and the other two girls, who were older, were the teachers. They decided to teach the catechism to my sister and me and other neighborhood kids, so I got home reciting the catechism. I was eight or nine years old and I had memorized: "Who killed Jesus? The Jews killed Jesus." And that was how, line by line, by memory, the girls who went to the Catholic parochial school learned the catechism. When my parents heard that, they had a fit. They asked me if I knew what I was saying. No, I had no idea what I was saying.

Marjorie: Why didn't they send you to another school? Why did they decide to leave you there? Do you think it was beneficial for you in some way?

Silvia: I never thought that it could have consequences. It was part of my daily life. I assumed that things were like that, that these things happened to me and everyone else. I only had two or three friends from school; the rest of my friends were Jews, outside school. Saturdays and Sundays I spent the better part of my time with my Jewish friends. They were all going through the same thing. The Hebrew school that existed in Viña del Mar only went up through the sixth grade. The only Hebrew school that offered high school classes was in Valparaíso. We lived in Viña and I think it was more convenient to go to a school that was near us. It was a bigger school and considered better, educationally speaking. The school in Valparaíso didn't have a schoolyard; it was a smaller school, with fewer opportunities, and my parents thought it was more important for us to learn English. Of course I disagreed with my father on this and I would never speak English with him at home. This made him deeply angry, but it was one of the few rebellious things I did. I did it on purpose. I thought, Dad wants me to speak English and therefore I am not going to say a single word to him in English.

Marjorie: What does your identity as a Chilean Jew or a Jewish Chilean mean to you?

Silvia Zeldis Testa

Silvia: While I was growing up, I felt very Chilean at school. I felt Chilean and Jewish. Jewish even though at home no one was extremely religious. There was no kosher food or anything like that. But we still observed the traditions, and went to the synagogue. Since all my friends were Jewish, it was easy to feel comfortable with that. I even belonged to Maccabee and went to Maccabee camp when I was twelve or thirteen years old. I was in charge of a group of kids. I participated actively until I was fourteen or fifteen years old. So I felt Chilean and Jewish. The fact that my grandparents had emigrated from Europe seemed accidental. It never seemed important to me that my Chilean roots were not too deep. My mother was Argentinian and for us Argentina and Chile were like the same thing because my mother's family was in Argentina. We spent summers in Argentina. So I felt myself to be Chilean but at the same time it seemed fine to me to feel a bit Argentinian. Now, the rest of South America is foreign to me—Bolivia, Peru, Brazil, to say nothing of Colombia and Venezuela. To me they might as well have been in North America. But Chile and Argentina, and Uruguay, too, felt in my mind like where I lived. It was only much later that I began to talk with my grandparents about their origins and I realized that perhaps my background was not so much Chilean as European.

Marjorie: Do you think that coming from a Jewish family you were overprotected? Or do you think that has to do with belonging to a certain social class?

Silvia: While I was at the English school, I was overprotected. I was totally separated from society in general. I never took public transportation. I walked to school, lived in a good neighborhood. I saw there was a washerwoman who earned her living washing clothes. She came by to pick up the clothes at my house, took them away, and brought them back. There was a maid in the house although I never talked to the maids. I didn't know anything about how they lived.

Marjorie: That happened to everyone in your social class. In Chilean society in the 1960s, there was a strong division between social classes. The girls who went to private schools had no way of knowing that another Chile existed, submerged in the most desolate and desperate poverty. Many of the children of immigrants lived in glass bubbles, protected from public life. Your case is very similar to mine. I never took public buses to get to school either. I did spend time in the maids' room and I really enjoyed seeing the photos they had of their first communions. For me it was like entering another dimension, a wonderland of fairy godmothers in tulle dresses and floating veils. Curiously, it was there that I felt my otherness and I felt very separate from the world of those photographs.

Silvia: That was typical. That was Chile. Except that, for the last part of high school, for grades ten through twelve, my parents decided that they were going

189

to switch me to another school. The new school was the public high school. They made this decision partly because the private school where I was going was no longer such a good place. It did not offer me much on the upper levels, the higher grades. And secondly, I think that my parents realized that the people I met there were members of an elite that really did not know what they were doing and were also very materialistic. All people talked about in school were the newest car and the most recent vacation trip. Now we were in a very good economic situation, but I never thought of myself as rich or thought we had money to throw away. We traveled to visit our family in Argentina, we took vacations, but that was due to my father's work and I always assumed that I was going to have to work someday, too. I never imagined that I was not going to work, so I changed schools. For the first time I realized that when the school required a fee for something, not everyone could pay that fee. They hardly ever asked for fees for anything. I realized that we all walked around in blue uniforms, but my uniform was better quality than other girls' uniforms. Very few other girls had as many books as I had.

Marjorie: So the high school made you learn a little about the other Chile? You realized that you and other people who lived like you were existing inside a glass bubble.

Silvia: Totally. Now whether or not this relates to being Jewish, I don't think so. I think that that was more related to social class. What I did find important in my Jewish upbringing was the importance given to individual effort, to studying and working. Despite living in this Chilean upper class, my mother dreamed of my being a professional. They always encouraged me to study, and for me there was no conflictive choice to be made between having a family and studying. It didn't seem like a problem to me.

Marjorie: Tell me more about your university experience.

Silvia: During the third year at the university we began to go to the hospital and people began to call me "Doctor." We had to prepare the medical histories of our patients and do physical exams, but I knew I was not the doctor. People asked me for advice and help. At that point one has to make certain choices that are quite personal. It would have been so easy to believe myself to be a doctor. Society gave me that title, and I was only in the third year of medical school. It was the first time I had put my hands on a patient and they were already calling me "Doctor." We were all so young. This went to the heads of many of us, and I'm not sure whether there was a conscious effort on the part of the professors to deflate us a bit and humble us a little and make us realize that we were not doctors yet. They should have told us that the fact that people put their lives and

Silvia Zeldis Testa

their trust in us was a gift, not a right. I do not remember hearing this as a part of my education, but I felt that should have been included. I felt very humble because the problems people told me about and the solutions they requested from me were beyond my ability to give. That's when my eyes were opened to the importance of social and economic problems in people's health. I am not sure that everyone really understood this.

Marjorie: What was your experience in medical school like? Was there any connection between this experience and your Jewish experience?

Silvia: Well, the war in Israel in 1967,[1] the year I entered the university. I came from a girls' school where this never would have been discussed in public. All of a sudden pamphlets began to appear. It turned out that I was the only Jewish woman first-year student. The medical school was new then, and it was growing. There were only three years of classes. But in the third-year class there were three Arab students who of course were two years older than me and were involved in political activity against Israel. Suddenly, there I was, the only Jew in the whole class of twenty-some people. I think there was another Jewish student in the second year, but somehow it fell on me to defend Israel. So I remember that well, having long conversations with my father to educate myself since I had never taken the time to read much about history. I had never needed to, really. Even though they had yelled "Jew!" at me once in a while during my school years, it had never been on an intellectual level. It was always totally on an emotional level. When they called me Jew right out like that it was because they were jealous of me. But now here, suddenly, I was plunged into discussions among university students. The experience was not only one of, "I am going to defend Israel," but I also had to defend Judaism and even myself as well. I had to do this, and I was tremendously ignorant. I found out what politics and politicking were like. Describing events selectively and distorting them for political motives. Many of these people wanted to be president of the university and hold offices and positions and thus had underlying political motives, political circumstances. I think the university is where politicians are formed. I found it incredible that people could tell barefaced lies against Israel, against other people, say that they represented the majority without having any kind of real majority vote. The topic had never really come up for a vote. For example, they wanted to print an official manifesto of the Valparaíso medical school in favor of the Arab countries. I don't remember whether they published it or not, but to say that they had a majority vote in favor of bringing it out was a lie.

Marjorie: Silvia, your time as a medical student coincided with the social and political upheavals of Salvador Allende's presidency. How did this affect you?

Silvia: We were beginning to read about what was happening in Europe and in France.[2] All this in the third year at the university, and then for the fourth, I transferred to Santiago. When I entered the third year, my last year in Valparaíso, everything was already polarized. People talked about being Communist or anti-Communist. At that time, to be a Communist was to be a total extremist. I remember my father opening my eyes for me on many occasions, saying, "Silvia, you're not hearing their own opinions when they speak; there is someone who is feeding them information about what they should say and what they need to speak about. Pay close attention as to whether that is the best for the university, for the school, for the city, or whether this has a political significance that goes beyond local matters. Don't just pay attention to the local, but see beyond it."

Marjorie: And that is what you did not know how to recognize, whether what they were saying had political connotations or not?

Silvia: Looking back at it now, I think there were political agendas everywhere, but at the time, I always felt innocent and I could not believe that people could have political motives and that it might not matter to them whether they damaged the medical school or the University of Chile in Valparaíso for the sake of political ideas that transcended the local. I had been brought up all my life in Viña and I was not really Chilean. I was from Viña, and very provincial. The newspaper had one page of international news. I never read the Santiago political news. Later, when I moved to Santiago, I realized that I belonged to something bigger and that this in turn was part of an even larger picture and so on. In my years in Viña del Mar, all this was shocking to me because my world was Valparaíso, for me the important place was where I was living. And so, later on, when I read your book and spoke to my grandparents, I could understand what it meant to people to have grown up in a small place, thinking that this was the world.

Marjorie: The main reason for your family's immigration to the United States was a desire to advance professionally, but, nevertheless, you immigrated to the United States during a volatile era—between Allende's socialism and Pinochet's military dictatorship. Silvia, tell me something about your motives in coming to North America. Did you choose the United States?

Silvia: The time when we came was a moment when we were finishing up a phase in our lives there and were about to begin a new phase. It was not political except that we did not want to educate our children under the military system. I think that socially things worked out in a way that these various motives combined, but we did not feel obliged to come, we knew that we could always go back. But there was never any reason to go back. Very few things took me by surprise. Of course I missed being surrounded by the adults I was used to having close by. I needed adults with experience because I felt so young. I missed my parents and my parents-in-law, especially during the weekends, because we had always gotten together with them.

My daughter was three and a half years old and she missed them a lot. I suffered not so much for myself as for her. I felt somewhat guilty about her sadness. The main reason for coming here was the professional aspect. We had studied medicine in Chile, using the same textbooks as here. In fact, we had been reading many of the journals directly in English because we didn't care for the translations and we could see there what was happening in medical fields in the United States, which did not relate much to what was happening in medicine in Chile. It was another level. In the United States there could be a higher level in part because health problems were different. We were interested in the type of medicine we saw in the journals, and we became aware that we were being left behind. We came to Boston by chance; we decided to take turns and not both go through training at the same time. For me, the first big decision I had made in my life was to decide to be a housewife for as many years as necessary. I thought it would not be for longer than three years. It ended up being five. Before we came, I had made that responsible decision to dedicate myself to my family. At that point we had one daughter, and the three of us came. We arrived full of enthusiasm, knowing that this was a different society. In fact, lots of people told us that Boston was the cradle of racism and they didn't understand why we were going to come live here. In a city of four million inhabitants, we were sure we would find friends. We came with the positive attitude that we were going to be able to work and study. We were excited about the whole medical aspect. Boston is one of the most attractive centers for studying medicine. We were young enough to be able to adapt to the fact that we were immigrants.

Marjorie: Silvia, which country do you call yours now?

Silvia: I've just been thinking about that because I have gone to Chile as a tourist and I have tried to think what it would be like to live in Chile again, and I've tried to figure out where I would feel more comfortable. I think that I feel more comfortable in the United States.

(Translated from Spanish by Mary G. Berg)

RUTH BEHAR

194

November 12, 1956	Born in Havana, Cuba
May 4, 1961	Leaves Cuba and settles in Kibbutz Gash, Tel Aviv, Israel
June 6, 1962	Arrives in New York City; lives in Brooklyn with maternal grandparents during the summer and then in apartments in Queens
1974	Attends Wesleyan University in Middletown, Connecticut; meets future husband, David Frye
1977	Graduate school in anthropology at Princeton University
1980–1981	Lives and studies in Santa María del Monte in León, Spain
1982–1985	Lives and studies in Mexquitic, San Luis Potosí, Mexico
1983	Receives doctorate in anthropology
1986	Moves to Ann Arbor, Michigan; son, Gabriel, born; publishes *The Presence of the Past in a Spanish Village* (Princeton University Press)
1991	Begins travel to Cuba on a regular basis
1993	Publishes *Translated Woman: Crossing the Border with Esperanza's Story* (Beacon Press)
1994	Promoted to professor in the department of anthropology at the University of Michigan
1995	Edits *Bridges to Cuba*, an anthology of Cubans of her generation on the island and in the diaspora (University of Michigan Press); Co-edits *Women Writing Culture* (University of California Press)
1996	Publishes *The Vulnerable Observer: Anthropology That Breaks Your Heart* (Beacon Press)

At the turn of the century, Cuba served as a way station for European Jews intent on emigrating to the United States. Once they obtained entry papers, they left Cuba. Because of this, a visible Jewish community in Cuba did not form until the 1920s, when U.S. immigration tightened its policies and closed its doors to a variety of people, including Jews. European anti-Semitism and the outbreak of war brought a new wave of Jews to Cuba in the late 1930s. By 1950, around 16,500 Jews had settled in the urban area of Havana, with a few thousand living in rural settlements.

At the end of World War II, immigration restrictions relaxed, allowing Cuban Jews greater access to the United States. As a result, the island's Jewish community decreased to ten thousand by 1951. At the time of Castro's Communist revolution, in 1959, the Cuban Jewish community was comprised of Jewish immigrants of Eastern European and Sephardic descent who had made the island their permanent home. Most of these Jews, engaged in the economic sectors Castro sought to nationalize, did not support his regime. In the early 1960s, 70 percent of Cuba's Jews left the country for the United States, Israel, Puerto Rico, Mexico, Venezuela, and other Latin American nations. It was during this diaspora that five-year-old Ruth Behar emigrated with her family to Israel and then to New York.

Ruth Behar, born in Havana, Cuba, in 1956, is a friend and immigrant of my generation. When I converse with her, I feel as though her stories and mine fit together like pieces of a jigsaw puzzle. Together, we might create a recognizable whole. Ruth is as obsessed with Cuba as I am with Chile, and both of us are fascinated by the European homelands of our parents.

During two years of correspondence, Ruth and I shared family and professional stories. We also shared our passion for poetry and exchanged poems in our letters. I took the liberty of correcting her Spanish and she did the same with my English. This conversation, a continuation of that correspondence, took place in Saratoga Springs, New York, Chicago, and at my home in Wellesley.

Marjorie: Do you think there is something specific about the Jewish immigration experience to this country that makes it different from all the others?

Ruth: For me it's not just being Jewish, but being Jewish-Cuban ... I am a certain kind of Jew. I speak Spanish. I am a Jew from the Caribbean, so that's what always made the experience unique for me. So when my family moved to New York, we did not fit into the Jewish community because we spoke Spanish and Ladino.[1] That made a big difference.

Marjorie: When we both arrived in the United States, we were very young. We did not speak English and did not have a community or a support group. How did you integrate into society those first years?

Ruth: Well, it was interesting. I always gravitated toward other immigrant children, so that when I was a child, a little girl, my very first close friend was from Belgium. She was Jewish too, Dina, my closest friend from about age nine until I was eleven or twelve. We were very, very close friends. We had the Jewish identity in common; we were both immigrants. We had both come to the United States when we were around five years old. I felt a bond with her. At the same time, my parents had a group of friends, a group of Cuban-Jewish friends that always saw each other, every weekend.

Marjorie: They were all Cuban-Jewish?

Ruth: Yes, in New York. They would see each other every weekend. I kept a diary when I was ten years old and I would write down almost every weekend that we would get together and have Cuban sandwiches. [Laughs.] And so, the language . . . I think the important thing was that we had the Spanish; really, Spanish was the language of our family and our little community.

Marjorie: So your identification with other Jewish immigrants as a child was almost nonexistent? Did you feel empathy with, let's say, somebody who was from Holland or Poland who was Jewish?

Ruth: I came to feel that more as I grew older. I mean I always had Jewish friends. I had a friend named Ruthie (people called her Ruthie and me Ruth to distinguish us). She was a next-door neighbor. She was Jewish and a close friend, too, but Dina was a special friend because she was a Jewish immigrant and she felt a connection to the country she had left behind. In fact, she would go back to Belgium regularly. Her grandparents still lived in Belgium and she would say to me how lucky I was to have all my family nearby. Then, later on, when I was eleven, we moved to another neighborhood in Queens and there I became close friends with a Vietnamese French girl and I admired her tremendously. There what I felt was the connection to the fact that she, like myself, was a mixture. She had two identities and she spoke French. Her mother was French and her father was Vietnamese. And I had the Jewish and the Cuban in me. I admired her tremendously. In fact, I adored her.

Marjorie: You have told me you still feel like an immigrant. Why is that? You had a great education and therefore most people would say that you are a privileged, mainstream person.

Ruth: Even after all of these years, I always feel . . . but then it's also maybe the anthropologist in me because anthropologists are always people who don't feel at home where they are, and that's why they have to go to other places. So that's one of the things that drew me to anthropology—I did not feel quite at home anywhere and wanted to go elsewhere. I always felt that everything felt borrowed. I don't feel that places belong to me. But maybe that's good. I did not have this sense of ownership about places. I just feel that this is wonderful, this wonderful place is a loan to me . . . it's given to me as a gift, it's borrowed. I may have to give it back some time and that is one of the things I talk about in my writings. I have a story about losing my suitcase when I went to New Hampshire and how I thought about what a suitcase means, having to pack a suitcase and take *everything* you have in that suitcase. If you are lucky. Maybe you won't be able to take a suitcase, maybe it will just be the clothes on your back. But the idea that you may have to leave or decide what it is you have to put in the suitcase . . . that everything might have to be reduced to a suitcase . . .

Marjorie: Do you feel like you are an exiled person or an immigrant? The metaphor of the suitcase is so much a part of your writings and your spirit.

Ruth: It is a mixture of both. I feel maybe that it would be pretentious for me to be an exile because, as you said, I have had lots of privileges here. An exile for me seems like a position of principle. You're an exile because you don't believe in something that has happened in your country. With me, it was really my parents who were the exiles and then I am the daughter of exiles. So what am I? Can I claim to be an exile too? Would that be pretentious? Am I really an immigrant child then? Lately I have been wanting to identify myself as an immigrant, because an exile is somebody who never arrives. And so I want to try to arrive. I am here and that is what I must now try to claim.

Marjorie: Do you claim some kind of ownership of this country? Or could you leave the United States and feel as if you had never lived here?

Ruth: Sometimes I feel that . . . I have feelings like that . . . When I am in Cuba, at times I think, "You know, I really could live here," and then I think about that. But at the same time, when I am here, in the United States, I think this is really where I want to be. Sometimes it happens to me in the most prosaic of situations, like when I am on a bus . . . in the U.S. And then you talk to the person next to you and they are from another country, and you start recognizing the immigrant past that we all have. For example, in Michigan, sometimes I think "Oh, this is the most homogeneous place. It's so American," but then you really talk to people and you find out, for example, Gabriel is on the soccer team and one of the team managers, I thought he was "just an American," but I talked to him and it turns out his grandparents are Lebanese. You know, and I had just put him into the American category, and he has this Lebanese background. Or I go to a camp trip with my son's class and I am talking to a woman who I think is American and it turns out that her background is Greek and you think, you have to open yourself to not assuming that, "They are all the Americans and I am the immigrant." We all have these home cultures, these other cultures within us, and I think sometimes I am so ready to assume that other people lack that. You make personal contact, you find that they have other places within them too.

Marjorie: I remember one of the few stories my father told us of when he was a young medical student at the University of Chile, in Santiago. One of his many foes told people not to speak to him, a landless Jew. The emblematic condition of the Jew as an errant, lost, and wandering soul has been part of the Western collective imaginary. But we have to examine this concept in greater depth. That is why I ask my friends what place they consider their homeland.

Ruth Behar

Ruth: I think about that a lot because, you know I don't want to be a nationalist and I don't like the idea of "homeland or death," which is the Cuban motto. Homeland or death, I think that is terrible. I don't want to be a nationalist in any way, any kind of nationalist for any nation.

Marjorie: But, don't we need something we can call home? What is home to you?

Ruth: Different things. Home is my desk. It is my books. That's definitely home to me. When I am at my desk with my books I am home. It is not so much a country. I have to have books. The books I have read and loved and the new books that I am reading. Books are very important. Also, interior spaces are very important to me. My house is really home because it has everything I have brought back from the places where I have been. And now I collect art work from my friends in Cuba and all of that surrounds me. So, you sort of make home, these interior spaces, which are important to me. When I was in Miami, I felt very much at home because I had the ocean, I had my grandmother, and I had the Spanish language. I love that. I love being able to hear Spanish, to speak Spanish, and I felt very at home among the Cuban community there. Everybody had a story, a tragic story, about loss and separation, about mourning. And the Cuban sense of humor. I feel very at home with that Cuban sensibility of making fun of everything.

Marjorie: Ruth, when you speak about your interior landscape where you collect memories, you are very Cuban. How do you reclaim the past? What makes you so different that you write about Cuba?

Ruth: I don't know. The one thing I say a lot is that I feel that I owe my life to Cuba. That if my family hadn't gone to Cuba in the 1920s they would have definitely perished under the Nazis. My mother's family was originally from Poland and Russia; my father's family from Turkey. My father's family might have been OK, but not my mother's . . . Those members of the family who did not migrate to Cuba died during the Nazi invasion. So I know that would have been my fate too. Or actually, I would not have been born. And so, Cuba gave me my life, saved my life. Nobody else in my family looks at it that way. I look at it this way . . . Cuba was our refuge.

Marjorie: Then it is inevitable that we talk about nations as refuges, but I want to speak to you about the migration and history of your family. Your family really ventured into the unknown.

Ruth: My grandparents were Jews who settled in Cuba because anti-Semitic immigration laws in the 1920s kept them out of this country. So I am Cuban because I am Jewish. But I am also Jewish because I am Cuban. The two diasporas are intertwined for me. I was able to calmly make my way through the Holocaust Museum in Washington, but when I came upon those piles and piles of suitcases, I fell apart weeping. And yet I am always traveling, packing or unpacking a suitcase.

Marjorie: Is travel for you a familiar encounter with the land and the ancestors? Is it also a way to renew ties? Here I am thinking about your return trips to Cuba and your involvement with young writers and painters.

Ruth: Well, maybe that is why I love going to Cuba so much, because I can connect there. There is no problem, you know? In the U.S. it is always a problem like, "Am I really Cuban? Am I really Latina? Am I really a woman of color?" I mean, I want to be with women of color. I think it is a privilege that I could be with a group of women that are black. I am "of color" here, but I'm not black. Women who are black could include me in their group, but then I also have to acknowledge, "Wait a minute, I haven't had to deal with the kinds of racist issues that black women deal with, so can you accept my being part of this group?" Those are my worries, but if they accept me, then I want to be there, and so I am glad that being Cuban gives me the possibility of being a woman of color in this country. But I know that in Cuba I am not a woman of color. I am a white woman, but I can be Jewish *and* Cuban in Cuba. As an anthropologist I worked in Spain and in Mexico and I was always afraid to tell people I was Jewish.

Marjorie: In Spain and Mexico, places that you have visited and written so much about?

Ruth: Yes. In Spain because I worked in a little village in northern Spain that was very traditional and very Catholic and I went there as a very young woman in my early twenties and I thought that as an anthropologist what I had to do was to be like them. So I would go to church. I would attend mass. I learned to recite the rosary, you know, and I did not tell people that I was Jewish and I went back several times and I kept thinking, "Now I will tell them. Now I will tell them." But I did not. I suffered mainly because I thought I was being dishonest with these people who had given me so much of their time and their lives and I had never been straight with them.

Marjorie: Do you think they would have rejected you?

Ruth: I don't know. I really don't know. What I feel bad about is that I hadn't done it from the beginning, and then it was something that ended up weighing on me. Should I or shouldn't I? I felt like a *conversa*, you know, in Spain, hiding . . .[2]

Marjorie: Ruth, your Cuban family does not really exist anymore. It has forged a new identity. How do you feel about going back to your *nana*, the woman who cared for you as a child?

Ruth: Wonderful. I want to write about her. She is one of the most important people to me in my whole life, because we left when I was so young. She knows me.

Marjorie: Tell me about that relationship.

Ruth: She never stopped thinking about me, which is the other amazing thing. And she told me stories about when I was a little girl that my mother never told me, so she has a knowledge of me because she was the one who was with me when I was a little child, day after day, not my mother. There are things that she knows about me that are very strong and very important.

Marjorie: So going back is a way of recapturing that past for you?

Ruth: Well, that and being all the things I am without contradiction. Like I am Jewish, that is fine. I am Cuban, that is fine too. They know my father was of Turkish background and my mother was Polish and Russian and it is OK. Cuba is also very special. I bet the revolution had a lot do with that. The level of political awareness and social awareness is very strong there. People understand that there was a Jewish immigration and people understand the past and it's not something strange to them. Maybe if I was in a very tiny town in the mountains of Cuba it wouldn't be like that, but in Havana . . . Havana is very cosmopolitan.

Marjorie: What about this country? It is supposed to be a country of immigrants, but it seems to not understand them.

Ruth: It's because things here are reduced to black and white racial politics. And then, also it's the desire to order and rationalize the world. So there are these boxes and the boxes don't allow for multiple identities; they only allow for a single identity at a time.

Marjorie: So, do you have conflicting identities all the time? Immigrant, Jewish, Cuban, professor . . . Does the immigrant experience enrich you and also maybe drive you crazy?

Ruth: I don't think it drives me crazy . . . I think it is a source of energy, actually. Because I was young, the trauma is more, "Can I recover it?" instead of, "Did I lose it?" I was so young, I think that the trauma is having been a child, an immigrant child, who did not know English and I was just put in a public school where I had to figure out how to make it. My parents could not help me.

Marjorie: Did they put you in the "dumb class"?

Ruth: They put me in the "dumb class" in second grade and I was with the slightly retarded children, the slow learners, and also with a Japanese immigrant boy. But I think that was good for me, because I decided that those kids were kids just like me too. They weren't better or worse, they were just kids. So I think that's what I am grateful for. Compassion is very important to me, that's what I strive for, to be compassionate.

Marjorie: Then maybe being an immigrant has allowed you to have a certain awareness . . . to place yourself in someone else's skin. That happens to me constantly and I feel a strong kinship with the boat people and the displaced women in refugee camps. This empathy is also part of what you call compassion.

Ruth: Yes, yes. I also think that there is a lot of compassion in this country if you can connect with certain people and certain groups. For example, a friend of mine had an incredible conference last year at Michigan. It was about disability—art and disability. There was a woman who had no arms and she was a spectacular performance artist. She came out naked and said: "Here I am, you can examine me just the way the doctors did. See my disability?" And it was so strong, because I went to this conference and a few days later I had to go to Cuba and I thought, this is amazing, this country has given me something— *this* country. This could not have happened anywhere, I mean, anywhere else, this desire to have compassion. I was so moved, I gave a talk there, because I broke my femur at the age of nine in New York and I was in a body cast for a year, I was in bed the whole year and could not walk.

Marjorie: A whole year?

Ruth: And so it gave me a sense of what it might be like to be disabled. The nurses did not want to help me because they said, "Forget it, if she doesn't walk, she doesn't walk." Then, finally I had a tough nurse who forced me to learn to walk when I was terribly afraid, and because of that experience, I have always had a lot of compassion for people with disabilities, especially those involving walking. You know, I had the body cast so that my legs would grow at the same rate and I was only nine, so they thought if they only put the cast on one leg it might end up shorter than the other. Whenever I see people who have that problem, with one leg shorter than the other one, and they are wearing this big heel, I think, "That might have been me." I see someone with an amputated leg and I think, "That might have been me too." The experience gave me a sense of compassion. So I gave my paper at this disability conference and I thought, "What are these people going to think? I'm not disabled anymore." I saw people who had problems with their legs . . . all the things I had been terrified of and there they were. They were great artists, great writers, and great people and I thought they would think I was just some stupid person complaining about a broken leg. And they came and spoke to me. I thought that was compassionate of them. They could have said, "You're not the one with the real disability," but they did not do that. They came up to me and said, "That was good. That spoke to me." So that was compassion. I thought to myself, "This is really where I want to be." I see things like that. And it was really very strong for me because I was going to Cuba afterwards and thinking, "Cuba is really my country," but I had been at this event and that was wonderful too. I really couldn't have experienced this anywhere else.

Marjorie: Do you think being an immigrant allows you also at one point to really love the country you have to live in?

Ruth: That's interesting. You know, I rebelled against that attitude because that was definitely my parents' attitude.

Marjorie: To be thankful and grateful?

Ruth: To be very thankful, to always say, "Thank you, thank you, thank you." And I guess I rebelled against that and said, "Yeah, but why are we here?" We're here because we symbolized the triumph of capitalism, so we were handy for this country; we were handy immigrants to have, so I don't have to be thankful. They used us since we were symbols for them of the cold war struggle between capitalism and socialism. So why do we owe anything? I felt that for a very long time, the rejection was very strong. I rejected my parents' attitude and therefore America. I did not want to accept this country because I did not want to be a patriot. I think of myself as very disloyal to institutions and countries. I don't want to have to salute any country. And with my parents it was so strong, especially with my father . . . I mean he loves to wear U.S.A. T-shirts and things like that.

Marjorie: Kind of like Matilde Salganicoff . . . her mother sent her tapes of Argentine national anthems. So, your father feels he is a patriot, but an American patriot?

Ruth: Totally. My father does not realize he is being discriminated against. He speaks with a very strong accent. He is viewed as a Latino. He looks like García Márquez. He has this big mustache and he has just a lot of Cuban/Latin American style about him. All that comes from the Sephardic part of his identity, which has become very important to him in the last few years. But he does not realize that he is being discriminated against when he is treated as less than a full citizen. He does not see that. It is denial, he wants to accept this country so it will accept him.

Marjorie: And you? Have you totally accepted this country?

Ruth: I think I am getting close to accepting it more.

Marjorie: Because of your age?

Ruth: Age might have something to do with it, but I tell you, I was very, very enchanted by Miami and I thought well, this could be the place for me because it's here but it's not really here. It's a place that has Spanish as its language, there's a whole way of being Latino or Latin American. There is a way of not following the rules there that I like . . . Plus, there is the ocean . . .

Marjorie: Now I can get closer to ask you what I have always wanted to know. This is a question I constantly ask. Tell me Ruth, what city would you like to sleep in?

Ruth: I don't know which city I would choose, maybe Havana, but also New York, where I grew up, and maybe Ocean Drive, in Miami Beach. I have good memories of vacations at the beach, and Istanbul, which I visited a few years ago, I was fascinated by it. Madrid is full of memories for me, especially the Museo del Prado, the basement where I used to go see Goya's black paintings. I would like to, if possible, mix and match my favorite streets in various cities and create my own geography.

Marjorie: Maybe you would choose Havana then?

Ruth: Havana would be nice. I had a very strange response when I went to the Jewish cemetery in Guanabacoa, which is right outside of Havana, and I thought, this is where I would want to sleep eternally. That is where I want to be buried. I had that feeling when I saw the cemetery . . .

Marjorie: Of all the places that you have loved, the cities and the people, what makes you feel most nostalgic?

Ruth Behar

Ruth: We are not supposed to want to be nostalgic. It's sort of a bad thing, but I don't know. I sometimes feel nostalgia for those early immigrant years because the family was very close. We all lived in the same apartment building. My family was all there, my parents, me and my brother, Mori, my grandparents, my aunts and uncles, my cousins. We were all in one building. Sometimes I am nostalgic for those years when that unity was so strong. My parents, my brother, and I have really broken down as a family. This country broke us down. It's a lot of different things. It's very complicated. For example, with my brother I felt that everything, for a long time, depended on me. I had to make the phone calls, I had to visit him, and I reached a point where I got tired and I said, "If you want the relationship *you* keep it up now." And it all kind of fell apart.

Marjorie: Who are you, Ruth? Do you define yourself as an immigrant? In what landscape do you feel free? I have made a certain peace with myself by accepting the fact that I do not belong and in that I have some freedom.

Ruth: All those things—being Jewish, Cuban, U.S. immigrant, and an anthropologist too—everything is there in me in a very poetic way. I don't always identify with the discipline of anthropology, but I identify with the poetry of anthropology as an identity of never being quite sure if this is where you want to be. What I am trying to learn now is how to be in the present . . . because I am so swept up by memory. I get lost . . . I think that being an immigrant is always about thinking about the past, being in the past, and to finally stop being an immigrant, you have to be willing to be in the present.

Marjorie: What does it mean to be in the present?

Ruth: To be in the present is to be where you are. To be in whatever place you are and accept it as it is. This is it . . . It means to be part of a community. I think, for me, it's a search for ways to identify with people that I am convinced at the beginning I have nothing to do with . . . that's what I have been striving for.

Marjorie: Do you think being in the present means being able to say, "enough of being the outsider"?

Ruth: I think so . . . I think it's a little bit of that, also getting over a certain kind of snobbiness that I think I had—maybe this is too strong—but aloof. I was aloof, I would go off and think . . .

Marjorie: Is this shyness too?

Ruth: Shyness too, yes. Maybe it was a fear that you won't have something to give. There is always that insecurity that you feel and at the same time (you will understand this since you are a writer too) I have a need for solitude, but sometimes other people take that away from you. Sometimes you really *want* that distance. What I find is that if you connect with people, they give you so much. They give you their stories and that's what you want as a writer . . . you want their stories. If you keep putting a distance, you don't get the stories and you want them . . . they are all interesting. I think I used to be very small-minded, I used to think only *some* stories were interesting and now I think *all* stories are interesting, and that I underestimated people I met and I did not think they had anything to give me and they do. I think that's what has been important to me now. I think that is making me a better writer, that I am *willing* to see everybody's story as interesting.

Marjorie: Also, you are willing to give everyone a chance. I also want to ask how being Jewish has influenced you. What does it mean for you to be Jewish?

Ruth: Many things, so many different things . . . It's hard to know where to start with that. Definitely the Sephardic part of my identity is strong because it means being able to link being Jewish with speaking Spanish. So that is very important to me: the identity. Sephardic music and poetry gives me a lot of energy, and when I went to Turkey a few years ago, I picked up on a lot of Sephardic poetry written in Ladino and that was extremely important to me, to have that, and to know it goes back so many centuries. It's not just from Cuba, in fact, it is older and it goes back to Spain. And also that connection to Spain and being a Jew from a Spanish-speaking country is very strong. So even when I am speaking Spanish, it reminds me that I am Spanish, too, because I have that from being Jewish more than anything else. I do also have, and this I have learned in this country, the tradition of Jewishness and social justice being things that are linked together. It has nothing to do with religion, but again, with the desire for compassion and community and so I have learned from reading and meeting Jewish people in the U.S. who are on the left and who have taught me a lot. At home we maintain certain rituals. David loves to make bread, so he makes challah. Every Friday he makes challah and I light the candles. I want to at least have that, those small but significant traditions.

Marjorie: What do you think about when you light the candles?

Ruth: Just gratitude for life. Life, light . . .

Marjorie: So you are grateful for Gabriel and the things of the earth?

Ruth: Gabriel and David. It's the three of us when we do that. I am connecting with them. I am grateful to them and what they give me. My two "boys" and

Ruth Behar

definitely connecting with that longer tradition. I am also fascinated by the Old Testament, the stories fascinate me, and that's important. Hebrew still has a kind of power over me.

Marjorie: The language? The prayers?

Ruth: The language, the look of the language, the letters. When I see something in Hebrew . . . and Ladino is very wonderful because it's Hebrew letters, but it's Spanish, and these Hebrew letters are saying something to you in Spanish. It's an amazing thing . . . It's powerful. It's gorgeous. It's wonderful and the chanting for me always is emotional and moving, particularly what moves me in the whole Jewish calendar, in the liturgy, is the Abraham and Isaac story of Rosh Hashannah.

Marjorie: Of the sacrifice?

Ruth: That sacrifice of Isaac always, always, always moves me tremendously, emotionally; it's very strong for me. My problem with Jewishness is that the way my parents taught it to us was always very . . . it was an obligation . . . *un compromiso.* Cuban Spanish has that sense of "duty" and obligation. We have to do this because other people want to know if we are doing it. So, for example, my brother does not want to have anything to do with Jewish practice.

Marjorie: Is he married? What is his family life like?

Ruth: Yes, he is married to a Jewish woman from Philadelphia who is very connected to her Jewish identity, but he . . . because it was always something that was very much for other people . . . You were not doing it because you loved it, but because if you did not do it, what would the others say . . . It was such a bad way of doing things. We did so many things like that. My parents were very much into obligation, and so the beauty of Jewishness seemed so forced. They did not show their love for it, or so it seemed.

Marjorie: So are you again rebuilding that in your own house with David and Gabriel?

Ruth: I am trying with Gabriel. He goes to Hebrew school, which he does not love, but I notice when he does not think I am listening he hums songs that he has learned in Hebrew school. So, it's hard because I don't want to force it on him, but I don't want him to grow up ignorant either. The most beautiful thing happened when we were in Miami for a semester's visit. I had decided not to put him in Hebrew school there because there were so many new things to cope with, a new public school . . . My grandmother said that she had a friend

207

who had been a Hebrew school teacher. She was eighty-eight years old and she started teaching Gabriel. Once a week we would go to Frida Salesky's house in Miami and it was a beautiful experience for her, for Gabriel, and for me. She taught him prayers; hers is the old school, where you repeat it and repeat it and at first Gabriel hated it, but by the time he was done, he loved it, and she kept saying to him, "You are my last student. You are my last student." She didn't want me to pay her. She did not want any money. She said, "I will not teach for money." I asked her if I could make a donation in her name to the Cuban-Hebrew synagogue and she said yes. And I made a donation that was much bigger than she thought it would be and she was very, very honored. That was beautiful. I thought it was a great way to bring Gabriel to Hebrew, to Jewishness, to this gift from this old, old woman who could barely see. It was a strain for her to do this, her health was not great, and she gave him a great gift. I kept telling him that this was a gift: "Gabriel, you have to recognize this because you got this from such an older person." And he did. He was very loving with her and that made me feel good, knowing that there was such a special bond between that older generation (someone who had migrated from Cuba) and Gabriel, born here in Michigan.

Marjorie: How do you dream and where do you return to when you think about your childhood?

Ruth: I dream in two languages—English and Spanish. But for the most part it's images that I remember and some hard-to-define things like desire and fear. A Sephardic Jew can always return to Spain and feel some nostalgia. It happened to me, although returning is always somewhat bitter (you'll see in my essay "The Story of Ruth"). I return to the Sephardic songs and they always bring up strong emotions. I think that we return to that language—Ladino—to the ancient Spanish, tender, sad, and which was maintained in Turkey and other countries to which the Spanish Jews moved when they were exiled.

Marjorie: In your book you are a "translated woman." How do you feel about yourself, about living in multiple identities?

Ruth: Well, it's hard because, is there an original? I mean, that is a question that people are asking. There is a book by a Cuban poet called *Translations without Originals* and now I think, well, which is the original? I mean, if we all exist in translation, what am I worried about? I think just communication is an act of translation. You cannot be inside of me, I cannot be inside of you . . . We have to translate feelings, experiences, longings . . . all of that. So any effort at language, communication, or art is translation. It's all translation.

EPILOGUE

I have finished inscribing the conversations for this book, taking leave of these traveling companions as I board the plane to Santiago. Once again, I am airbound for Chile, the country I know best and love most. This can be an ambivalent love affair, for sometimes I feel like a stranger in Chile: I have been absent for so long. Yet Chile is the one place where no one asks me where I am from. And when I return, my grandmother Josefina is there to greet me. My grandmother, with her halo of golden braids, stayed behind in Chile, cultivating familial memories and preserving my past. Because of her, I know that my adolescence was real.

Even during the years of the Pinochet dictatorship, when people and conversations were frightened and covert, my grandmother—present, ceremonial, eternal—would greet me. For me, neither Chile nor my memories would exist without her. She is as solid and permanent as the rocks of the Chilean coast. She meets me at the airport and takes me home with her, telling familiar stories again and again, so that I will not forget. Yet, as the years pass, those stories seem to slip by, no longer belonging to me. Sometimes even her voice, her language seem foreign, as though the beloved words are spoken by a person I have never met.

But now I step out onto the balcony of my grandmother's house, where often at night I would linger in the garden, steeped in the fragrance of lavender flowers just come into bloom. At this balcony I had learned to push myself up on my hands and peer over the shrubs at a wider world, catching a glimpse of the mountain peaks among the mists. Even now the mountains are illuminated, and again I see women dressed as brides and widows descending from the peaks. At this moment I know for certain that I have returned—that images, signs, dreams from my past may disappear from time to time, but always reappear.

My grandmother comes up to me perplexed. She looks at me accusingly as she did when I was little, accusations I hold dear because she loves me. She scolds me because I am not wrapped in my shawl, I have been outside for too long, I will catch a cold. I go inside with her, my arm around her shoulders that seem smaller to me with each visit.

I return to my bedroom, where a hot water bottle awaits me, and pull layers of covers over myself as once I did in the cold Latin American winters. This is my place. I recognize myself not in the objects but in the certainty that I have been here, have stood on these wooden floors, have gazed at these shelves. I know where to find the switch for the night-light, and turn it on. Illuminated, I recover my past. Here in this stone house by the sea, a house inhabited by a very old woman, all the places of my childhood are restored to me.

This house, like all others, has ghosts. Tonight I feel the presence of Carmen Carrasco Espindola, a wealthy woman who lost her family and her fortune in an earthquake in the 1940s. After this, she became my grandmother's companion and servant for a quarter century. When I was a child, she brought me wonderful birthday gifts: miraculous leaves and herbs, sedatives for peace, jasmine for desire, and laurel for perseverance. She brought me living and dead chickens, and wild fruits that clung to my palate and puckered my lips like sweet and dangerous poisons. And for one birthday, this woman, unschooled and barely literate, gave me a notebook. "Here you will find happiness," she said, "and you can record the essence of your dreams."

I loved that notebook with its rough covers like the bark of ancient trees. I seeded it with letters, inscribing syllables of longing and anger and pain. I recorded acts of love long before I experienced them and wove stories about my future. In my grandmother's kitchen, Carmencha and I would watch one another, I hunched over my seedbed of dreams while she chopped onions. Aware of her gaze, I knew that she willed my notebook to contain the steps of angels, the secret of the river after a rainfall.

At night, she would rub my neck tenderly, bless me in ancient languages, kiss my hands and my notebook. Secretly, she would make the sign of the cross over me because she feared that I would be carried off to hell. And when she wasn't looking, I would draw a Star of David on her forehead.

That battered and magical notebook is beside me tonight, and I rest my words and my face upon it. Writing is a singing river, and I thank each one of you for joining your voices with mine.

Notes

Zezette Larsen (pp. 13–36)

1. Sephardic Jews have roots in the Iberian peninsula (in contrast with Ashkenazic Jews, who hail from Central Europe). Sephardic Jewry followed the tradition of Babylonian scholars, as opposed to Palestinian scholars, and developed separate customs, which saw a great flowering in medieval Spain. When the Jews were expelled from Spain in 1492 by the Inquisition, Sephardim moved their culture to the Middle East and North Africa. Today they account for approximately 20 percent of the Jewish population.

2. Malines, also called Mechelen, was a camp built by the Nazis in Belgium in October 1941 as a detainment center for Jews going on to death camps in Eastern Europe. Malines saw twenty-six transports of over twenty-five thousand Jews between August 1942 and its liberation by the Allies in July 1944.

3. The so-called "death marches" were attempts by the SS (Schutzstaffeln, Hitler's "protection squad.") The SS were formed as a security arm of the Nazi police to protect high-ranking Nazi officers. A racially elite group, the SS were distinguished by their black uniforms and their adoption of the death's head as their trademark symbol. They tried to evacuate the inmates from Polish camps so as to prevent their liberation by the advancing Soviet troops in January 1945. Thousands of Jewish women were forced to march barefoot in the snow to the Ravensbruck camp; those who lagged behind were shot on the roadside.

4. "Adults" were treated differently from children in the death camps. As the Jews filed out of trains onto waiting ramps, SS doctors would divide them up into two groups: those who would be used for labor and those destined for immediate slaughter. Children almost always were placed in this second group. According to survivors' testimony, at Auschwitz-Birkenau children were even cremated alive when the gas chambers were slowed up in the later years of the war.

5. Zezette here refers to the genocide, or "ethnic cleansing," of Bosnian Muslims by the Serbian government in the early 1990s. The echoes of the Holocaust are amplified by Central Europe's repeated role as a theater of human destruction.

6. Zezette here refers to the mass slaughter of the Tutsi racial group by the Hutu party in power in the African state of Rwanda in the early 1990s. Unlike the Jewish Holocaust, in which the concealment of religion could possibly have meant escape, the victim Tutsi were publicly marked—physiologically, they appear much taller and thinner than the ruling Hutu.

Notes

7. Russian and Soviet laws have distinguished Judaism not as a religion but as a separate nationality. Anti-Semitism was condoned by Stalin as politically expedient. While Jews comprised less than 1 percent of the general population, Stalin's fear of their allegiance to the newly created state of Israel was such that it fostered the active obliteration of Yiddish culture in the early 1950s. Russian Jews of the post-Stalin era remained under many of the same restrictions and bans placed on their culture as an ethnic minority. Antagonism between Jews and the government continues to be deep-rooted, as evidenced by events such as the rally against anti-Semitism in St. Petersburg in 1991.

8. A former U-boat commander in World War I, Martin Niemöller became a Lutheran pastor in 1924. He was a major figure in the Nazi resistance movement, forming both the Confessional Church and Pastors' Emergency League. Niemöller was arrested in 1937 and was later imprisoned at Dachau. After being rescued in 1945, he traveled to the United States to address audiences, often ending his speeches with the following well-known words: "First, they came for the socialists, and I did not speak out because I was not a socialist. Then they came for the trade unionists, and I did not speak out because I was not a trade unionist. Then they came for the Jews, and I did not speak out because I was not a Jew. Then they came for me, and there was no one left to speak for me."

Elena Ottolenghi Nightingale (pp. 43–71)

1. On September 1, 1938, the Council of Ministers decreed the deportation of Jews who found refuge in Italy after 1919. On September 2, 1938, it issued a decree forbidding Jews to study or teach in any institution. On November 17, 1938, legislation passed to prohibit marriage between Jews and Aryans; to prevent Jews from serving in the army, working in the government, working in municipal service, and employing Aryans; and to confiscate Jewish property—among many other provisions.

2. The Shema is a prayer declaring the unity of God, consisting of three passages from the Torah and recited in the evening and the morning. It was not uncommon for the Shema to be recited in bed as an additional blessing.

3. Giuseppe Mazzini (b. 1805, Genoa; d. 1872, Pisa) spearheaded the Italian national revolution of 1848. After his death Mazzini was regarded as a symbol of Italian freedom and idealism.

4. Rosh Hashanah is the Jewish New Year, celebrated as a two-day festival in autumn, the central ritual of which is the sounding of the shofar (ram's horn). Yom Kippur is, literally, the Day of Atonement: the most solemn date on the Jewish calendar, it is usually observed with a twenty-five-hour fast.

5. Charoset is a paste usually made from nuts, fruit, and wine used to sweeten the bitter herbs during the Passover seder. It stands as a symbol of the mortar used in the building projects upon which Israelites were forced to labor in ancient Egypt.

6. Mussolini's March on Rome, a political and military operation occurring October 27–29, 1922, was intended to frighten King Victor Emmanuel III and conservative government officials into bringing the Fascists to power.

7. Gabriel Heatter (b. 1890, New York; d. 1972, Miami) was a well-known radio news commentator. He hosted programs for the Mutual Broadcasting Company in the 1930s and 1940s, such as "Behind the Front Page" and "We, the People."

212

8. Amnesty International is a grassroots activist group founded in 1961 dedicated to the preservation of the rights of political prisoners and the abolition of extrajudicial cruelties.

Susan Bendor (pp. 79–84)

1. Yad Vashem is an Israeli national institution devoted to the memorialization and documentation of the Holocaust.

2. Labor camps, the Forced Labor Services, or Munkaszolgálat, were brigades of political unreliables such as Jews and Communists used to aid the Hungarian army in projects of national interest. Those drafted into these labor brigades were sent for long periods to remote locations, such as the Russian front.

3. Raoul Wallenberg (1912–1947) was a Swedish diplomat who worked to save the lives of Hungarian Jews in Budapest at the end of World War II. He was later imprisoned by the Russians, and it is believed that he died in his cell.

4. During Passover, the Seder table is set with a full cup of wine reserved for the prophet Elijah, who is the Messiah's herald; near the end of the meal, the front door is opened to welcome Elijah as a gesture to indicate that Passover is a time of security for Jews who have been delivered. Chad Gadya is the name of an Aramaic song allegorizing the plight of the Israelites that is sung at the conclusion of the Seder.

5. The *yahrzeit* is the anniversary of a relative's death. A candle is burned for twenty-four hours as a symbol of mourning and a fast is sometimes observed.

Matilde Salganicoff (pp. 107–124)

1. *Porteño* denotes something or someone native to Buenos Aires.

2. The Bolshevik war refers to the Russian Revolution of 1917. The word *bolshevik* means "member of the majority" and was the term used to describe a follower of Lenin, who led the radical faction of the Russian Social Democratic Workers' Party. The Bolsheviks eliminated opposition and from 1918 became known as the Communist Party.

3. Machu Picchu is the largest and best-preserved example of the imperial architecture of the Incas in Peru. Its rediscovery by Hiram Bingham in 1911 attracted the attention of scholars to the Incan culture of the Andes. The site's most prominent feature is its series of agricultural terraces, which were designed to produce goods for the capital at Cuzco.

4. Matilde is referring here to Carol Gilligan's book *In a Different Voice : Psychological Theory and Women's Development* (Cambridge, Mass.: Harvard University Press, 1982).

Renata Brailovsky (pp. 131–136)

1. Kristallnacht, "Night of the Broken Glass," refers to the events of November 9 and 10, 1938, sparked by the assassination of diplomat Ernst Vom Rath in Paris by a Polish Jew. According to government figures, 815 Jewish shops and 76 synagogues were leveled,

Notes

and a further 191 synagogues were set aflame. Although engineered to seem a spontaneous action, it was in fact a nationwide effort orchestrated by the Nazi regime to speed up Jewish emigration from Germany and Austria.

2. Kindertransport was a German word for a train full of Jewish children being sent out of the country before 1939 for safety. Other European countries—such as Belgium, England, and Sweden—placed the children with families for the duration of the war.

3. *Pastel de choclo* is a typical Chilean food made of corn. It is really like a baked pie.

Susan Rubin Suleiman (pp. 146–157)

1. Georges Bataille (1897–1962), French poet and fiction writer. An early supporter of surrealism, his work is noted for its violence and eroticism.

2. Reference to the turmoil of May and June 1968 in Paris at the universities, which were plagued at the time by overcrowding and high enrollment, dim prospects, and job insecurity for graduates. The student revolts that took place on the campuses of Nanterre and the Sorbonne culminated in the "night of the barricades" on May 5, but these only sparked greater political uprisings. By the month's end, nine million workers were on strike.

Katherine Scherzer Wenger (p. 173)

1. Borough Park is a Brooklyn neighborhood that developed during the 1920s, attracting a mostly Jewish population.

Silvia Zeldis Testa (pp. 191–192)

1. Reference to the Six-Day War between Israel and Egypt, Jordan, Syria, and Iraq. It lasted from June 5 to June 10, 1967. Israel emerged victorious, having reclaimed the West Bank, the Sinai Peninsula, and the Golan Heights.

2. The student revolts in Paris in 1968 caused a sensation among other Western cultures; see note 2 for Susan Suleiman.

Ruth Behar (pp. 196–201)

1. Ladino: a creole language spoken by Sephardic Jews with its origins in Spain.

2. A *conversa* is literally a convert. In this context it is a term for a former Jew turned Christian, wishing to conceal Jewish identity from the Inquisition.

University Press of New England publishes books under its own imprint and is the publisher for Brandeis University Press, Dartmouth College, Middlebury College Press, University of New Hampshire, Tufts University, and Wesleyan University Press.

Library of Congress Cataloging-in-Publication Data
Agosín, Marjorie.
Uncertain travelers : conversations with Jewish women immigrants
to America / Marjorie Agosín; edited and annotated by Mary G. Berg.
   p. cm. — (Brandeis series on Jewish women)
ISBN 0 – 87451 – 945 – 4 (cl. : alk. paper)
1. Jewish women—United States Interviews.   2. Immigrants—United
States Interviews.   3. United States—Ethnic relations.   I. Berg,
Mary G.   II. Title.   III. Series.
E184.36.W64A35   1999
305.48'8924073—dc21   99 – 30391